THE HIGH-YIELD ALTERNATIVE TO CDs

Mortgage Securities

THE LOW-RISK ALTERNATIVE TO STOCKS

DANIEL R. AMERMAN

PROBUS PUBLISHING COMPANY
Chicago, Illinois
Cambridge, England

© 1993, Daniel R. Amerman

ALL RIGHTS RESERVED. No part of this publication may be reproduced, stored in a retrieval system, or transmitted, in any form or by any means, electronic, mechanical, photocopying, recording, or otherwise, without the prior written permission of the publisher and the copyright holder.

This publication is designed to provide accurate and authoritative information in regard to the subject matter covered. It is sold with the understanding that the publisher is not engaged in rendering legal, accounting, or other professional service.

Authorization to photocopy items for internal or personal use, or the internal or personal use of specific clients, is granted by PROBUS PUBLISHING COMPANY, provided that the U.S. $7.00 per page fee is paid directly to Copyright Clearance Center, 27 Congress Street, Salem, MA 01970, USA; Phone: 1-508-744-3350. For those organizations that have been granted a photocopy license by CCC, a separate system of payment has been arranged. The fee code for users of the Transactional Reporting Service is 1-55738-477-0/93/$00.00 + $7.00.

ISBN 1-55738-477-0

Printed in the United States of America

BB

1 2 3 4 5 6 7 8 9 0

Dedicated to my wife and companion, Laurie,
for putting up with me;
with many thanks to the good friends who
gave of themselves so generously on this project.

Table of Contents

Chapter	Title	Page
Preface:	A Visit to the Bank	vii
1	The Professional Investor's Secret	1
2	Reversing the Mortgage to Build Wealth	9
3	Surviving Inflation and Taxes	21
4	The Many Benefits of Monthly Payments	33
5	The Five Layers of Safety	41
6	Comparing Stocks to Ginnies and Fannies	49
7	Meet Our Helpers	63
8	Unlocking the Mystery of Prepayments	73
9	Mastering the Four Faces of Prepayments	87
10	Figuring Out Premiums and Discounts	105
11	Same Prepayments, Opposite Results: Discounts, Premiums, and Rate Changes	115
12	The Pitfalls and Pleasures of Topping the Prepayment Curve	133
13	The Surprising Truth about Price Risk	143
14	Minimizing Yield Risk: The Real Story	155
15	Accumulating Wealth the Safe Way	173
16	A Hidden History of Success	189
17	Buying Mortgage Securities	199
18	Winning with Mortgage Securities	215
Investor Checklist		227
Appendix		231
Glossary		233
Index		241

Preface

A Visit to the Bank

Looking in the mirror, I straighten my tie. My certificate of deposit matures today; it is time for me to reinvest the money. Deciding I now look respectable enough for a trip to the bank, I drive all the way downtown to the main branch.

What an impressive sight! My bank is in an old stone building with tall, carved columns all across the front. The bank across the street occupies a tall, smoked-glass and steel tower with its name on the top. Both are imposing structures. A thought crosses my mind: I wonder how much it cost to build my bank?

I push my way through the heavy front doors of the bank. They are more difficult to open than most because of all the brass and thick glass. Inside, an opulent vista awaits me, and I pause for a moment to admire the view before proceeding across the cavernous lobby. Look at all that marble! The floors, the walls, the interior columns, the teller counter, there is marble everywhere! The bankers themselves are well dressed—tailored dark suits with tasteful accents on the women, and the men are wearing conservative dark suits over their starched shirts. I glance down—good thing I am not wearing my blue jeans.

Over on one of the walls, I see a large sign with a lot of numbers on it. I walk over to take a close look, and this is what it says:

Anybank, USA

Passbook savings	3.00%
30-day CD	3.65%
1-year CD	4.00%
5-year CD	5.50%
Home Mortgage Loans	9.00%

Hmmmm, that is a lot of numbers. How do they compare for the $25,000 in savings I need to invest? Fortunately I have a calculator with me, and I figure out how much I would earn with each investment (see Figure 1).

Preface

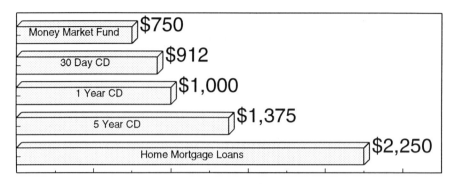

Figure 1
Annual Earnings on a $25,000 Investment

Well, looks like there is no question about it. My $25,000 invested in the mortgage loans would earn $2,250 per year in interest. Why, that is *three* times the $750 I would earn with passbook savings, and almost *twice* the $1,375 I would earn with the highest-paying certificate of deposit! Confident in my decision, I get in line to see the next desk person. After all, I am an investor this time, and not just a depositor in the teller line.

"Next."

"Good morning. I would like to invest my money in those 9.00% mortgage loans."

"Oh no, sir," she says. Shaking her head in exasperation at my ignorance, she explains, "9.00% is the rate we loan money out at, we don't pay 9.00% interest rates. Would you like a 3.00% savings account instead? How about a 4.00% one year CD?"

Embarrassed and disappointed over my misunderstanding, I excuse myself without investing my money and I go back over to the sign. So the bank will pay me $750 per year on my savings when I lend to them, and will charge me $2,250 per year when they lend to me. The source of the bank's money for the grand building, the artwork, and all that marble is becoming clear now: I'm the source:

Bank earns 9.00%:	$2,250
Bank pays 3.00%:	- 750
Bank keeps 6.00%:	$1,500

My eyes keep returning to the interest rates displayed on the wall. I am just not very happy about the savings or CD rates, but the mortgage rate still looks good. If there were only some way to cut the bank out of the middle. I have better uses for that money than buying marble columns or country club memberships for bankers.

I could go ahead and loan the money directly to someone who needs a mortgage to buy a house, but how would I find them? How could I make sure that I was collecting the money for the mortgage every month? How would I get my money back if the homeowner stopped paying me?

If only there were a simple way to invest in mortgages, so I could invest as much as I want to, when I want to.

If only someone else were there to make the mortgage and collect the payments so that all I had to do was deposit a check each month.

If only there were a safe way to invest in mortgages, with the federal government guaranteeing the full payment of mortgage principal and interest, under an even better insurance program than the government offers to depositors at FDIC-insured banks.

There is of course a way to do all of that and more by investing in the mortgage-backed securities (MBS) market. Little known or understood by most of the investing public, a quiet revolution has been taking place in the financial marketplace over the last decade: the trillion-dollar growth of the mortgage-backed securities market. Offering an unbeatable combination of exceptional safety, unusual simplicity, and attractive yields, mortgage securities have been immensely popular with professional investors. So popular that there has been little need to attract individual investors.

Safety, Simplicity, Yield

There has been another revolution over the last decade: the increasing number of individuals who are finding themselves required to make difficult investment decisions. An unprecedented number of us are leading healthy and active lives as retirees, with many of us relying upon income from our investments to make ends meet. There are even larger numbers of us who are of working age and are having to assume responsibility for managing our own IRAs, Keoghs, and self-directed retirement accounts. All together, there are 50 million or more of us in the United States currently making our own investment decisions. Decisions that are critically important in determining how we will live our lives. Decisions for which most of us have little training or preparation regarding complex alternatives that we often do not understand.

High interest rates, rising bond prices, and a long bull market in stocks eased the difficulty of our investment tasks in the 1980s, but the investment climate of the early 1990s has created a baffling dilemma for many of us. Interest rates are at their lowest levels in decades, and our traditional safe favorites such as money market funds and short-term CDs no longer pay us enough to live on; with yields less than the rate of inflation, they are an unattractive way to save for retirement. Gold, silver, oil & gas partnerships, junk bonds, real estate tax shelters—too many high-flying fads have soared and then crashed for most of us to chase after the new fads. Stocks have done well, but many of us remember that the stock market moves in both directions, and are leery of risking everything in a market that already stands at record highs. Where do we go?

Where to Invest with Interest Rates Low and Stocks Sky-High?

In the pages that follow, we will be discovering an investment alternative that delivers to us an unparalleled combination of safety, simplicity, and yield. We will find out how we can use the high-yield, monthly-pay characteristics of mortgage securities to survive inflation and taxes and safely build wealth over time. We will learn about the Five Layers of Safety, the giant friends of the mortgage security investor, and the stark contrast between stocks and mortgage securities. We will unlock the mysteries of the Four Faces of Prepayments, and unravel the relationships between prices, yields, and prepayments. We will then link together these simple building blocks and learn the surprising truth about the powerful performance of safe mortgage securities during times of level, falling, *and* rising interest rates. In doing so we will discover the reasons why professional investors around the world have developed a near-insatiable appetite for the uniquely desirable risk/return characteristics of mortgage securities, and thereby fueled the explosive growth within a decade's time of the mortgage securities market from an obscure backwater to a titan larger than the corporate bond, municipal bond, or even bank commercial lending markets.

Most importantly, no degrees in finance will be required, and no prior knowledge of investments will be needed for our exploration of mortgage securities. We will not need to understand balance sheets, projected earnings, price/earnings ratios, intangible assets, or depreciation schedules. What we will need to do is simply to think like homeowners who have mortgages, and if we can do that, we will have the knowledge we need to master these most personal of investments.

1
The Professional Investor's Secret

Most of the investments in the United States are purchased by a relatively small group of highly trained men and women whom few of us have ever met. This small group consists of the investment managers for the nation's insurance companies, pension funds, investment companies, trust companies, banks, thrifts, and mutual funds, who collectively have over $10 trillion currently invested.

The world of these professional investors is entirely different from that of the individual investor. This is a world of huge sums where it is routine for $100 million to move on a phone call, and where $5 million is often referred to as "and change" in pricing discussions. The world of the institutional investor is also a place of precision, where results are measured to the last dollar on an often daily basis, and managers live and die by the basis point (one hundredth of one percent in yield). Postgraduate degrees in disciplines such as finance, economics, and mathematics are the norm for these investors rather than the exception, and they have instant access to vast amounts of information through research analysts and computerized databases.

With all this money, information, and expertise one would expect these investors to be entering into sophisticated, esoteric investment strategies far better than anything available to those of us who are not professional investors and do not have huge sums of money to invest. Surprisingly however, one of the favorite investments of institutional investors over the last decade is no more complicated than our own home mortgages. What are the secrets of these obscure-sounding securities? Why are mortgage-backed securities the professional's choice?

Mortgage-Backed Securities: The Unknown Giant

Ask the average person on a street corner to talk about investments and almost everyone will mention stocks. Quite a few will talk about mutual funds and bonds. Experienced investors may talk about growth funds, defensive stocks, and tax-exempt bonds. More-aggressive investors may even talk about their (probably expensive) experiences with tax shelters, futures, and options.

What very few individual investors will talk about is investing in mortgage-backed securities (MBSs), as most people are not familiar with these obscure sounding investments. Unfamiliar does not mean unimportant however. As the table below shows, the mortgage-backed securities market is in fact larger than many other better-known markets.

Total Amounts Outstanding, March 1992

Total mortgages	$4,071 billion
Total mortgage-backed securities	1,293 billion
Total corporate bonds	1,071 billion
Total tax-exempt obligations	1,110 billion
Total bank commercial loans	712 billion
Total consumer loans	776 billion

Source: Federal Reserve Bulletin

That the mortgage market dwarfs so many better known markets such as corporate bonds, tax-exempt bonds, and even bank commercial loans, may at first seem a surprise. The important thing to remember is what the mortgage market is: it is the financing for most of the real estate owned in the United States, including almost all the homes, apartments, and office buildings. From this perspective it is easy to understand why the market is so large.

Mortgage-Backed Securities: Safer Than CDs?

What could be safer than money in the bank? Well, money invested in Ginnie Maes for one thing (also called Government National Mortgage Association Mortgage-Backed Securities, or GNMA MBSs). While Certificates of Deposit (CDs) issued by FDIC-insured banks and Ginnie Maes are both guaranteed by the full faith and credit of the federal government, Ginnie Maes are guaranteed under a better insurance program for the investor. Two significant advantages that Ginnie Maes hold over CDs are:

1. The insurance on CDs is limited to $100,000 per investor per bank; there is *no limitation* on investor holdings of fully insured Ginnie Maes.
2. CD insurance is for payment of principal and insured interest up until the time the banking institution is taken over, interest earnings are then lost until payment is received. Payment is generally timely, but there is no guarantee as to how quickly you will receive your money. Ginnie Mae insurance guarantees *timely* payment of full principal, and payment of full interest through the principal payment date.

Table 1.1 compares the safety of mortgage-backed securities and GNMA MBSs.

Table 1.1
Safety: Bank CD Versus GNMA MBS

Investment	CD[1]	MBS[2]
Insurer	FDIC	GNMA
Federal government guarantee	Yes	Yes
Insurance limit	$100,000	None
Interim Interest paid	No	Yes

[1] *Certificate of deposit* [2] *Mortgage-backed security*

Mortgage-backed securities are long-term investments and do carry market risk if early liquidation is needed or desired (see Chapter 13). Not all mortgage-backed securities are directly federally insured, most are *indirectly* federally insured as a result of their issuance by quasi-governmental agencies (see Chapter 7 and the Glossary at the back of this book). That said, mortgage-backed securities are among the very safest investments available today, and are much safer than stocks, corporate bonds, futures, options, partnerships, most tax-exempt bonds, and almost any other investment you care to name other than U.S. Treasury bonds.

Mortgage-Backed Securities: Extraordinarily Simple

Ginnie Mae MBSs; Freddie Mac PCs; Fannie Mae MBSs; amortizations; weighted average lives; prepayment shifts; guarantors; servicers; originators. Are these familiar terms? Probably not. Are they simple to understand? Yes!

There is a crucial difference between the complex and the familiar. Stocks, bonds, partnerships, and options are "familiar" to many investors, yet are highly complex even for finance Ph.D.'s. Some examples of familiar complexities are:

- If you buy IBM stock, do you have an informed opinion about how the processing speed of their new midrange computer stacks up against the competition? What is the market share trend in their personal computer division? How well hedged are earnings against the impact of foreign currency fluctuations? Is the pension fund overfunded or underfunded?

- If you buy bonds, what is the debt service coverage ratio? What is an indenture? Have you ever read an indenture? What technical defaults trigger mandatory redemptions in your investment's indentures?

- If you buy futures or options, what is volatility? What is the difference between the delta and gamma of an option? What is Black-Scholes valuation?

All of the above are examples of familiar investments that are too complex for most nonprofessional investors to fully understand and evaluate. Instead, investors must make a "leap of faith" that whoever is advising them knows the complexities and is evaluating them correctly. Such "leaps" can be very expensive for investors who receive bad advice or did not understand all the risks involved:

Stock risks include:

- Market risk
- Industry risk
- Company risk
- Interest rate risk
- Bankruptcy risk
- Dividend risk
- Earnings growth risk
- Foreign competition risk
- Technology risk
- Regulatory risk
- Currency risk
- Lawsuit risk
- Environmental risk
- Many other risks

In marked contrast, mortgage security risks involve only:
- Interest rate risk
- Price Risk
- Prepayment risk

Stocks and Corporate Bonds Are Familiar, But Complex. Mortgage Securities Are Obscure, but Simple. While mortgage securities are not familiar to most investors, they are generally quite simple to understand. To invest intelligently in mortgage-backed securities, we do not need to know how to read balance sheets and income statements, we do not need to read two-hundred-page bond indentures, and we do not need to understand the effects of changes in perceived volatility upon the time value of money.

If we can understand our own home mortgages, and what factors increase or decrease the chances that we will prepay our mortgages, then we can understand mortgage-backed securities.

Mortgage Backed Securities: Necessary High Yield

Mortgage-backed securities occupy a niche all by themselves in the universe of risk/return combinations available to investors. Stocks, junk bonds, many types of partnerships, futures and options speculation—all of these investments have potential higher returns than mortgage-backed securities; however, all also carry the risk of a *total* loss on investment.

The niche that mortgage-backed securities occupies is that of the highest yielding *safe* investments; that is, those investments that have very high *credit* quality. Credit quality measures the likelihood that principal and interest will be paid, with those investments that have the highest credit quality available receiving "AAA" or "Aaa" (usually referred to as "Triple A") ratings by Standard & Poor's and Moody's.

Very few investments qualify for the elite "Triple A" rating. It is rare for even the best-known or seemingly wealthy corporations to be judged this safe (Boeing, Citibank, General Motors, IBM, McDonald's, and Sears do not have Aaa ratings on their debt), and fewer than one in five state governments receive that rating. Yet, almost all mortgage-backed securities receive this highest ranking of credit safety.

Table 1.2
Purchasing Power of Government-Insured Investments

	Yield	35% Taxes	Inflation	Purchasing Power
30-day CD	3.0%	−1.1%	−4.0%	−2.1%
1-year CD	4.0%	−1.4%	−4.0%	−1.4%
10-year treasury bond	7.5%	−2.6%	−4.0%	0.9%
Ginnie Mae MBS	8.5%	−3.0%	−4.0%	1.5%

Another risk for investors is that of purchasing-power risk: will after-tax earnings on the investment equal or exceed the inflation rate? See Table 1.2 for an illustration of after-tax purchasing-power risk.

Table 1.2 illustrates the dilemma that confronts even the most safety minded and conservative of investors: There is no "risk free" way to invest money. While short-term government-insured investments may not face the credit risk of a loss of principal and interest or the market risk of long-term investments, on an after-tax, after-inflation basis they often have a negative rate of return, leading to a steady erosion of purchasing power for the investor.

The great appeal of mortgage-backed securities is that they are usually the highest-yielding of the government-insured investments (very-long-term Treasury bonds will occasionally yield more, but such securities have far greater interest rate risk), and are one of the few ways available to earn the "necessary high yield" required to beat inflation on an after-tax basis, without risking a total loss of investment.

Mortgage-Backed Securities: The Professional's Choice

At about this point the skeptical investor (and all investors need to be skeptical) should be asking a question about mortgage-backed securities: "If there are so many of these things out there, and if they are so safe, and if they have such high yields, how come my stockbroker isn't constantly trying to sell them to me? Why don't I get phone calls interrupting my dinner pitching mortgage-backed securities like I used to get for penny stocks, silver futures, or oil and gas partnerships?"

The answer is quite simple: mortgage-backed securities are such a favorite of professional investors that the market doesn't need you, the individual investor,

The Professional Investor's Secret   7

or particularly seek your money. Pension funds, insurance companies, foreign banks, U.S. banks, and savings and loans have all developed almost insatiable appetites for the desirable risk and return characteristics of mortgage-backed securities, and purchase virtually all of the supply available. This is not a matter of any kind of conspiracy by the big guys to keep the good investments from the small investors, it is simply a matter of economics and convenience.

Bad investments:
- Are difficult to sell
- They come looking for you

Good investments:
- Are easier to sell
- You have to look for them

Issuers of mortgage-backed securities, as well as the investment banks that distribute them, are like anyone else: they want to do as little work as necessary. If they have a choice between selling $300 million in mortgage-backed securities to ten pension funds and insurance companies within half a day; or of using 3,000 stockbrokers to call 50,000 individual investors over a period of two weeks, common sense dictates they will choose the half-day alternative. Economics dictate that it is cheaper to sell to financial institutions at commission rates of 1/50 of 1% to 1/8 of 1% ($200 to $1,250 per million sold) rather than paying stockbrokers 1/4 of 1% to 5% commissions ($2,500 to $50,000 per million sold) to sell to individual investors.

This is not to say that the mortgage-backed securities market is closed to individuals, however. As common sense would suggest, the easy investments that come looking for you are all too often the bad ones that no one else will buy. The best investments usually have to be looked for and the finding may require some work. This is exactly the case with mortgage-backed securities. They are a superior investment for many individual investors and fortunately they are easy to understand; unfortunately it may take some looking to find the right ones for you.

As you go though this guide, there will be some new names and concepts for you to learn. Just remember as you go:

- MBSs are as SIMPLE as home mortgages.
- MBSs are SAFE.
- MBSs are the HIGHEST YIELDING of the government-insured investments.
- MBSs are the PROFESSIONAL'S CHOICE for good reason.

2
Reversing the Mortgage to Build Wealth

"Only invest in what you know and understand."
"But I don't know anything about mortgage-backed securities."

Yes, you do! You may not be able to properly value a stock unless you understand corporate finance and mathematical models for dividend valuation. You may not be able to judge the merits of an oil and gas limited partnership unless you are a geologist with a keen understanding of global politics. You may not be able to evaluate wheat and soybean futures without a knowledge of the ins and outs of long-range weather forecasting.

If you can understand your own home mortgage, you can understand mortgage-backed securities, because that is really all that mortgage-backed securities are: groups of home mortgages financing the residences of people like us. When we purchase a mortgage security, we are buying a share of a pool of mortgage loans, which were extended to a group of average people who were buying homes (see Figure 2.1).

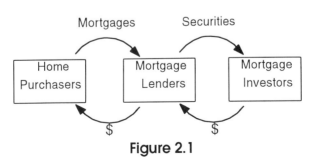

Figure 2.1

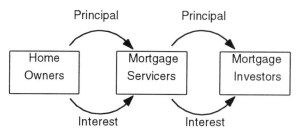

Figure 2.2
Monthly Cash Payments

With our purchase, we are essentially taking over the role of mortgage lender, as we have now provided the money that the lending bank or mortgage company originally loaned to the home purchaser. Like any lender, we made the loan so that we would be repaid not only the principal (amount) of our investment, but also the interest. Since we provided the money, we are now the people who collect the homeowner's payments of principal and interest (see Figure 2.2).

There are several added layers of protection for us as investors, but they do not change what we are doing: we in combination with other investors are lending home buyers their mortgage money, which then entitles us to be paid by them on a monthly basis. Mortgages are something most of us have personal experience with, and which most of us can easily understand. This understanding places us in a very advantageous position when we invest in mortgage securities. We can sift through investment alternatives and decide for ourselves which investment is best for us, thereby placing us in command of our own financial future. In order to achieve this understanding and mastery of mortgage-backed securities, there is one key item we must always keep in mind: We are now the lender instead of the borrower, and that means we are *reversing the mortgage*.

Reversing the Mortgage

What is bad for the homeowner is good for the
mortgage investor (and vice versa).

What is bad for the homeowner and good for the mortgage investor? There are a number of beneficial mortgage investment characteristics that we will look at in this section, but a good place to start is interest payments. A popular personal financial management technique that has received a lot of attention is that of sending in some extra money with your mortgage payment every month. The

Reversing the Mortgage to Build Wealth

reason for doing so is that every dollar of principal paid early can save several dollars in later payments. To illustrate this, the following table shows an example of a fixed-rate mortgage:

Example Mortgage

Maturity:	30 years
Interest rate:	9.00%
Initial amount:	$100,000
Monthly payment:	$804.62
Total payments:	$289,663.20

(360 months × $804.62)

The rationale behind paying principal early can easily be seen when looking at the example in the table. Every dollar borrowed must be paid back with $2.89. By paying back the dollar early, the extra dollar and 89 cents in interest is saved.

By *reversing the mortgage,* the mortgage-backed security investor can completely turn this relationship around: now for every dollar initially invested, $2.89 is received back, almost a three-to-one return.

Equally or more important than the amount of return is the type of return, this three to one return is a *contractual* return instead of the *speculative* return that might or might not be earned by investing in stocks or real estate or the like.

Compounding Wealth

Most people have seen various examples of the power of compound interest like that in Table 2.1, and many have trouble believing that such numbers are real, that this mysterious "magic" can really work for them. You may not have realized it, but if you have ever made a mortgage payment, you have already put this magic to work for you!

Table 2.1
The Magic of Compound Interest

Value of $1.00 Invested in 1900 at a 10% Yield
(Monthly compounding)

Year	Value	Year	Value
1910	$ 2.71	1960	$ 393.52
1920	7.33	1970	1,065.28
1930	19.84	1980	2,883.76
1940	53.70	1990	7,806.46
1950	145.37	2000	21,132.41

Though total mortgage payments may equal only about three times the money borrowed in the previous example, sending in extra money early does save you much more than three times the extra money paid, as is illustrated by the example below. Everything is the same as in our previous 30-year, 9.00% mortgage example, except that now we send in an extra $1,000 with our first mortgage payment.

$100,000, 30-Year, 9% Mortgage

Extra payment in Month 1	$1,000
New mortgage payoff date	28.6 years
Number of $804.62 monthly payments saved	17.1
Cash savings	$13,758
Return on "investment"	13.8 to 1

What is happening here? Why do we get a 13.8-to-1 savings instead of the 2.9-to-1 savings we might expect from our first example?

A related mystery lies in a problem that most homeowners are familiar with: in the first 5 to 10 years that they own their home, it seems like almost no progress is being made in paying down their mortgage. Virtually all the money goes to paying interest, and the mortgage is paid down at a snail's pace. Using our 9.00% mortgage example, only $54.62 of our first $804.62 payment goes to pay mortgage principal. At this rate, how can we ever pay off our $100,000 mortgage?

Years to Pay Off $100,000 Mortgage

Mortgage amount	$100,000
First month's principal payment	$54.62
Number of $54.62 payments in $100,000	1,831
Years to pay off mortgage	153??

The answer to each of these questions lies in the magic of compounded interest, a powerful investment tool that lies within every mortgage amortization, and which is equally available to the mortgage investor and the homeowner. For what every homeowner is doing when making monthly mortgage principal payments is *buying a mortgage*. We as homeowners are buying our mortgages back from our mortgage lenders, using the magic of compound interest to repay our mortgages in 30 years instead of 153 years. We as mortgage investors can use the magic of compound interest to increase our return on investment on mortgages from three to one up to as much as fifteen to one or more.

Reversing the Mortgage to Build Wealth 13

To understand this better, let us take a closer look at how mortgage payments work. A fixed amount of money is required to be paid each month by the homeowner, $804.62 in our example mortgage. From the monthly payment, interest is first paid out: one month's interest at an annual rate of 9.00% on $100,000 is $750 in our example mortgage. All remaining cash is then applied to the payment of principal on the mortgage, which is $54.62 for the first month in our example. In essence, we are *purchasing* $54.62 of our own mortgage back from the mortgage lender.

Mortgage Principal Payment: Month 1

Mortgage payment	$ 804.62
Required monthly interest payment	-750.00
($100,000 × 9.00%) ÷ 12	
Cash available to repurchase mortgage	$ 54.62

In order to see how the magic of compound interest works, let us look at Month 2. Here again we have $54.62 available within our mortgage payment to purchase mortgage principal, but we also have an additional $0.41 available in interest savings from the mortgage principal we repurchased the month before. Therefore in Month 2 we are able to repurchase not $54.62, but $55.03 of our mortgage, for a cumulative total of $109.65.

FORTY-ONE CENTS??? This is the magic of compound interest? Looking at our second month only, it is hard to become too excited about this wonderful wealth-building technique. How could an extra 41 cents possibly reduce the payment period on our $100,000 loan from 153 years down to only 30 years, thereby saving us 123 years of $804 payments? As hard as this may be to believe, our 41 cents does in fact save us about $1.2 million, and it accomplishes this miraculous task through *stretching, stacking,* and *snowballing.*

Stretching

The first thing to keep in mind about our 41 cents in interest savings is that it is not a one-time occurrence. Once mortgage principal is repurchased, then the interest savings from that particular repurchase *stretch* out to reappear in every one of our monthly payments from then on, as is shown in Figure 2.3.

Within the 30-year period shown above, the *stretching* of our 41 cents saves us $147.19, a very nice savings for a single $54.62 principal payment. Looking at the mystery of our 153-year amortization, adding 41 cents to each principal payment has the effect of reducing our repayment period by 2 years to 151 years. Obviously there must be a lot more to this compound interest magic than *stretching* alone.

Figure 2.3
STRETCHING Interest Savings

Stacking

The next component to keep in mind is that more than one principal payment is being made. Indeed, a new principal payment is being made each month. Each one of the principal payments then produces its own *stretched-out* stream of interest savings, as is shown in Figure 2.4. To calculate the interest savings available in each month, we must then *stack* up each of the *stretched* interest-savings streams.

As is shown in Figure 2.4, each month our interest savings is 41 cents greater than the month before, and our *stacking* of these savings continues to build until by the end of 360 months (30 years) we are saving $147.19 in *stacked* interest each month. Over 30 years, this combination of *stretching* and *stacking* saves us $13,137 in mortgage interest. Together, adding *stacking* to *stretching* brings the expected number of years required to pay back our $100,000 mortgage from 153 down to 48 years. But one more important factor is still missing.

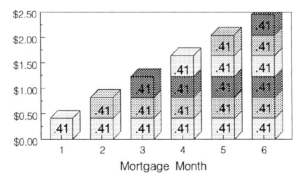

Figure 2.4
STACKING Interest Savings (Before Snowballing)

Reversing the Mortgage to Build Wealth 15

Snowballing

Compound interest is also referred to as interest on interest, and this is where our savings can really start to *snowball*. Our first $54.62 in purchased mortgage principal starts very slowly down the hill, picking up 41 cents in interest our first month. In Month 2 we pick up another 41 cents from the stretching of our first month's interest, and we stack on another 41 cents for the second month's principal purchase. We have now picked up a total of $1.23, and our snowball begins to gather speed. The interest on our interest starts to kick in as we save 1 cent on the $1.23 our interest savings have purchased, and *our speed increases to 42 cents per month*. (See Figure 2.5.)

By the beginning of our second year (see Figure 2.6) our "snowball" has increased in size by about 10% from $54 to $59 in monthly principal purchases, and we are picking up speed at the rate of 44 cents per month. *Stretching* and *stacking* provide most of the progress as our mortgage principal "snowball" slowly picks up size and speed during the early few years. While month-by-month progress may seem slight, an important milestone is reached by month 94 (year 7): our "snowball" has more than doubled in size. The interest on our interest is now purchasing $54.82 in mortgage principal every month, more than exceeding the $54.62 we have been contributing.

Our speed has doubled as well, and our principal purchases are now increasing at the rate of 81 cents per month. Because of this increase in speed, we reach our next milestone in half the time, tripling our "snowball's" size to $165.06 in principal purchases per month by the 149th month (Year 12). From this point forward the compounding of interest in combination with the *stretch-*

Figure 2.5
STACKING Interest Savings (After Snowballing)

16 Mortgage Securities

ing and *stacking* of interest savings from our previous purchases causes our mortgage purchases to *snowball* faster and faster: 83% of our monthly principal purchases ($325.79) is coming from interest on interest by Year 20 (Month 240), and interest on interest accounts for $500 per month by Year 25. Finally, by the end of the 30th year of our mortgage, our snowball has increased in size to $744.01 per month, with interest on interest accounting for $689.39 per month.

Yes, 41 cents per month, through a combination of *stretching, stacking* and *snowballing,* has indeed reduced the time to pay off our $100,000 loan from 153 years to 30 years, saving us $1.2 million. This seeming magic is not just theory, but occurs every time we make a mortgage payment, though perhaps without our knowledge of all the underlying details.

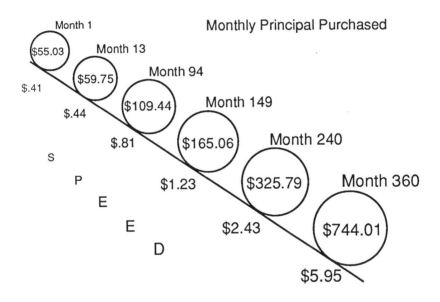

Figure 2.6
SNOWBALLING Interest Savings

Investor Benefits

The mortgage security investor also benefits fro*m stretching, stacking,* and *snowballing;* indeed, as investors we can reap far greater rewards than we can as homeowners. The first way in which these principles affect us as investors can be found by *reversing the mortgage.* The contractual schedule upon which the mortgage investor is paid is driven by the principles of *stretching, stacking,* and *snowballing;* for the investor is of course on the receiving end of each homeowner payment. The investor receives what the homeowner pays out—an even monthly cash flow that is virtually all interest payments in the early years, with rapidly increasing principal repayments decreasing the loan balance in the latter years. No harm is done to the investor by the "magic" of compound interest, the investor receives full interest until principal is paid, and then that principal is available to meet current cash needs or for reinvestment.

It is through reinvestment that we as mortgage investors can turn *stretching, stacking,* and *snowballing* to our own advantage, and exceed the benefits enjoyed by the homeowner. Let us recall that earlier we said that what the homeowner was really doing was purchasing a mortgage (from their lender), using $54.62 per month. This is the literal truth of what the homeowner is doing, for if we compare the effects of *stretching, stacking,* and *snowballing* between

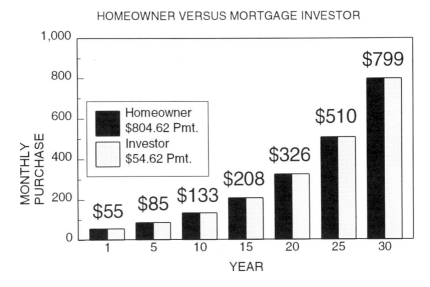

Figure 2.7
Monthly Principal Purchase Comparison

the homeowner's payments, and an investor investing and reinvesting at the mortgage rate, then we have an exact match (see Figure 2.7).

As Figure 2.7 demonstrates, the principal amortization of a mortgage is *exactly* equal to the investment growth that a mortgage investor can achieve through monthly investments in mortgages equal to the homeowner's small *first* principal payment ($54.62), so long as the interest rates are the same. The results achieved by the homeowner repurchasing principal and the investor purchasing mortgage securities on a monthly basis are identical. There is however one crucial distinction between the homeowner and the investor, which works strongly to the investor's advantage. The homeowner is fighting an uphill battle to repay a very large debt with monthly payments, and uses the magic of compound interest to pay off $100,000 in debt with $289,663 in *total* payments ($804.62 × 360), with $189,663 of the cash going to meet the crushing interest burden that comes with being heavily in debt.

In *reversing the mortgage,* the mortgage investor is not fighting any debt, but is free to use the combination of *stretching, stacking,* and *snowballing* to multiply wealth. Freed from the debt burden, our investor accumulates wealth over our 30-year example at almost 15 times the rate at which a homeowner can amortize debt. Whereas the homeowner pays $804 per month over 30 years to pay down a $100,000 mortgage, the mortgage investor does not have to pay the initial $750 a month in interest, and can accumulate $100,000 with monthly savings of only $54, about one fifteenth of the homeowner's payment. Instead of the homeowner spending $289,633 to repurchase $100,000 while *paying* interest, the investor through *earning* interest turns $19,663 in savings into $100,000 in ending wealth through the magic of compound interest combined with the certainty and high monthly yields of mortgage investing.

Another way to see the benefits of using *stretching, stacking,* and *snowballing* to build wealth rather than pay down debts can be found by taking our example full $804.62 monthly mortgage payment and using it to buy 9.00% mortgages instead of paying down a 9.00% mortgage (see Figure 2.8).

The same amount of cash that we would use to repay the example 30-year, $100,000 mortgage will compound to almost 15 times that amount if all of that cash is used for interest-earning mortgage purchases rather than paying down mortgage principal with what is left after interest charges.

Reversing the Mortgage to Build Wealth 19

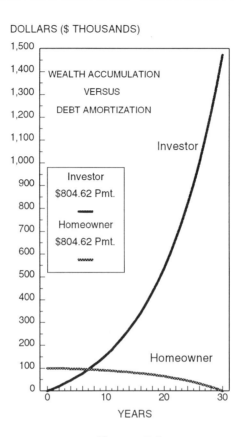

Figure 2.8
Wealth Accumulation Versus Debt Amortization

Just as the mortgage investor has the ability to build wealth through the use of consistent level monthly payments, the mortgage investor can also, like the homeowner, capture the benefits of lump-sum payments. As the example below demonstrates, the investor can access the wealth-multiplying advantages of single payments through the reinvestment of cash as received:

Reinvesting Cash From Mortgage Payments

The Mortgage
    Borrow $100,000
    Pay back   289,664

Reversing the Mortgage
    Invest $100,000
    Receive back   289,664

Reversing the Mortgage and Compounding the Interest
    Invest $ 100,000
    Value in 30 years   1,473,058

There is of course no guarantee that the magic of compound interest, in conjunction with reversing the mortgage, will work exactly as planned. There are no guarantees that a 9.00% reinvestment rate will be available; and as we will see in the next chapter, taxes may substantially reduce the compounding effect, and inflation may eat up much of the apparent benefit. It is also unlikely that all the home mortgages will remain outstanding for thirty years, indeed it is highly likely that most will prepay within 7 to 15 years (see Chapters 8 & 9).

That said, the fact remains that by *reversing the mortgage* we as mortgage investors can take what is a frustrating problem for most homeowners and turn it into a powerful tool for achieving financial success. The homeowner faces the frustrating problem of paying large mortgage payments that in the early years barely make a dent in mortgage principal owed; and through reversing that problem we have a means of increasing wealth through contractual investing by a factor of 3 times, 5 times, 10 times, or even 15 times the original investment!

# 3
Surviving Inflation and Taxes

"A dollar saved is a dollar and fifty-four cents earned."
—*Benjamin Franklin, updated for inflation and income taxes*

To spend a dollar, we must often earn a dollar fifty or more. It is not what we earn that is important, but how much we keep after federal, state, and local taxes.

Neither a penny nor a dollar will buy us as much today as they would have 10 or 20 years ago, let alone 30 or 40 years ago. It is not how much money we will possess in the future that is important, but rather how many things that money will purchase for us.

In this chapter we will take a look at taxes and inflation, and see how they eat away at seeming profits and wealth accumulation. We will compare a mortgage to a government-insured certificate of deposit to see how each withstands taxes and inflation. We will find that these twin scourges do reduce our apparent wealth accumulation with mortgage securities, but when compared to the devastation inflicted upon other government-guaranteed alternatives by inflation and taxes, we will see why seeking higher-yielding alternatives such as mortgage securities is a necessity for most investors.

Taxes

A significant benefit to being a homeowner and making payments on a mortgage is the tax-deductible nature of mortgage interest payments. Indeed, for many families their mortgage interest payments are their single largest tax deduction. In *reversing the mortgage,* unless we are investing in tax-exempt bonds collateralized by mortgages, we must pay taxes on the interest income that we receive from our mortgage investments (although taxes may be deferred through

21

holding our mortgage investment in an IRA or other tax-deferred retirement savings plan).

Paying taxes is not pleasant, and taxes do certainly reduce the amount of spendable cash that our investments generate for us. When we are looking to our investments purely to provide current income, we find that taxes do not change the percentage advantage that mortgage-backed securities hold over bank CDs, Treasury bills, and other government-insured investments. Simultaneously, we also find that while taxes *reduce* the dollar benefit that we enjoy over some other investments, including taxes *increases* the relative benefit to us from our investment in mortgage securities, and the motivation for learning about them.

To see why this is the case, let us go back to our example of a typical 9.00%, 30-year mortgage, and compare it to a 4.00% certificate of deposit. This time, let us assume a combined federal, state, and local income tax rate of 35%:

Before and After Tax Earnings Comparisons

$10,000 Investment	4.00% Bank CD	9.00% Mortgage	Dollar Advantage	Ratio
Pre-tax earnings	$400	$900	$500	225%
After-tax earnings	260	585	325	225%
	(2.60%)	(5.85%)		

The above example demonstrates that the relative advantage of higher-yielding mortgages remains constant. We are still receiving two and one quarter times as much income from the mortgages as we are from the CD, even though the dollars received decline significantly after income taxes are paid.

Taxes have certainly reduced the cash advantage that mortgage securities holds over CDs. Our annual income advantage has gone down from $500 per year to $325, a significant sum for those who are living on a fixed income.

Yet it is for those of us who are living on fixed incomes that the after-tax yield advantage enjoyed by mortgage securities becomes the most important (see Figure 3.1). The fewer dollars that we have, the more important each additional dollar becomes in maintaining our usual or desired standard of living. The couple who can no longer afford country club dues or overseas trips with a 4.00% yield may have difficulty affording trips to see the grandchildren or medical bills with a 2.60% yield; the importance of increasing an after-tax 2.60% to 5.85% can exceed the benefits of increasing a 4.00% yield to a 9.00% yield.

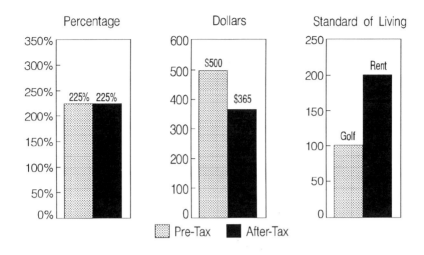

Figure 3.1
Mortgage Security Advantages Before and After Taxes

There is a greater tax impact upon those investors who are investing for the future in order to accumulate wealth. Taxes have a straight proportional effect on *stretching* and *stacking,* just as they do on current income. If taxes are at a combined 35% level, then our *stretching* and *stacking* incomes are each reduced by 35%. *Snowballing* is a different matter, however. Our interest upon interest component is the most critical aspect of long-term investing, and the speed with which our wealth *snowballs* can be slowed down substantially by the impact of taxes, as is illustrated by the example mortgage in Figure 3.2.

Three items of crucial importance to those who wish to accumulate wealth through *snowballing* interest payments are illustrated in Figure 3.2:

1. Because of the effects of the interest rate in determining how fast our wealth will snowball, we gain wealth with higher-yield investments at a faster rate than a simple comparison of yields might indicate. By way of analogy, if we look at *snowballing* as rolling down a hill, the interest rate is what determines the steepness of the slope. As any of us who have ever rolled down a hill know, doubling the steepness of the slope increases the speed with which we roll by considerably more than twice.

    So it is with the accumulation of wealth. While our example mortgage may "only" yield a little more than twice what our example CD yields, its higher rate means that it *snowballs* much faster than twice as fast as

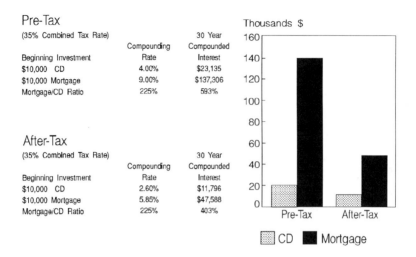

Figure 3.2
Impact of Taxes

the CD. Over 30 years, the mortgage builds almost *six times* the increased wealth that the short-term CD does; our mortgage investment profits are almost *fourteen* times our original investment (including the return of our original investment, we are ahead almost 15 to 1), while the CD earns a little more than *double* our original investment in profits.

2. Because taxes reduce the rate at which our wealth *snowballs,* they reduce our wealth accumulation by a larger amount than we might expect. In the example in Figure 3.2, 35% taxes reduce our ending increase in wealth by 65%, with our ending compounded interest plunging from $137,306 to $47,588. Because the 4.00% CD investment has less snowballing speed to lose, the addition of 35 % taxes reduces compounded interest by "only" 49%.

3. Even after including the damaging effects of income taxes, there are still huge advantages to be gained by investing in mortgages for those of us who are building wealth for the future. While the degree of our snowballing advantage is reduced by taxes, we still maintain a significant advantage over CDs relative to the rate at which wealth accumulates. Mortgages maintain a 4-to-1 one advantage over CDs in the example shown in Figure 3.2, a towering advantage that can spell the future difference between comfort and subsistence.

Inflation

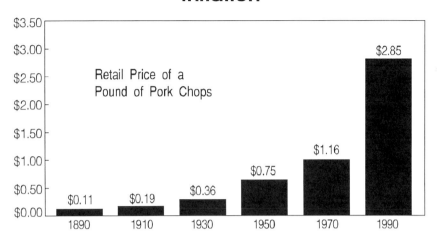

Figure 3.3
The Cost of Inflation: Retail Price of a Pound of Pork Chops

As we all know (but sometimes forget), money by itself is meaningless. What really counts is what our money will do for us. What can we buy? Where can we live? What can we eat? Where can we go? How much security do we have? Since 1939, in every year except two, a dollar has on average purchased a little bit less of most things than it did the year before. From 1970 to 1990 inflation (as measured by changes in the Consumer Price Index) decreased the value of the dollar by an average of 6.26% per year; from 1980 to 1990 the dollar has decreased in value by an average of 4.72% per year.

Adjusting for inflation will substantially reduce many of the wealth-building advantages of mortgage investments that we have seen in this chapter so far. But, as we will also see, inflation is one of the strongest reasons for investing in mortgage-backed securities, as these securities may be the only effective way to build wealth on an after-tax, after-inflation basis while maintaining the peace of mind that comes with government-insured investments.

One of the problems with inflation is that no one can predict its severity on a long-term basis with any degree of accuracy. However, for the sake of discussion, let us make the assumption that inflation into the future remains constant at the relatively modest rate of 4.00%. Using our example CD and mortgage investments, we can quickly look at the effects of inflation upon simple yields (see Figure 3.4).

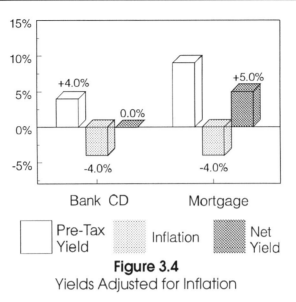

Figure 3.4
Yields Adjusted for Inflation

Inflation has the effect of quickly wiping out the entire yield of a bank CD in the example, a result that is neither random or unrealistic. Indeed, it is quite common for the yields of short-term government securities or bank CDs to approximate inflation. As is shown in Figure 3.5, mortgage rates are far more consistent in staying ahead of inflation than 3-month Treasury bills.

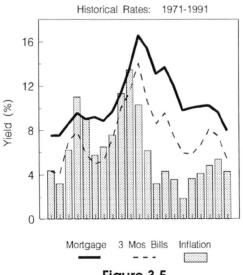

Figure 3.5
Mortgages, T-Bills, and Inflation

Surviving Inflation and Taxes

Before drawing the conclusion that short-term government-insured investments are a good way of at least keeping up with inflation, the impact of taxes must also be taken into account (see Figure 3.6).

After accounting for both inflation and income taxes, most investors in high-grade, short-term securities are merely incurring a steadily increasing loss in purchasing power over time. While their savings may give the appearance of growth (particularly if income taxes are paid from other sources), in reality they are slowly losing the purchasing power of their savings to the ravages of inflation and taxes.

Viewed from this perspective, the higher yields associated with mortgage-backed securities become not a greedy or risky play for increased income, but a vitally necessary investment strategy, if we as investors are to at least maintain the value of our savings, and hopefully build real wealth. With mortgage securities we do usually have the earning power to pay taxes and keep up with inflation, and build real wealth, albeit at a slower rate than we would if it were not for inflation and taxes.

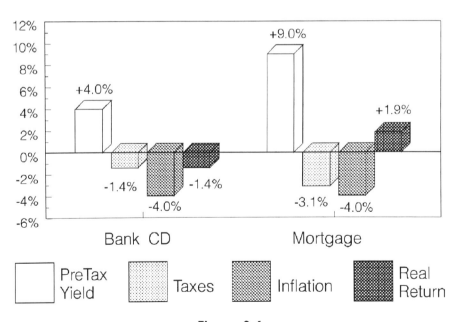

Figure 3.6
Real Returns After Inflation and Taxes

Special Tax Considerations

Tax rates are not the same for everyone, and many of us have different tax rates for different investments. If we are looking purely at current income from our investments, then any changes in tax rate are strictly proportional; that is, if our tax rate is one third lower than the next person's, then we just pay one third less in taxes on otherwise equal income. If however we are investing in mortgage securities as part of a wealth-accumulation strategy, then changes in tax rates have a disproportionate effect on the amount of wealth that we can accumulate. This difference in the amount of accumulated wealth is caused by the impact of taxes upon snowballing interest earnings, as we looked at earlier in this chapter. The impact of taxes upon snowballing varies widely, however, depending on the actual tax rate, as is shown in Figure 3.7.

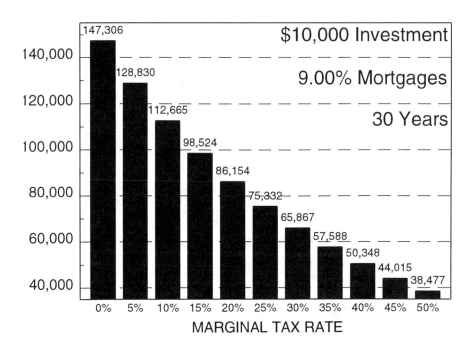

Figure 3.7
The Impact of Tax Rates upon Wealth Accumulation

Returning to our analogy of rolling down a hill, each time we lower our tax rate, we increase the steepness of the hill, and our accumulation of wealth increases much faster than our decrease in taxes. This means that the lower our tax rates are, the greater the advantage to us of investing in mortgage securities.

There are several interesting practical conclusions that can be drawn from this investment principle. The first has to do with the popular perception that the rich can earn more on their money than the middle-class, small investors. This is true, so long as the small investors are sticking to low-yield, high-safety investment strategies such as investing in short-term CDs and money-market funds. However, the small investor can turn this relationship on its head by following the lead of institutional investors and purchasing higher-yield, high-safety mortgage securities, particularly in low tax states. The Washington State farmer who is in a 25% federal tax bracket, can over 30 years outperform by 42% the New York City financier who is in a combined 38% bracket *by investing in identical securities.* The New Hampshire waitress in a 15% bracket who is investing her $10,000 inheritance can outperform by 96% the Los Angeles attorney who is paying a combined 40% in income taxes.

The Little Guy CAN Win

As impressive as the (percentage) wealth accumulation advantages are for small investors in low tax brackets, the most impressive performance by far is achieved through not paying a current income tax on our investments. If we can allow all of our interest earnings to compound first, and then tax them later, we can nearly triple our ending wealth relative to what we would accumulate if we had to subtract out 35% combined taxes on our earnings on an ongoing basis. Fortunately, there are literally tens of millions of us who do have the ability to do just that and compound our earnings on a tax-deferred basis through our tax-deferred retirement plans: IRAs, Keoghs and employer-sponsored, self-directed retirement plans.

Turning Hundreds into Millions

Mortgage securities are an excellent retirement wealth accumulation vehicle for the safety-conscious or prudent investor, and use of these securities within a retirement savings plan allows us to fully capitalize upon the most advantageous features associated with investing in mortgage securities. As an illustration of how well this can work, let us take a look at Table 3.2, which shows the wealth accumulation of a 25-year-old who puts $200 in his or her IRA each month for 40 years at a 9.00% rate, retires at 65, and then draws down that money each month for 20 years. Assuming that our investor deposits $200 each month, and invests at a 9.00% rate, we find the following:

Monthly savings	$200
Years of savings	40
Total savings payments	$96,000
Investment rate	9.00%
Wealth at retirement	$936,264
Years to drawdown	20
Monthly drawdown	$ 8,424
Annual drawdown	$101,086
Total retirement cash	$2,021,715

Savings of $200 a month toward retirement, if invested and reinvested at 9.00% for 40 years, is sufficient to pay out a little more than $2 million over a 20-year retirement period. In this example, we are getting $21 back in retirement income for every $1 saved. Not bad, but what about inflation and taxes?

Let us add two more assumptions to our example: constant 4% inflation and a 20% tax bracket upon retirement. Let us assume that our monthly savings payments increase at a 4% annual rate, that all our future drawdowns are taxed at the 20% rate we might expect a retiree to pay, and that we draw down our savings at an increasing rate when we retire so that we are living on level income, *after* inflation:

Surviving Inflation and Taxes

	Inflationary Dollars	Constant Dollars
Monthly savings	$200-$957	$200
Years we save	40	40
Total money we save	$232,213	$96,000
Investment rate	9.00%	9.00%
Wealth at retirement	$1,481,635	$308,608
Years of retirement	20 (41-60)	20 (41-60)
Monthly drawdown	$9,855-$21,524	$2,046
Total retirement cash	$3,585,783	$491,055
After-tax retirement cash	$2,868,627	$392,844

Surviving Inflation and Taxes 31

When we fully adjust for inflation, we find that our now-increased total of $3.6 million that we have for our retirement is worth "only" about $491,000 in today's dollars, after discounting for inflation. While this is a major reduction, it still represents a 5-to-1 increase over the $96,000 in inflation-adjusted dollars that we saved. We are able to turn our 40 years of inflation-adjusted $200 a month savings into 20 years of a $2,000 a month inflation-adjusted retirement (though we are actually drawing down $21,000 a month in future dollars 60 years from now in order to provide a current $2,000 a month living standard).

Taxes do reduce our income, but deferring taxes eliminates their negative impact on *snowballing* and allows us to accumulate several times more wealth than we would otherwise be able to. Even after the payment of taxes and a cumulative, long-term inflation that is powerful enough so that a future dollar is worth less than 10 of today's cents, we see that investing in mortgage securities under the assumptions shown can allow us to accumulate significant real wealth through tax-deferred savings plans, a 4-to-1 increase in the example shown. If we include the value of our current tax savings, then the likely reduction in tax rates that we will experience at retirement can boost our benefits even further. Assuming a current 35% combined tax rate, our $96,000 in inflation-adjusted savings only costs us $62,400 in after-tax dollars, compared to our $393,000 in after-tax retirement cash, this means that we have enjoyed a *real,* after-tax, after-inflation return of more than 6 to 1, while maintaining the safety of having our savings in government-guaranteed investments. With mortgage securities, we cannot only survive inflation and taxes, we can prosper.

The exact performance shown in the preceding examples is based upon all of the assumptions working exactly as shown. Change the assumptions, and the performance changes; it is highly unlikely that future performance will exactly follow any uniform set of assumptions, or that someone who invests their tax-deferred savings in mortgage securities for exactly 40 years will realize precisely a 6-to-1 increase in after-tax, after-inflation wealth. In practice we know that investment yields, inflation, and tax laws all change frequently over time, and are highly unpredictable over the long term.

What is important is the relationships that we have explored between yields of different investment types, inflation, and taxes. We do know that during the period from 1971 to 1991 inflation compounded at an average rate of 6.21% per year, and that 3-month Treasury bills averaged 7.53%. Anyone who was on average in a 18% or higher tax bracket and consistently invested in 3-month Treasury bills during those years would have had a negative real rate of return, after taking into account inflation and taxes. The unfortunate truth is that short-term, high-quality investments such as Treasury bills, money-market funds, and short-term CDs all often have negative after-tax real rates of return over long periods of time.

We do know that from 1971 to 1991 Freddie Mac mortgage purchase yields, net of servicing, on 30-year mortgages averaged 10.61%, or about 171% of the inflation rate during that period. Mortgage securities offer a slightly lower return than mortgages themselves, but we do know that based on past history it is reasonable to expect mortgage securities to exceed inflation on an after-tax basis, allowing us to safely build wealth in real terms.

We also know that the accumulation of wealth through monthly-pay, high-rate investments such as mortgage securities is acutely sensitive to tax rates. For this reason, mortgage securities perform particularly well when held by small investors who are in lower brackets, or when held within tax-deferred retirement savings plans. Within such plans, if the past is indicative of the future, we can build real wealth through investing in safe mortgage securities. Even if the past is not a particularly good predictor of the future, for the reasons we explore in depth in later chapters, mortgage securities do hold persuasive advantages over alternative high-quality investments for the long-term accumulation of real wealth.

4
The Many Benefits of Monthly Payments

*"I really don't feel like paying my mortgage this month.
I think I'll just skip it."*

What would be your reaction if a friend, your son, or your daughter-in-law made a statement like that? Would you be shocked that they could be so irresponsible? Would you be surprised that they would think they could get away with something like that? Would you feel an obligation to try to talk them out of doing something so stupid? One of the few certainties in life is that if there is any possible way of doing it, most people will make their mortgage payments each and every month.

The requirement to make monthly mortgage payments or face losing your home can be a terrible strain on the homeowner who is experiencing financial difficulties, but when you *reverse the mortgage* the strain turns into a wonderful advantage: we as mortgage investors are assured of getting our payments each and every month.

Reversing the Mortgage
Homeowners PAY each and every month
Investors ARE PAID each and every month

Are Monthly Payments a "Hassle"?

As homeowners and consumers we are all used to the monthly ritual of sitting down and writing out the bills, paying the monthly interest and a small principal payment toward our home mortgage, auto loan, and credit card. Common as this practice is for consumers, it differs substantially from "normal" practice for stocks and bonds, where dividends and interest are generally paid quarterly or semiannually, and principal is paid only at maturity. Some in the investment world who have grown accustomed to these traditional payment patterns for investments say that the monthly payments associated with mortgage-backed securities are a disadvantage for the investor. The argument has been advanced that monthly payments are an inconvenience because they may come in sooner than needed, and may require the investor to spend unnecessary time searching for a reinvestment for the "early" receipt of the money.

The real "problem" with monthly investment payments is not one of inconvenience however, but of unfamiliarity and change. A close look at the investment implications of monthly payments reveals that this perceived disadvantage is in fact a useful advantage to the investor, for monthly payments increase income and flexibility!

As every college finance student or investment professional knows, the sooner an investor receives any predetermined sum of money (interest payment), the better off that investor is.

To see why this is the case, and how the monthly-pay aspect of mortgage securities can benefit each of us personally, let us consider three example investments, each with a "simple" yield of 9.00%. Simple yield is annual interest payments compared to money invested, so if we had 9.00% simple yield on a $100,000 investment, we would be receiving $9,000 a year in interest payments from our investment. Three common ways in which we might be paid interest are: semiannually for most taxable or tax-exempt bonds; quarterly for stocks (actually dividends instead of interest); and monthly for mortgage-backed securities. The distribution of payments to us in the first six months of our investment are shown in Figure 4.1 for a 9.00% simple yield on our $100,000 investment under each of the payment frequencies discussed.

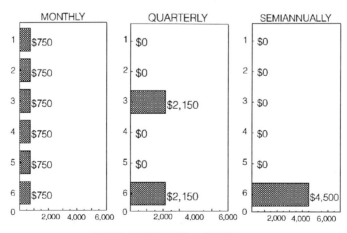

Figure 4.1

The Many Benefits of Monthly Payments

The first of our advantages is the flexibility to meet unexpected cash needs. What happens if our furnace suddenly needs to be replaced during our first or second investment month? Or if we lose our paycheck, or if one of our children has an urgent need for emergency cash? We have no extra cash available under the semiannual or quarterly payment alternatives, but we do have $750 to $1,500 available with the mortgage investment. What if we need money in Month 3, or Month 5? In each case, there is at least as much money available under the monthly-pay method as under the more conventional quarterly or semiannual payment alternatives, and we usually have more money available. The monthly payment method is clearly the most flexible of the three. To the extent that there is less likely to be a need to liquidate principal in order to meet unexpected cash requirements, the monthly payment method may also be the most convenient alternative of the three.

Another kind of flexibility has to do with our ability to adapt to an ever changing investment environment. Monthly receipts of cash allow the mortgage security investor to quickly adapt to changing market conditions, and to immediately reinvest interest payments as well as principal payments at the new rate level. The danger of being mismatched with the current market is called interest rate risk, and monthly payments gives us as mortgage investors on average a 1 1/2-month advantage over the quarterly-pay investor in reinvesting interim interest payments; on average we have a 3-month advantage over the semiannual pay investor. Interest rate risk can work for us or against us, what matters is whether we want to take on that uncertainty. With monthly-pay mortgage securities that uncertainty is reduced. As we will see in later chapters, monthly payments are one of the several reasons why mortgage securities hold far less interest rate and price risk than do other investments of equal maturity.

Monthly Payments Reduce Interest Rate Risk

Monthly interest payments not only give us greater flexibility and less interest rate risk, but they also can significantly increase the total income that we realize. Because we receive interest income earlier than with many alternative investments, we are able to earn additional interest income upon the interest already received. To see how this works, in Table 4.1 we will revisit our investment principles of *stretching* and *snowballing*.

Table 4.1
9.00% Interest Payments with 9.00% Compounding

	9.00% Semiannual (Bonds)	9.00% Monthly (Mortgages)
Month 1		
Security interest	$ 0	$ 750
Interest on interest	0	0
Month 2		
Security interest	0	750
Interest on interest	0	6
Month 3		
Security interest	0	750
Interest on interest	0	11
Month 4		
Security interest	0	750
Interest on interest	0	17
Month 5		
Security interest	0	750
Interest on interest	0	23
Month 6		
Security interest	4,500	750
Interest on interest	0	29
Months 1-6		
Security interest	4,500	4,500
Interest on interest	0	85
Total Interest Earnings	4,500	4,585
Year 1		
Security interest	9,000	9,000
Interest on interest	203	381
Total Interest Earnings	$9,203	$9,381

The Many Benefits of Monthly Payments 37

If we look at *stretching* only, which is our interest income from the security itself, then we have two different-looking interest streams that add up to the same thing. We receive one payment of $4,500 from the bond investment in the first six months, versus six $750 payment from the mortgage, which all add up to $4,500. The advantage to us of monthly payments is found in the entries labeled "interest on interest," which we have also been referring to as *snowballing*. Because we receive $750 with our mortgage investment five months before we receive any cash from the bond investment, we are able to reinvest that money. We earn an extra $5.63 in Month 2, an extra $11.29 in Month 3, and so forth, until we have accumulated an additional $85 by the end of the first six months, and an additional $178 by the end of the first year.

Professional investors are keenly aware of the importance of payment frequency, and because of the ability to earn additional interest income from monthly payments, they do not consider a 9.00% simple yield on mortgages to be at all the same as a 9.00% simple yield on bonds. Professional investors use a mathematical equation to convert mortgage interest rates to what is called a "corporate bond equivalent" yield (CBE yield). The use of CBE yields creates a level playing field, where investments with different payment frequencies can be compared fairly. Plugging the conversion formula into our example we find that a 9.00% mortgage yield is equivalent to a 9.17% bond yield.

Seventeen hundredths of one percent? Doesn't that seem like an awfully minor amount to be worried about? Perhaps it is, and for many investors the only appropriate conclusion may be that something is better than nothing, that monthly payment frequency provides that extra something and is an advantage, and leave it at that. The dollar difference, $178 (in the first year) on $100,000, is not overwhelming, however if our goal is accumulating wealth, or building toward retirement, we have already seen that small yield differences can *snowball* over time to become significant differences in ending wealth. This is also true of our yield enhancement from monthly payments, with the degree of enhancement depending upon on the amount of time that the *snowballing* has to work its magic within, as shown in Figure 4.2.

As can be seen in the right-hand column of Figure 4.2, our first year's $178 advantage has turned into over $1,000 within 5 years and almost $10,000 within 15 years, and we earn an extra $70,000 with monthly payments over a 30-year period (almost a quarter of a million over 40 years). Two factors are working together to cause this rapidly rising increase in profits: our total wealth is *snowballing* rapidly, and the yield enhancement of monthly payments is itself *snowballing* in importance relative to our stated security yield, driving our percentage profit increases resulting from monthly payments up from 1.9% in

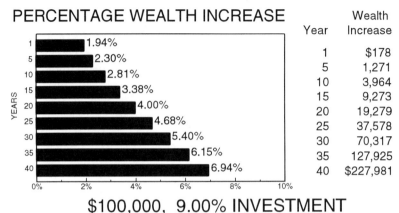

$100,000, 9.00% INVESTMENT
Figure 4.2
Monthly Pay Benefits

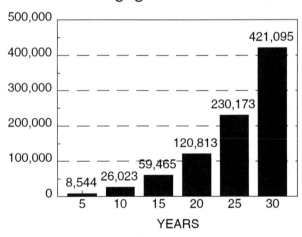

Figure 4.3
Wealth Advantage

the first year to 5.4% by the 30th year, as is shown in the graph at the left of Figure 4.2.

The advantages to building wealth with mortgage securities rather than bonds become even more obvious when we add in the yield differences between bonds and mortgage securities. An 8.00% bond may seem to be a reasonably close alternative to a 9.00% mortgage. Should we go to the trouble of learning

The Many Benefits of Monthly Payments 39

about mortgage-backed securities, or just leave these minor differences to the professionals? Our answer to that question can be found by comparing how we build wealth under two alternatives: purchasing $100,000 in 8.00% bonds and reinvesting semiannually in more 8.00% bonds, versus purchasing $100,000 in 9.00% mortgage securities and reinvesting monthly in more 9.00% mortgage securities (see Figure 4.3).

As we can see, a percent here, a few hundredths of a percent there, and all of a sudden we are talking about real money! Investing over time in order to accumulate wealth is very much about margins and fine-tuning, with tiny percentage differences in return potentially meaning the difference between a comfortable retirement and just getting by. The *snowballing* of monthly payments can help provide the necessary margin we need to achieve our financial goals, at the same time as they are increasing our cash flexibility and decreasing our interest rate risk.

5
The Five Layers of Safety

"My broker says this stock should double in less than a year!"

"Silver is at its lowest level in ten years, and through futures I can control $10,000 of silver with only $2,000 down!"

Do the above statements intrigue you? Or do they scare you? Why worry about a percent here and a half a percent there when we can double our money in the stock market? Or triple our money in real estate? Or quadruple our money with futures speculation?

No question about it, mortgage-backed securities are BORING compared with many investment alternatives. If what you are really looking for is exciting investment alternatives, put this book down and book a flight to Las Vegas, it will be cheaper and more entertaining than playing the futures market.

Stocks, real estate partnerships, and particularly futures and options speculation all carry the *possibility* of far higher returns than can be achieved through investing in mortgages. But they also all carry the possibility of a major or total loss on investment if they do not perform as hoped for. The limitations and advantages inherent in investing in mortgage-backed securities by *reversing the mortgage* can easily be seen:

Reversing the Mortgage
Homeowners contract to pay full principal
and interest, no more and no less.
Investors contract to *receive* full principal
and interest, no more and no less.

If you as a homeowner get a big raise at work, does your required monthly mortgage payment go up? If the value of property in your neighborhood rises, does your mortgage payment go up? If you lose your job and have to take a lower-paying position, or if the value of houses in your neighborhood declines, does your required monthly mortgage payment reduce?

The answer to all of the above questions is "of course not!" Yet these are exactly the kind of risks that we as investors take when we invest in stocks or real estate. The value of our investments and our earnings will rise and fall with company profits and real estate values, and will depend on the complex relationships between our investment, its competitors, its industry, and the state of the economy.

Mortgages are a contractual relationship. We as homeowners know that we have to make our monthly payment with no contingencies and no excuses. The only way we can avoid making our contractual mortgage payments without losing our home is to pay off our mortgage in full. In *reversing the mortgage,* we as investors know that we will receive our contractual mortgage payments in full for each mortgage underlying our mortgage-backed security until each mortgage has been paid in full. We are not completely insulated from all investment risks, but we are protected from most of the risks that we face with most other investments.

False Comfort

Mortgage-backed securities are certainly not the only *contractual* investments available that legally agree to pay back full principal and interest. Corporate bonds, municipal bonds, notes from general partners—all of these are contractual investments that often carry substantially higher yields than mortgage-backed securities. Many of these investments may even seem safer than mortgage-backed securities, representing obligations of major corporations or (supposedly) superwealthy individuals. You may often hear investors make statements like, "These partnership notes are guaranteed by a billionaire, why I saw his picture in *Time* magazine just last week" or "That company has stores all over the country, including one just down the street. I'm sure that they can pay their bonds back." But, as many unfortunate investors have found out in recent years, that is not the case. "Household name" tycoons and major corporations go bankrupt with surprising regularity.

The "safety" of billionaires—infamous insolvencies:
- Nelson Bunker Hunt
- William Herbert Hunt
- Alan Bond
- Robert Campeau
- Donald Trump
- Robert Maxwell (Estate)

The Five Layers of Safety

The "safety" of major corporations, insurers, and issuers:

- Washington Public Power Supply System ($2.25 billion in AAA-rated municipal bonds)
- Public Service Company of New Hampshire
- LTV
- Texaco
- Southland Corporation
- Manville Corporation
- Circle K Corporation
- Drexel Burnham
- Executive Life Insurance Company (AAA-rated GICs and municipal bonds)
- Mutual Benefit Life Insurance Co. (AAA-rated municipal bonds)
- Trans World Airlines
- Revco
- Olympia & York
- Eastern Airlines
- Greyhound
- Continental Airlines

Real Safety

In sharp contrast, as Table 5.1 shows, mortgage-backed securities have compiled a perfect safety record for investors.

(Please note that unless otherwise specified, whenever we use the words "mortgage-backed security" or "mortgage security," we are referring only to standard, fixed-rate, 30-year Ginnie Mae Mortgage-Backed Securities (MBSs), Freddie Mac Participation Certificates (PCs), and Fannie Mae Mortgage-Backed Securities (MBSs). These are the most common of the mortgage securities, are generally the easiest to understand, and are especially suitable for nonprofessional investors. There are, however, numerous other kinds of mortgage securities available, with a wide range of investment characteristics and risk profiles. Before purchasing any mortgage securities, please read Chapter 17, and make sure that what you are buying is indeed what you believe it to be.)

Table 5.1
Mortgage Security Default History

	Total Issued	Defaults
Ginnie Mae MBSs	$700+ billion	$0
Freddie Mac PCs	$600+ billion	$0
Fannie Mae MBSs	$600+ billion	$0
Totals	**$1.9+ trillion**	**$0**

The Five Layers of Safety

To understand better why mortgages are such a safe investment for us, we need to *reverse the mortgage* and examine the many levels of protection that we as mortgage-backed security investors enjoy. The first level of protection we benefit from is creditworthy borrowers.

As all of us who have gone through the process of purchasing a home know only too well, not just anyone can get a mortgage. Regardless of whether the lender is a bank, a savings and loan, or a mortgage banker, the hopeful borrower is going to have to *prove:*

- Adequate income to pay both the mortgage and other normal costs of living.
- A good to excellent credit history of paying other bills on time.

Anyone shopping around for a mortgage quickly discovers there is often a surprising level of uniformity in the underwriting standards that various lenders utilize in making their mortgage-lending decisions, at least in comparison to the wide range of lending philosophies evident in credit-card lending, auto lending, business lending, and other types of loans. The reason for this uniformity is that most mortgage lenders currently make mortgage loans on the basis of being able to later turn those loans into mortgage-backed securities. In order to convert a mortgage loan to a mortgage-backed security, the loan must meet an exacting set of underwriting standards that have been proven over the decades to minimize credit losses. When we *reverse the mortgage,* the rigorous criteria that each mortgage borrower must meet in order to get their loan ensures that we as mortgage investors are investing only in loans to borrowers who have been thoroughly screened, and who long standing credit tests based on decades of experience with millions of borrowers have shown are likely to be excellent credit risks.

Reversing the Mortgage
Protective Layer 1: Creditworthy Borrowers

The prospective homeowner must have a good income and good credit, so the mortgage investor is secured by good income and good credit.

The second fundamental level of protection that we enjoy as mortgage investors is that even if all the credit checks and income verifications fail, the mortgage is secured by a property worth more than the loan itself.

Many couples have scrimped and saved for years in order to come up with a large enough down payment to be able to purchase their first home. Many other couples have sweated out the arrival of the all-important appraisal report

The Five Layers of Safety

prior to being able to close on their intended home, waiting for an independent professional to confirm that their purchase is indeed more valuable than the loan being made. When we *reverse the mortgage*, we as investors are assured that the homeowners have the extra motivation that providing a substantial cash down payment gives a borrower, in addition to the protection we receive from being secured by a property worth more than the mortgage itself.

Reversing the Mortgage
Protective Layer 2: More Valuable Property

The homeowner must use a cash down payment to purchase a home more valuable than the mortgage, and the investor is secured by a home that is more valuable than the mortgage.

The third level of protection that shields us from risk is that of insurance: mortgage insurance, title insurance, and property insurance. Some form of mortgage insurance must generally be purchased by the home buyers unless they are contributing at least a 20% cash down payment ($20,000 cash on a $100,000 home). Those home purchasers who qualify often use the relatively low-cost government insurance offered through the FHA (Federal Housing Administration) and the VA (Veterans Administration). Under these programs the federal government guarantees that they will repay the mortgage *investor* (not the homeowner) almost all of remaining balance of the mortgage and the associated interest, should the homeowner default. If the homeowner or mortgage does not qualify for FHA or VA insurance, then more-expensive private mortgage insurance (PMI) must be purchased.

Mortgage Insurance Is Paid for by the Homeowner, and Benefits the Investor

A closing cost that all mortgage borrowers are familiar with is title insurance. The prospective homeowner must pay for a title search to be done, and then for an insurance policy to be issued, before the mortgage loan is made. While the homeowner does benefit from this policy, the primary purpose of the policy and the reason for its mandatory nature is to ensure that the mortgage *investor* will have good title to the home should they need to foreclose upon it.

Title Insurance Is Paid for by the Homeowner, and Benefits the Investor

Another familiar expense to the homeowner is that of homeowner insurance. While the homeowner insurance is in the name of the homeowner, does benefit the homeowner, and is paid for by the homeowner, it must be noted that the *primary* beneficiary on a homeowner policy is always the mortgage lender. In the event of a fire or other catastrophe that results in a total loss, the homeowner does not receive *one penny* until the mortgage lender has been *paid in full*.

Property Insurance Is Paid for by the Homeowner, and Benefits the Investor

In summary then, you as a home purchaser must obtain and pay for multiple levels of insurance protection before you can get a home mortgage, even though you are not the main beneficiary of such policies. *When we reverse* the mortgage, we as mortgage investors are protected by multiple layers of insurance, though we have not paid for any such policies.

Reversing the Mortgage
Protective Layer 3: Layers of Insurance

The homeowner must *pay for* mortgage insurance, title insurance, and property insurance.

The mortgage investor is *protected by* mortgage insurance, title insurance, and property insurance.

Where are the mortgages that make up mortgage-backed securities located?
 (a) Anchorage, Alaska
 (b) Miami, Florida
 (c) Bangor, Maine
 (d) San Diego, California
 (e) All of the above

Who owes the money on these mortgages?
 (a) Doctors
 (b) Steel workers
 (c) Bankers
 (d) Truck drivers
 (e) All of the above

The answer to each of these questions is of course "(e) all of the above." This is our fourth level of protection as mortgage-backed securities investors, that of national diversification. From coast to coast most homes in every town in the United States are financed through mortgages. Owing money on a mortgage is as American as apple pie, and is exceedingly common among the middle-aged, middle class who make up most of our country.

When we *reverse the mortgage,* this means that our mortgage investments are secured not by any single home, individual, or corporation, but by the

The Five Layers of Safety 47

American economy as a whole, indeed, the strongest portion of that economy. Persons from every segment of the country borrow money to purchase homes. The jobs they hold are in every segment of the overall economy, and collectively we are secured by this economy.

Reversing the Mortgage
Protective Layer 4: National Diversification

> Mortgage BORROWERS hold jobs in every industry in every city in every state—they ARE the economy.
>
> Mortgage INVESTORS are secured by every industry in every city in every state—we are secured by the American economy itself.

With the bleak assessments that we are always hearing in the media about the economy and its future, some might question whether being secured by the economy is desirable. What if there is a recession? What if there is another oil embargo? What about the budget deficit and the trade deficit?

Not to worry. Mortgage-backed securities have been around since 1970, have weathered multiple recessions, have withstood the oil embargo, deficit crises, the real estate crises in Texas, Louisiana, and Oklahoma, and have never defaulted on a single security. Numerous investment fads have come and gone and over the past 22 years, and no agency (Ginnie Mae, Freddie Mac, or Fannie Mae) mortgage-backed security has ever defaulted. The combination of national diversification and the first three levels of protection make these securities among the very safest of investments, safer than any one company, or industry, or even any one state government.

Ultimate Safety

The truly pessimistic investor might ask what would happen if:

- The homeowners lose their jobs and can't make their payments (negating protection level #1).
- The local housing market crashes and the houses can't be sold (negating protection level #2).
- The mortgage insurance companies all go bankrupt (negating protection level #3).
- The same things happen in every town across the country (negating protection level #4).

In such an environment, almost any other investment is likely already to have sustained major losses or defaulted. Widespread major unemployment would likely be the result of huge corporate losses and bankruptcies, which would have decimated the stock market. The crash in housing values would have devastated real estate investments. Nationwide economic catastrophe would force many municipal bonds into default. Yet, even under this economic doomsday scenario, mortgage-backed securities would still be paying full principal and interest because of their fifth protection level: federal government sponsorship and guarantees. Ginnie Mae (GNMA) is a federal agency whose obligations are directly guaranteed by the U.S. Treasury. Freddie Mac (FHLMC) and Fannie Mae (FNMA) are quasi-governmental agencies whose obligations are considered implicitly guaranteed by the Treasury.

Reversing the Mortgage Protective Layer 5: Government Guarantees

Congress created all three agencies (see the Chapter 7 for more information on these agencies) for the specific purpose of providing federal guarantees to mortgage investors. The intent of the guarantees is to bring more investors into the mortgage market, and thereby lower mortgage rates for borrowers. These programs have been an outstanding success. The federal guarantees have kept a steady supply of money for mortgages at reasonable interest rates flowing into our housing system, regardless of investment cycles and current economic conditions. We as investors directly benefit from the unparalleled protection of the five layers of mortgage-backed securities protection. These protections, in combination with the yield advantages discussed earlier, are what give mortgage-backed securities their unique place in the investment world: the highest-yielding portion of the safest family of investments.

(If we want to be even more pessimistic, a theoretical case can be made that Ginnie Mae mortgage securities are of higher credit quality than U.S. Treasury bonds. Given the continued growth of the national deficit and the growing burden of interest payments on that debt, the unlikely chance that the federal government might renounce its debts at some time in the future cannot be entirely discounted. If such a doomsday scenario were to occur, Ginnie Maes would only have lost their guarantor, but not the mortgage pools that are the source of their payments. Treasury bonds would have lost both their guarantee and source of repayment.)

6
Comparing Stocks to Ginnies and Fannies

Comparing shares of common stock to mortgage-backed securities is not like comparing apples to oranges; the differences between the two types of securities are so great that apples to ice cream or oranges to meatloaf would be more apt comparisons.

Common Stock

Shares of common stock are ownership interests in corporations, and as shareholders in a company we are exposed to all of the uncertainty faced by that company. This uncertainty can be either good or bad. The corporation's new and improved widget could revolutionize the market, and double or triple the value of our investment in a few months. The corporation could land a fat new long-term contract, leading analysts to increase their earnings and growth estimates, and the price of the stock could double in a few weeks. The company could enjoy a long, sustained growth in market share and profitability that leads to a quadrupling in share price within just a few years. The stock market as a whole could enjoy a major rally, or enter a new phase of a bull market, and our stocks could get pulled up 15%, 20%, even 30% in price in less than a year (such as in the rallies of 1935, 1975, 1982, 1985, and 1991). Common-stock investments can earn large profits very quickly

All of those very good things could indeed happen when we purchase shares of stock. Unfortunately, just as many and more bad things could happen to us as well. The company's new and improved widget could prove uninspiring or even defective, causing share prices to plummet. Negotiations with the unions over a new contract could collapse into a bitter battle that ultimately forces the company into bankruptcy and makes our shares worthless. A product produced decades ago could turn out to be dangerous, and a class-action lawsuit could wipe out the company. Or, a downward run in the market could turn into a rout, and we could lose 20%, 30%, even 40% of our investment value in a few hours to a year, as happened in 1903, 1907, 1917, 1920, 1929-31, 1937-38, 1939- 40, 1946-47, 1961-62, 1966, 1969-70, 1973-74, and 1987. Common-stock investments can incur devastating losses very quickly.

Mortgage-Backed Securities

Mortgage securities have contractual payments and offer predictable responses to unpredictable markets. With mortgage-backed securities, we know exactly how much principal will be paid back to us, and we know exactly what interest rate we will earn on that principal until it is paid back. We do not know which direction interest rates will go, but we know if market rates *rise* a certain amount, then the value of our investment will *fall* by a reasonably certain amount; and we know that if market rates *fall* by a certain amount then the value of our investment will *rise* by a reasonably certain amount. We don't know exactly when prepayments will return our principal to us, but we have a pretty good idea. We also know that these prepayments will almost certainly *rise* when market rates *fall*, and almost certainly *fall* when market rates *rise*.

In contrast, the nature of performance for individual shares of common stock is such that even professional investors have no certainty about what is going to happen. Part-time investors who have not studied investment finance may have no idea what is likely to happen. We have an idea of how we expect the stock to perform and why we bought it, and we now have an ownership interest in the company, and that is the end of our certainty. The number of things that can go better or worse than we expected is truly almost infinite, and to accurately approximate the amount of money that we will earn is nearly impossible. There is no principal amount that will be paid back; what we can sell our stock for in the future is totally dependent on future company performance and market conditions. While our stock is more likely than not to move with the overall market, it may also be down in an up market, or up in a down market. Even our dividends are far from assured, they can be increased, decreased or suspended, by the company's board of directors at any time. Individual common stocks pay unpredictable amounts and offer unpredictable responses to unpredictable markets.

Stocks do not so much face *different* risks than do bonds and mortgage securities; what they face are *additional* risks. Fundamentally, the same kinds of equations[1] drive stock valuation as bond or mortgage valuation: determining the value today of future expected cash payments, after adjusting for risk. As stocks pay dividends but not principal, their reaction to interest changes is like the very longest term bonds[2] with much larger price swings than mortgage securities for a given change in interest rates. There are, however, so many other factors affecting stock prices that their reaction to interest changes can be obscured by numerous other factors, such as changes in earnings growth estimates.

Clearly the risk and return characteristics of common stocks and mortgage securities are entirely different. The purchase of the shares of any individual company is always an investment with no guarantees; yet most knowledgeable financial planners routinely recommend the purchase of common stocks as the most suitable long-term investment strategy for individual investors. Why is this so, and is there even any need for us to consider a long-term investment strategy other than stocks?

Long-Term Historical Performance of Stocks

A number of well known studies by various researchers have shown that investing in the stock market has historically been an outstanding investment strategy over the very long term. Roger Ibbotson & Laurence Siegel[3] calculated that $1 invested in common stocks in 1925 would have grown to $21.77 by the end of 1988, and that if we reinvested dividend income as received over that time period, then our total would be $406.46. This return over 63 years is equal

---

1 Both dividend valuation (stock) and bond valuation models calculate value through discounting future expected cash flows. Dividend valuation models also incorporate a growth component, which can offset changes in the interest rate component; however, if there is no change in the growth or cash components, then a given change in discount rates will trigger a larger stock price change than bond price change.

2 The lack of maturity means that stocks are technically valued as perpetuities, with an infinite future revenue stream.

3 "Stocks, Bonds, Bills, and Inflation: 1989 Yearbook," by Ibbotson Associates, Inc. from *The 1990 Dow Jones-Irwin Business and Investment Almanac.* Chicago, 1989, pp. 266-267.

to a 10.0% annual rate of return,[4] an extraordinary rate of return over that long of an investment horizon.

When compared to the compounded returns of long-term bonds, short-term bonds, and inflation, then the historical yield advantages of common stock become even more apparent (see Figure 6.1).

As we discussed in earlier chapters, Treasury bills and short-term bank CDs generally do little better than inflation over time, on an after-tax basis such investments often end up with negative real rate of return, even though every penny of principal and interest is paid. Long-term treasury bonds do better, yet as we see in Figure 6.1, their performance pales in comparison to common stock.

It is this type of study that accounts for the common opinion among many financial planners and experts that common stocks are the premier investment of choice for long-term savings, representing the best way to beat inflation and taxes. Indeed, it is not unusual to see this opinion phrased as a statement of fact rather than as a probability or likelihood, though written advertising will almost always contain a disclaimer that future results will not necessarily equal past results.

There are strong reasons why common stocks should outperform bonds, certificates of deposit, mortgage securities, and other "safe" investments that guarantee the return of full principal and interest to the investor. Stock ownership gives investors the ability to own their share of the private enterprise component of our economy. This direct participation gives the investor a way to benefit from the sustained real growth of our economy, and to profit from the earnings of our nation's corporations, earnings that generally have a far greater ability to withstand the damaging effects of inflation.

"Stocks are ownership interests in the economy."

The difficult question to answer about stocks, however, is whether stocks will perform as well in the future as they have performed in the past. We would be foolish to invest in anything else if we could be certain that stocks will also be the best long-term investment in the future. Should we be looking

---

[4] This and all other long-term growth and return averages in this chapter are based upon internal rate of return calculations of the necessary annual yield for the beginning value to compound to the ending value. These yields may vary substantially from a simple average of annual historical yields.

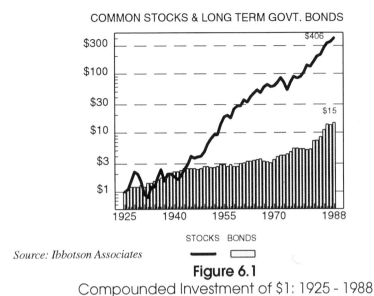

Source: Ibbotson Associates

Figure 6.1
Compounded Investment of $1: 1925 - 1988

for alternatives such as mortgage securities for long-term investing, or should we consider only stocks? In answering this question, let us first take a closer look at the past.

An Erratic History

Figure 6.2 tracks the annual closes of the Dow Jones Industrial Average (DJIA) from 1900 to 1990.[5] Two conclusions about the long-term behavior of the DJIA are immediately apparent from an examination of the chart:

1. The long-term trend of the market is clearly upward, as the Dow Jones climbs from 50 in 1900 to 2634 at the end of 1990, an increase of 52 times the original index.

2. The climb of the market has not been a smooth rise, but a jagged series of sharp increases followed by plunging declines.

---

[5] The DJIA consisted of 12 stocks prior to 1914, changed to 20 stocks in 1914, and changed again to the present 30 stocks in 1928. The calculated index itself changed as well in 1914, and pre-1914 closes have been multiplied by 71.15% in order to compensate. The individual stocks that comprise this average have also changed numerous times over this period.

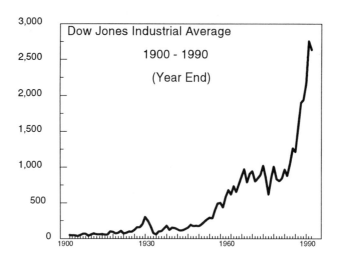

Figure 6.2
Dow Jones Industrial Average 1900 - 1990

The erratic progress of the DJIA, even over the long term, can be illustrated by looking at two 50-year investment periods that began only 9 years apart:

A Comparison Of 50-Year DJIA Returns

Period	DJIA Begin	DJIA End	Growth Rate	Total Growth
1928-1978	300	805	1.99%	168%
1937-1987	121	1939	5.71%	1504%

Clearly, much depends on whether we begin our comparison period in a bull market and end it in a bear market, as we do in the 1928-1978 example, or whether we begin in a bear market and end in a bull market as we do in the 1937-1987 example. Another problem with long-term studies is that most people do not invest in the market for 50, 60 or 90 years at a time; instead, their long-term savings are often invested for 10, 20, or 30 years.

One way to deal with these problems of bias in selecting starting and ending years, as well to analyze different possible 10- to 30-year investment results over a much longer period of time, is to consider *all* the possibilities. Some investors begin and other investors end investment programs in every year, so to account for the wide range of individual performances, we must consider a wide range of beginning and ending dates. Searching out all of the possible 10- to 30-year investment periods that have occurred between

Table 6.1
10- To 30-Year DJIA Growth Rates (Price Changes Only)

	Number of Incidences	Percent of Total
Negative growth rate	111	7.4%
Growth rate less than 1.0%	197	13.2%
Growth rate less than 2.0%	346	23.2%
Growth rate less than 3.0%	528	35.4%
Growth rate less than 4.1%	745	50.0%
Growth rate 6.0% or higher	465	31.2%
Growth rate 10.0% or higher	67	4.5%
Total investment periods analyzed		**1491**

1900 and 1990, we find that there were 1,491 possible long-term investment periods, over which investors could have realized 1,491 different investment portfolio returns (see Table 6.1).[6]

Table 6.1 demonstrates that while over the last 90 years it has been likely that most investors achieved positive long-term price gains from their stock investments, such price gains were not at all certain, and achieving substantially positive price gains was even less certain. True, 93% of the time if we held stocks for between 10 and 30 years, then the value of our stocks on average increased, yet this statistical likelihood may have been small consolation for the 7% who experienced long-term price losses.

About one-eighth of the time, investors received less than a 1% long-term annual return from price gains on their investments, and they realized less than a 2% growth rate almost one-fourth of the time. Investors received less than a 4.1% long-term annual return from price gains half the time, and a greater than 4.1% return the other half of the time. The chances of sustaining a 6% or greater annual growth rate over the long term were less than 1 out of 3. Historically

---

[6] This chart was calculated by taking the annual close of the Dow Jones Industrial Average for each year between 1900 and 1990, finding every possible combination of beginning and ending closing averages that are 10 or more years apart but no further than 30 years apart, and then calculating an annual internal rate of return such that the present value of the ending year close is equal to the starting year. By way of example, 1900 to 1910 would be a unique investment period, as would 1900 to 1911, 1960 to 1990, and 1980 to 1990; there are a total of 1,491 possible different 10- to 30-year investment periods between 1900 and 1990.

investors were 64% more likely (7.4% versus 4.5%) to achieve a long-term negative rate of return based on price changes than they were to realize a 10% or greater growth rate:

> ***The DJIA: 10- to 30-Year Investment Periods***
> Chances of negative growth rate   7.4%
> Chances of 10% or higher growth rate   4.5%

The record clearly establishes that while long-term stock price changes have historically been predominantly positive, they have been anything but certain or consistent. This is particularly true if we look at individual portfolios rather than market averages such as the DJIA. If the past is inconsistent over the long term, then how can we be certain about the future, even *if* the past is an accurate guide to the future?

Shrinking Dividends

The above analysis of historical growth trends in the Dow Jones Industrial Average may seem at odds with the graph that we saw in Figure 6.1 of the long-term study performed by Ibbotson & Siegel, where $1 grew to $406 over a 63-year period, realizing a 10.0% annual rate of return. This appears inconsistent with what we just saw, where a 10.0% or greater growth rate was observed less than 5% of the time. Part of the difference lies in the indexes observed (DJIA versus the S&P 500), and part lies in the years observed (1900 to 1990 versus 1925 to 1988), but most of the difference lies in what we were observing: price changes versus price changes, dividends, and dividend reinvestment.

If we look solely at price changes, then the $21.77 that Ibbotson & Siegel calculate as a 63-year return is the result of a 5.0% compounded rate of return, slightly greater than the 4.1% median from our multiple investment period analysis, but certainly within a reasonable range. The difference between the $21.77 ending value and the $406 ending wealth is all the result of adding dividends and reinvested dividends:

> **Compounded Value of $1.00 from 1925 to 1988**
> Stock price gains only $ 21.77
> Price gains and reinvested dividends $406.46
> **Ending wealth resulting from dividends**   **95%**

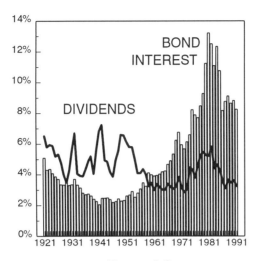

Figure 6.3
Historical Stock and Bond Yields

Without dividends our ending wealth would be reduced by 95% over the 63-year period studied by Ibbotson & Siegel.[7] While historical stock dividend yields are not as popular an item to track and graph as stock price changes, clearly they have great importance in determining ending investment results. Figure 6.3 shows how dividend yields have changed over time.

One of the many problems associated with using long-term past market projections to predict future market performance is readily apparent in the graph in Figure 6.3. The relationship between dividends and bond yields reversed in 1959, and this reversal has been greatly magnified during the decade prior to 1990. Common stock dividends historically provided substantially higher yields than bond interest payments, indeed during the critical two decades from 1930 to 1950, average dividend yields of 5.14% were almost twice the 2.62% average of bond yields (see Figure 6.4).

It was the compounding of these (relatively) high current cash payments that provided much of the necessary fuel that allowed stocks to so drastically outperform bonds. Fully half the advantage enjoyed by stocks over bonds during the entire period from 1925 to 1988 resulted from the yield differential enjoyed

---

7   This is not the same thing as saying that dividends contributed 20 times as much wealth as price gains, but rather that the compounding (snowballing) of wealth over 63 years is 20 times greater with two 5% yields (5% from price appreciation and 5% from dividend yields) combining to form a 10% yield, rather than one 5% yield compounding by itself.

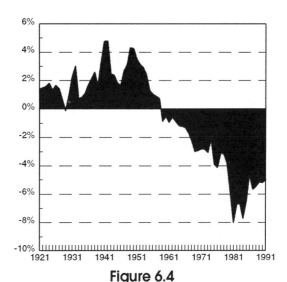

Figure 6.4
Stock Dividend Yield Advantage Versus Long-Term Govt. Bonds

by dividends prior to 1959 (generating a long-term stock index investment and dividend reinvestment model, with the substitution of historical bond yields for dividend yields prior to 1959, showed a 50% reduction in ending wealth compared with no substitution).

There are compelling reasons to study past markets, and compounded 4%, 5%, and 6% dividend yields were indeed an extraordinary wealth-creating mechanism during the long-ago days when long-term Treasury bonds yielded only 2% and 3%. Even without the benefits of high dividends, stock investments have outperformed bonds by a wide margin during most of the first 90 years of this century.

However, recent years have shown an entirely different relationship between stock dividend and bond interest yields: since 1980 long-term bond yields have continuously been at least 2 times as high as dividend yields—often 2.5 times as high. Indeed, with dividend yields at a historical low by the third quarter of 1992, we find that the sum of current dividend yields and long-term stock appreciation averages of 4% to 5% is now *lower* than the yield on mortgage securities or long-term Treasury bonds; implying that unless dividend yields rise or stocks appreciate at a higher than historical rate, they will be outperformed by the interest yields alone on bonds or mortgage securities. At the least, the use of decades-old dividend/bond relationships, whether from the 1930s or the 1960s, to predict investment results for the future makes little sense under modern market conditions.

Comparing Stocks to Ginnies and Fannies 59

The Problem with History

Can you imagine steering your car exclusively by watching your rear-view mirror?

- Avoiding the tree behind us, we run over the shrub in front of us.
- Swerving to avoid that shrub we just ran over, we now clip the side of a boulder.
- Pulling away from the side of the boulder behind us, we find ourselves on a long, flat, straight road.
- Pressing down on the gas pedal to take advantage of the great road, we sail off into space over the edge of a cliff.

The problem with basing our investment plans on historical performance is that we are using our rear-view mirror to steer our investments forward into an uncertain future. This is just as hazardous for our financial health as steering our car that way would be to our physical health.

Oil and gold were the keys to wealth in the 1970s, but a changing world left them far behind in the 1980s. Junk bonds and commercial real estate were two miracle investments through much of the 1980s, but both had gone bust by 1990. With perfect hindsight we know that stocks have been the investment of choice for six out of the first nine decades of the twentieth century, but this is no guarantee of success for the last decade of the century, or assurance that stocks will again be the secret to building wealth in the twenty-first century.

This is particularly true when we consider the real nature of the stock market. Despite all the numbers, graphs, and equations we use in attempting to decipher the market, the essence of the market is not the study of numbers in and of themselves. The U.S. stock market reflects the financial health and future prospects of the medium-sized and large companies in the United States, which are of course heavily influenced by the health and circumstances of the overall U.S. and world economies.

> "Stock performance comes from the economy, not numerology."

What our historical review of the market shows us is not that if we purchase stocks and hold on to them for at least 20 years we will achieve a 10% return. Rather it shows us that a nation that shifts from an agrarian to an industrial economy while winning two hot world wars and a cold one will have a healthy stock market. Our review of long-term investment periods did not guarantee us a 93% chance of rising stock prices if we hold on to our stocks for between 10 and 30 years. Instead, we learned that if we had invested long-term in an economy that was in transition from horses and buggies to space shuttles, from slide rules to laptop computers, and from telegraphs to satellites, then we would have made money from rising prices 9 times out of 10.

There will likely be numerous important changes in the coming decades that profoundly affect the risks and returns of our investment portfolios, including changing tax and business laws, evolving technologies that will change our lives in unimagined ways, and a radically different world market than has ever existed before. While we don't know what these changes will be or what the next 10, 20, or 90 years holds for us and the economy, there is one thing we can be certain of: we won't be repeating the last 90 years.

In summary then, our brief look back at some of the details underlying the extraordinary performance of the market over much of the past century has shown us that long-term stock gains and losses are erratic

Unquestionably, the predominate trend in the markets over the long term has been strongly positive. However, this is *not* the same thing as saying that so long as we are investing long-term, then increases in the market will always have earned us a large profit when we need our money, though the price record is often implicitly interpreted that way. A detailed historical look reveals that if we consider a long-term investment period to be between 10 and 30 years, then *negative long-term growth rates* have characterized 7.4% of the possible investment periods from 1900 to 1990; and there was a less than 2% annual growth rate almost 25% of the time. Far from being uniform, long-term stock price performance results have been highly erratic, with wide variations based upon differing purchase and sale dates. Relying on primarily positive trends is fine, unless of course it happens to be *your* retirement savings that are unfortunate enough to be invested in the market during a negative or low growth period.

High Dividends Are Both Crucial and Long-Gone

Looking at the impressive 406 to 1 total return that could have been achieved by purchasing a market portfolio in 1925 and selling it in 1988, we find that 95% of this ending wealth is based upon dividends and reinvested dividends. We also find that between 1930 and 1950, stock dividend yields averaged approximately twice the rate paid by Treasury bonds, that long-term bond yields did not exceed average dividend yields until 1959, and that the two yield types remained reasonably close throughout the 1960s.

Comparing Stocks to Ginnies and Fannies

Given the paramount importance of reinvested dividends and interest payments in determining ending wealth, and given that modern dividend levels are consistently between one third and one half of long-term bond interest levels, it is patently absurd to use reinvested dividend models that incorporate data from prior to the 1970s in order to judge the likely future performance of stock portfolios versus bonds or mortgage securities.

Leaving aside all the numbers, the trends, and the growth rates, the only performance characteristics of the stock market that we know with certainty are those of the past. We know that the economy and corporate performances in the years 2000, 2010, and 2020 are going to be quite different from how they were in 1930, 1960, or 1990. What we must be careful not to do is to blindly steer our investment portfolio toward the best investments of 1930, 1960, and 1990 without considering how different the road is that the current economy and stock market are traveling.

The stock market may do much worse in the future, or it may perform much better. Well-thought-out and reasoned guesses can be made, but such guesses carry no certainty. This takes us back to the heart of the difference between investing in stocks and investing in mortgage securities.

Certainty versus Uncertainty

- Will the purchase of an individual stock double your money or lose it all? *Nobody* knows.
- Will stocks outperform mortgage securities over the coming decades, or will mortgage securities outperform stocks? Again, *nobody* knows.
- Will you get your money back, and high interest too? With mortgage securities, *you know.*

7
Meet Our Helpers

If a corporate president decides to do a leveraged buyout of the shareholders and our high-grade corporate bonds turn into "junk" bonds overnight, what do we do?

If we own a municipal bond issued to finance a nursing home, and the nursing home stops making interest payments, what can we do?

If a corporate chairman decides to reward himself with a $100 million stock option plan for his performance in losing market share and cutting the value of our stock in half, what are we going to do?

When we invest in most types of securities, we are generally on our own. SEC regulation, accountant's audits, and brokerage due diligence are all intended to help investors. However once the securities have been issued, the SEC generally only gets involved with securities *fraud*. Brokers and accountants are hired and paid by the corporation that issued the stock or bonds. They do not stand between the corporate issuer and the investor, and in the event of trouble they tend to run for the sidelines as fast as possible, leaving investors to fend for themselves. Even huge institutional investors such as insurance companies and major pension funds have difficulty defending their interests as shareholders or bondholders against corporate managers who are pursuing their own selfish agendas, despite the institutional investors having financial and legal resources equal to or exceeding those of the corporation. Individual investors can all too easily find themselves in a one-sided David versus Goliath confrontation against corporate management, with the Davids only rarely winning the battle.

When we invest in mortgage-backed securities, however, our playing field is entirely different. As mortgage securities investors we always have at least two layers of professional intermediaries standing between us and the ultimate borrower (the homeowner): the originator/servicer and the guarantor. These entities, whom we will look at in this chapter, are generally large financial and governmental institutions that are contractually bound to look out for our interests on an ongoing basis. In the case of mortgage-backed securities, the Goliaths work for us!

We have expert underwriters performing all the checks necessary to ensure that good-quality mortgages underlie our investment. We have a seller who warrants that the underwriting was done correctly, and who agrees to repurchase the mortgages if it was not. We have a servicer to act in our behalf and process mortgage payments, to collect monies when homeowners are late with their payments, and to foreclose upon the homes if necessary to regain our investment. We have a government-chartered agency overseeing each of these services for our benefit, which will aggressively act on our behalf as necessary, and which guarantees that we will be paid our principal and interest in full regardless of whether the money can be collected from the underlying mortgages. Who are these helpers of ours?

The Originators

When we think of mortgages, we usually think of the companies who extend mortgage loans to homeowners, the lenders. These lenders can be banks, savings and loans, mortgage companies, or other financial concerns. As employees of mortgage lenders are the only mortgage "people" that homeowners usually meet or communicate with, and as the mortgage lender actually provides the money to the homeowner, many people think that their mortgages begin and end with these financial institutions. Years ago this was usually the case. Today your mortgage lender has often sold your loan before you ever close on your house, and may never have any intention of collecting the first payment. In our increasingly complex financial world, the former mortgage "lenders" are increasingly becoming mortgage *originators* instead. These banking and mortgage company originators perform the critical series of steps necessary to create (originate) a mortgage-backed security:

1. Find creditworthy mortgage borrowers.

2. Ensure that the first three layers of safety are firmly in place.

3. Close the mortgage loans and advance monies.

Meet Our Helpers 65

4. Warrant that steps 1 to 3 were performed correctly.
5. Deliver the loans to create the security.

The originating company works for our benefit as mortgage investors each step of the way. Through advertising and working with realtors, the originator finds prospective homeowners to whom we can lend money. The originator then goes through a rigorous multistep underwriting process to ensure that the first three levels of protection are all in place for us: good income and credit history, more-valuable property, and adequate insurance. The originating bank, thrift, or mortgage company closes the loan and advances the money to purchase the home. The originator then finds a guarantor agency (Ginnie Mae, Fannie Mae, or Freddie Mac) willing to securitize the loan, warrants to that agency that the loan has been properly created and all the necessary due diligence to verify the proper existence of the first three layers of safety was satisfactorily completed, and then delivers the loan so that the mortgage-backed security can be created for us to purchase.

Step 4, making warranties and representations that the loan was properly created with the necessary due diligence, may appear legalistic and obscure, yet it lies at the heart of a crucial distinction between the mortgage-backed security market and most other securities markets that works strongly to our advantage: mortgage originators guarantee their work. While these companies generally do not guarantee that the mortgage loans will pay properly, they do guarantee that if there is a flaw in the loan as a result of a warrantied underwriting mistake they made, they will buy the loan back or otherwise correct the problem. This simple-sounding step of making firm warranties, with contractual accountability to make good on mistakes, stands in marked contrast to the reaction of most stock or bond underwriters when a security they have sold turns out to have an unanticipated flaw.

In exchange for performing these services to facilitate our protection as mortgage investors, the originating bank, thrift, or mortgage company is paid by the homeowner. This payment can be direct in the form of "points" that are paid by the homeowner at closing, or it can be indirect in the form of creating a mortgage with a high enough interest rate that it can be sold at a price greater than the principal amount of the loan, with the originator keeping the difference.

The Servicers

"The check is in the mail, honest!"
—Everyman

The other type of organization that mortgage borrowers deal with directly is another helper of ours, the mortgage *servicer*. It is the servicer who works for us to gather, process, and then forward to us the mortgage payments each month so that we as mortgage investors are paid our contractual principal and interest. When homeowners are late with their mortgage payments, it is the servicer who mails out reminders on our behalf, then sterner reminders, and then makes firm telephone calls if necessary. If a homeowner is unable or unwilling to pay the mortgage, it is the servicer who goes through the foreclosure and sale process for the house so that we can get our money back. It is the servicer who ensures the house is kept insured and the taxes current, so that we do not lose the collateral securing our investments to fire or back taxes. The mortgage servicer:

1. Processes normal monthly payments.
2. Collects delinquent mortgage payments.
3. Forecloses upon defaulted mortgages.
4. Protects collateral (home) value.

The servicer used to generally be the originator as well, and it is still quite common for the originator to deliver the loan into a mortgage-backed security and retain the servicing "rights" to the loan, as such rights can be valuable in their own right. With increasing frequency, however, these servicing rights are also being packaged and sold separately from the loans.

The Agencies

Fannie Mae? Ginnie Mae? Freddie Mac? Weren't they characters in the "L'il Abner" comic strip?

These three friendly sounding names are the most common way in which people refer to the Federal National Mortgage Association, the Government National Mortgage Association, and the Federal Home Loan Mortgage Corporation (try saying those three or four times in a row and you will see why everyone uses the acronyms). Though perhaps not well-known, these government-sponsored "agencies" are three of the largest financial entities in the nation, and each was chartered by Congress for the purpose of helping to keep housing financing readily available and affordable for the public. Each agency accomplishes this goal by keeping we investors as happy as possible, so that we will keep investing money in mortgages.

The first agency to be established was the Federal National Mortgage Association (better known as Fannie Mae), which was chartered by an act of Congress in 1938 as a corporation wholly owned by the federal government. Fannie Mae was created in response to the financial turmoil of the 1930s, and the public mission with which Fannie Mae was charged was to help bring a steady supply of investor money into the mortgage marketplace so that mortgages would be available at reasonable cost to homeowners, regardless of where in the nation the homeowner might live.

In 1968, Congress split Fannie Mae into two parts, one portion of which stayed a wholly owned part of the U.S. government and was renamed the Government National Mortgage Association (Ginnie Mae), and the other part of which became a privately owned quasi-governmental corporation. Fannie Mae *is* privately owned now and its stock trades on the New York Stock Exchange. With total assets exceeding $155 billion, it is one of the largest corporations in the United States.

While private in some ways, Fannie Mae remained a government agency in a number of important ways. Five of Fannie Mae's eighteen directors are appointed by the President of the United States; the Department of Housing and Urban Development (HUD) and the Department of the Treasury each supervise Fannie Mae and exercise effective veto power over important decisions. The Treasury is authorized to spend up to $2.25 billion to support Fannie Mae through the purchase of Fannie Mae securities. The Federal Reserve is authorized to buy and sell Fannie Mae securities as a part of its implementation of monetary policy. Fannie Mae securities are generally given special treatment by financial regulators.

What this strange hybrid of private and public status (also referred to as "quasi-governmental") means for us as investors is that while Fannie Mae securities are not considered to be exactly identical to Treasury securities, they are so close that it barely matters, and Fannie Mae securities are therefore treated by the market as being of higher credit quality than the highest-quality state or municipal debt, corporate debt, or bank or insurance company guarantees. Technically, Fannie Mae securities are not guaranteed by the full faith and credit of the U.S. government, yet, due to Fannie Mae's government charter and regulation, the support of the Treasury, and most importantly because of the devastating impact upon the U.S. housing markets and economy that would be caused by a default, it is generally considered near unimaginable that the federal government would allow Fannie Mae to fail. Freddie Mac occupies a niche very similar to Fannie Mae's, as it also is a privately owned quasi-governmental agency. Because Ginnie Mae is a government agency, its securities *are* directly backed by the full faith and credit of the U.S. government.

In 1970, two changes took place in the mortgage markets that would have a far-reaching impact: the Federal Home Loan Mortgage Corporation (Freddie Mac) was chartered by an act of Congress, and the first mortgage-backed security was issued by Ginnie Mae. The initial mortgage-backed securities were comprised only of FHA and VA loans, however with the issuance of the first Freddie Mac mortgage-backed securities (called participation certificates, or PCs) in 1971, conventional loans were being included as well.

The issuance of the first Ginnie Mae MBSs and Freddie Mac PCs marked the start of a financial revolution, the birth of the modern mortgage-backed securities market. The revolution came with the addition of the three "S's" of mortgage-backed securities: *standardization, safety* and *simplicity*.

Standardization:
Standard Contractual Terms
Standard Delivery Terms
Standard Payment Terms

Standardization is a critically important advantage that we can gain by investing in mortgage-backed securities. There is no such thing as a "standard stock," a "standard corporate bond" or a "standard municipal bond." The rights and income accruing to each share of stock are governed by the particular corporation's unique charter and bylaws, the individual decisions of the members of the board of directors, and the laws of the particular state wherein the corporation is legally domiciled. Corporate and municipal bonds are also far from standard, as each individual bond issue is governed by the contractual terms of a trust indenture entered into between the issuer and the trustee bank. Individual bond issues have widely varying trust indentures, which means that bondholder rights vary widely from bond issue to bond issue.

Mortgage securities achieved standardization through the mechanism of the agencies (Freddie Mac, Ginnie Mae, or Fannie Mae) stepping in between the mortgage originators and sellers on the one side, and mortgage investors on the other side. Sellers are offered a standard purchase contract with standard terms, which the sellers enter into with the issuing agency. The agency then offers what is essentially a mirror contract to investors on the

Meet Our Helpers 69

other side, with the agency passing through what is received from the originator/servicer to the investor. The genius of this simple arrangement is that each seller is now dealing with a single buyer instead of thousands of buyers, and each investor is now dealing with one seller instead of hundreds of sellers (see Figure 7.1).

The standardized contractual documents that define what mortgage securities are and how they work provide us two important benefits: *knowledge* and *representation*. *Knowledge* because with mortgage securities we don't have to worry about the rules changing with each new issue, unlike corporate and municipal bonds and preferred stock. *Representation* because the quasi-governmental agencies control the writing of the documents that govern mortgage securities, not the originators, sellers, or servicers.

Concerning ourselves about who wrote the documents may at first seem trivial, but the practical implications for us as investors are far-reaching. When corporate or municipal bonds are created, all the "rules" that govern the relationship between the bond issuer and the bond investors are defined in an indenture and ancillary documents, typically constituting several hundred pages of legal fine print, which are then summarized in the disclosure documents: the indenture, or official statement. The bond issuer hires teams of attorneys and investment bankers and pays them large sums of money to generate documents such that every section, every paragraph, and every sentence in those hundreds of pages is written to ensure that the resolution of every foreseeable possible conflict between the rights of the issuer and those of the bond investors will be slanted in favor of the issuer, to the maximum extent allowable under securities regulations and rating agency standards. Is it any wonder that Goliath almost always wins?

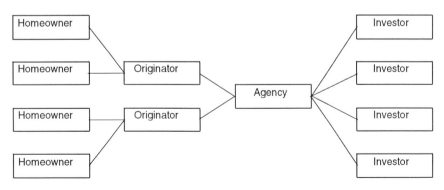

Figure 7.1
Standardizing The Mortgage: Purchases

The pooling and servicing agreements that govern mortgage securities were written from an entirely different perspective. To meet their congressionally mandated goals of attracting investors to the mortgage markets and keeping required investor yields (and mortgage rates) low, the agencies controlled and paid for the generation of standard documents that would be highly attractive over the long term for investors. Whether as originators or sellers and servicers, the financial institutions all must perform their contractual duties to exacting standards while guaranteeing their work, so that we as investors will get exactly what we are supposed to get, when we are supposed to get it. Who writes the documents is a matter of profound importance to us as investors, and a highly favorable aspect of the mortgage security market.

Safety and simplicity are also achieved through the agency stepping between the investor and everyone else involved in the transaction.

Safety

Safety is achieved by the investor entering into a contract not with a homeowner, and not with a servicer, but directly with the agency. Each agency, with their direct or implied government guarantee, directly obligates itself to pay the investor every month. *Simplicity* is achieved by the very same interposition of the agency between the investor and the others. No need to worry about whether the homeowners are making their payments on time, no need to worry about whether the servicer is doing its job correctly or is in financial difficulty, we as mortgage-backed securities investors can just sit back and receive our uninterrupted monthly series of principal and interest payments from the agency.

The structure of the new mortgage-backed securities was in many ways quite similar to the structure of closed-end mutual funds.[1] If we purchase a $50,000 participation certificate in a $5,000,000 pool financing fifty $100,000 mortgages, then we own 1.00% of that pool and we participate in 1.00% of all interest income and 1.00% of all principal payments paid to the pool, net of expenses. If the pool of 100 homeowners collectively pay $40,000 in interest payments and $20,000 in principal payments in June, then in July we receive $400 in interest (1.00%) and $200 in principal (1.00%). Another name for these securities is pass-throughs, for mortgage payments are passed from the home-

---

1 Mortgage-backed securities are more similar to closed-end mutual funds than to open-end mutual funds, as the issuers do not stand ready to redeem shares at a net asset value; rather, another investor must be found. They are even more similar to unit investment trusts, as no mortgages are traded once the security has been created.

owner to the servicer to the issuer (the agency), who then passes through the interest and principal to us, the investors.

The dollar item not included in the above example is that of expenses, and this is one of the key advantages of mortgage-backed securities investments. Standardization and government backing allow the total expenses for most mortgage-backed securities to total no more than 0.50% to 0.75% of outstanding mortgages per year, a bargain basement rate when we consider that this includes not only servicing and administration, but also an unconditional agency guarantee of repayment in full with interest. These expenses are taken out before setting the mortgage-backed security rate, so that a 8.50% Freddie Mac PC will pay exactly an 8.50% interest rate AFTER all expenses (the expenses have already been taken out from the 9.00% to 9.25% mortgages that probably underlie the 8.50% security). An example of how this works follows[2]:

On a 9.00% mortgage:
- Homeowner pays — $900 interest
- Homeowner pays — $100 principal
- Servicer keeps — $30 fee (0.3%)
- Agency keeps — $20 fee (0.2%)

On an 8.50% security:
- Investor receives — $850 interest
- Investor receives — $100 principal

The great advantage of the mortgage-backed securities to the agencies was that there was no longer any interest rate risk involved in funding mortgage purchases with bond sales. For a number of years the mortgage-backed security market grew relatively slowly. By the time that Fannie Mae joined the market with their first mortgage-backed securities in 1981, there were still less than $100 billion in outstanding mortgage pass-through securities. But the *standardization, safety,* and *simplicity* offered by mortgage-backed securities was proving irresistible to major institutional investors, and fueled by growing acceptance as well as the growth of the CMO and then Remic marketplaces, the mortgage-backed securities market grew more than tenfold during the

---

[2] Actual mortgage rates and outside fees may vary substantially, although the vast majority of the time these fees will total under 1.00%. However, some originators will occasionally use much higher rate mortgages in order to maximize servicing income, such as using 10.0% mortgages to create a 8.00% mortgage-backed security. This can lead to unpleasant surprises for the unwary investor, but can be helpful to the discerning investor. See Chapter 17 for more information.

1980s, with more than 1 trillion dollars' worth outstanding at the end of the decade.

Investments in mortgage-backed securities are even more suitable for individuals than for major financial institutions. Major investors have staffs of trained finance professionals to evaluate stocks, bonds, real estate investments. and so forth. They still prefer not to, however, because of the difficulties involved. For the investor who lacks such resources, standardization, safety and simplicity make an irresistible combination.

8
Unlocking the Mystery of Prepayments

How many people whom you personally know have paid off the mortgages on their homes after 30 years of payments? How many times have you known people to sell their house before paying off their mortgage? While it is not uncommon for a couple to pay off their mortgage prior to retirement, it is far more likely that any given mortgage will prepay long before maturity.

Indeed, historical experience indicates that only about 1 out of 20 newly originated conventional (nonassumable) mortgages will actually pay off at contractual maturity. The other 19 will *prepay* before maturity, on average about 7 years after origination. Even with assumable (primarily FHA & VA) mortgages that can be "taken over" by new purchasers of the home, it is considered likely that 17 out of 20 mortgages will prepay prior to maturity (average prepayment about 12 years after origination).

These prepayments can be a powerful advantage for us as mortgage investors. Despite the 30-year contractual maturity (at mortgage origination), the *effective* maturities of our mortgage-backed securities investments are far less. Partially, this is because of the amortizing nature of mortgages, with a little bit of principal being received back each month. Half of a 9.00% mortgage's principal is scheduled to be paid back to us by the 23rd year. The more important factor is prepayments. Typically we can expect to start receiving significant principal payments as a result of prepayments by the third year after mortgage origination, and combining the effect of prepayments and amortization, we find that if we invest in *new* 30-year conventional mortgages, we can expect to receive half of our investment *principal* back within 8 years (much faster if we are buying even 2- or 3-year-old mortgage securities).

Expected prepayments work strongly in our favor as investors, but expectations can change. Increases in interest rates tend to slow prepayments down, and decreases in interest rates tend to speed prepayments up. These increases or decreases in prepayments occur because of homeowners acting in their own best interests. When we *reverse the mortgage,* changes in prepayment speed almost always act against our interests as investors (prepayments in general are a positive feature, but *changes* in prepayments usually work against us).

> "Reversing the Mortgage: Homeowners prepay when interest rates are low, and don't prepay when interest rates are high. Investor mortgages are called away when rates go lower, and stay around when rates go higher."

Prepayments are what most distinguish mortgage-backed securities from other investments. In the chapters ahead we will find out:

- What are prepayments and where do they come from?
- What are prepayment speeds?
- What factors change prepayment speeds, and what is the impact upon us as investors?
- How can prepayment speed changes hurt our investments? Just how bad are the risks?
- Can we turn prepayments to our advantage?

The above may appear complicated at first glance, but this need not be the case. Remember, all that prepayments and prepayment speeds consist of are the average decisions of average homeowners. If you can think like a homeowner then you already understand every aspect of prepayments. The other important item to keep in mind when discussing prepayment *risk*, is to remember just what the risk is. Our risk is what the exact timing will be when we are repaid our principal *in full,* as well as the associated interest *in full.* Perhaps these are not bad problems to have in this age of Black Mondays, collapsing real estate empires and defaulted junk bonds.

Unlocking the Mystery of Prepayments

What Are Prepayments?

A mortgage prepayment occurs when a mortgage borrower (homeowner) makes a principal payment on his or her mortgage loan sooner than contractually scheduled. When we *reverse the mortgage,* prepayments return principal to mortgage-backed security investors faster than contractually scheduled. This early return of principal to us can be beneficial, detrimental, or unimportant, depending on current interest rate levels, the price paid for the mortgage-backed security, and our own particular financial situation and objectives.

Prepayments can take two forms, each having a widely different impact on the investor:

1. PREPAYMENTS IN FULL have a large initial impact, and change payments but not amortization.

2. PARTIAL PREPAYMENTS have a small initial impact, and change amortization but not payments.

Prepayments in full (also known as "liquidations") are almost always triggered by a change in ownership of the residence securing the mortgage or a refinancing of that mortgage. Moving to another town, moving to a larger or smaller house in the same town, divorce, death, fire and other casualty losses, and foreclosure are among the many events that trigger prepayments in full. The decline in interest rates during the last decade has been the recent leading cause of prepayments in full, as large numbers of homeowners have refinanced their homes to take advantage of the new lower rates.

When you as a homeowner pay off your mortgage because you sold your house, you use part of the sale proceeds to pay off the entire mortgage, and then you naturally make no further payments on that mortgage. When we *reverse the mortgage,* with this type of prepayment the entire remaining balance of that particular loan is paid to us as investors at one time, and we receive no further payments from that loan. As an example, if a $100,000 mortgage comprising 1% of a $10 million mortgage pool were to prepay in full, then 1% of the pool balance ($100,000) would be passed through to us investors as a return of our principal, and then future normal monthly payments would be reduced by 1% thereafter.

On the other hand, if you as a homeowner send in an extra $50, $100, or even $1,000 with your mortgage payment to prepay principal, then your future monthly mortgage payment does not change. As we explored in Chapter 2, what does happen is that the additional payment triggers *stretching, stacking* and *snowballing* changes, which accelerate the mortgage amortization and pay off the mortgage earlier than scheduled. When we *reverse the mortgage,* these partial prepayments (also known as "curtailments") are passed through in full to us as a return of principal, but they are generally barely visible to us due to their small size. However, over time these homeowner repurchases of mortgage principal will become increasingly visible as they accelerate the mortgage and shorten the number of mortgage payments that we as investors will receive.

For practical purposes, full and partial prepayments are lumped together, and all are treated as being full prepayments when projecting the cash-flow streams that determine mortgage-backed securities pricing, due to the overwhelming dollar preponderance of prepayments in full compared to partial prepayments. We will follow the industry norm from here forward, and treat all prepayments as if they were full prepayments.

Whether you or I or the guy across the street are going to prepay our mortgages in the next year is a guess. Accurately predicting the behavior of one individual can be a notoriously difficult task. However, the behavior of people in large groups is something that can be measured and then predicted with an often-surprising accuracy. Mortgage prepayments on a national basis are something that is highly predictable, and an understanding of the information gathered to date on how people prepay mortgages can be invaluable to the mortgage-backed securities investor.

The Federal Housing Administration has gathered and compiled such information for many years (see Figure 8.1).

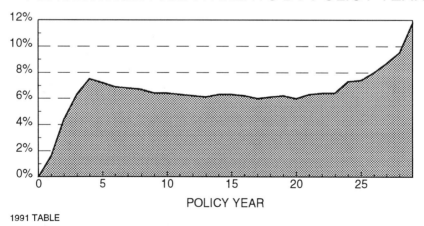

Figure 8.1
FHA Prepayment Experience

Unlocking the Mystery of Prepayments

The FHA "experience" chart in Figure 8.1 looks at prepayments over time, beginning on the far left at mortgage origination, and ending on the far right 30 years later at mortgage maturity. The height of the prepayment line represents the percentage of FHA loans that prepay in each year after origination, i.e., historical experience indicates that about 1.6% of the then-outstanding loans usually prepay in Year 1, about 4.4% usually prepay in Year 2, and around 6% to 7% prepay in each year from Year 3 to 25.

Think back for a moment on your own experience, and the experience of your friends and family: when and why did the moves occur? Likely, very few moves occurred in the first year or two of home ownership. People usually don't buy homes unless they plan on being there for a while. Still, plans change as time passes, transfers and job opportunities begin to take you to other cities, and by the third, fourth, and fifth years, job-related moves are at a steady and common level. This trend continues for a number of years until career-related moves begin to slow down; those who are likely to move have already moved.

Another form of moving is taking over by this point, that of lifestyle changes. Younger couples have children, get promotions, and move into bigger homes in more expensive neighborhoods. Older couples have more room and yard than they care to keep up, and move "down" to smaller homes. Neighborhoods change and deteriorate, some couples retire and move south, other couples divorce and sell the house, and the prepayments continue. All of these and other normal career and lifestyle changes are repeated a thousand times every day across the country. While the timing of each particular homeowner's move may be unpredictable, on a national basis such moves conform to a remarkably stable pattern, as Figure 8.1 demonstrates.

A limitation of the FHA statistics is that they are based upon *assumable* mortgages only. They are a good predictor for Ginnie Mae mortgage securities, which are composed exclusively of assumable FHA and VA loans, but a poor predictor for Freddie Mac and Fannie Mae mortgage securities, which are usually composed entirely of *nonassumable* conventional mortgages. Census bureau statistics from 1987 to 1988 indicate that about 18% of our population moves in an average year, though a disproportionate number of these movers are children and young adults. When we limit our look to owner-occupied households only, we find about 8.5% of those households moved in the previous year.

When we *reverse the mortgage,* as investors we can be confident that over time almost all the mortgages that underlie our mortgage-backed securities will in fact be repaid long before their contractual maturity. We as investors are likely to start receiving significant portions of our original investment principal back within three years even if we buy a security backed by brand-new mortgages.

Table 8.1
$100,000 Mortgage Cash Flow: Scheduled Versus Prepay

Year	Scheduled Amortization		10% Annual Prepayments	
	Payments To Investor	Principal Returned	Payments To Investor	Principal Returned
1	$9,157	$683	$18,693	$10,615
2	$9,161	747	16,763	9,544
3	$9,164	817	15,026	8,580
4	$9,169	894	13,464	7,713
5	$9,173	978	12,059	6,932
6	$9,178	1,070	10,795	6,230
7	$9,184	1,170	9,659	5,598
8	$9,190	1,280	8,637	5,030
9	$9,197	1,400	7,718	4,518
10	$9,204	1,531	6,892	4,058
11	$9,212	1,675	6,150	3,644
12	$9,221	1,832	5,482	3,271
13	$9,230	2,004	4,882	2,936
14	$9,241	2,192	4,343	2,635
15	$9,252	2,397	3,859	2,363
16	$9,265	2,622	3,423	2,119
17	$9,278	2,868	3,032	1,900
18	$9,293	3,137	2,681	1,702
19	$9,310	3,431	2,366	1,525
20	$9,328	3,753	2,083	1,365
21	$9,347	4,105	1,829	1,221
22	$9,369	4,491	1,601	1,092
23	$9,392	4,912	1,397	976
24	$9,418	5,373	1,214	872
25	$9,446	5,877	1,050	778
26	$9,476	6,428	903	694
27	$9,510	7,031	771	618
28	$9,546	7,690	653	550
29	$9,586	8,412	547	488
30	$9,630	9,201	453	433
Totals	$279,127	$100,000	$168,425	$100,000

Unlocking the Mystery of Prepayments 79

If the mortgages themselves are more than two years old, we are likely to start receiving significant amounts of principal back almost immediately, greatly increasing our flexibility and decreasing our vulnerability to changes in interest rates (see Table 8.1).

The rapid cumulative effects of prepayments upon the outstanding amount of principal and the way in which these prepayments fundamentally change the nature of mortgage investing are illustrated above. The mortgage is our familiar mortgage that we examined in Chapters 1 to 4, except instead of one $100,000 mortgage, we are assuming that we own a $100,000 piece of a large nationally diversified pool of 9.00% mortgages. We make the further assumption that 10% of the then outstanding mortgages in that pool prepay every year.

The "Scheduled Amortization" columns in Table 8.1 depict how the mortgages are scheduled to pay if there are no prepayments. Total payments to us as investors are relatively level over time, rising slightly as steadily smaller servicer and guarantor fees are taken from the level payments made by homeowners. We receive almost no principal in the first few years, but then as *stretching, stacking* and *snowballing* take effect, the principal comes in faster and faster. Half of our principal investment is received back by us during the last six years of the mortgage amortizations. Most of our cash comes from the many interest payments made over the long life of our investment.

When job transfers, growing families, and empty nesters are taken into account, a radically different kind of investment emerges, as the "10% Annual Prepayments" column on the right demonstrates. Initial cash flow is almost twice what was scheduled, as 10% of our outstanding mortgage investment prepays over the course of the year. Principal prepayments overwhelm and reverse scheduled principal payments. Now most principal is paid back within the first 4 to 8 years of the mortgage investment. Our cash flow and the dollar amounts of prepayments steadily decline over time as more and more mortgages have prepaid, even though the same percentage of *remaining* mortgages, 10.00%, prepay in each remaining year.

These normal types of prepayments are on balance highly beneficial to us as mortgage investors (refinancing prepayments are however another matter, as we will see in the next chapter). Cash is returned much more quickly to us than originally called for, allowing us to flexibly adapt to changing investment or lifestyle conditions. As they have such an important impact on the investor, understanding prepayments and how prepayment speeds are measured is therefore of paramount importance to us as mortgage-backed securities investors.

Prepayment Speeds

The simplest of the prepayment speed measurements is the Constant Prepayment Rate method (hereafter called the CPR speed).[1] Constant Prepayment Rate is another way of saying level prepayment rate; that is, if the CPR speed is 5.00%, then each year 5.00% of the remaining mortgages in the pool prepay; if the CPR speed is 10.00%, then 10.00% of the remaining mortgages in the pool prepay each year; and if the CPR speed is 20.00%, then 20.00% of the remaining mortgages prepay in each year (see Figure 8.2).

CPR speeds are easy for us to understand, particularly in the first year. If we purchase a $100,000 security that experiences a 10% CPR, then we can expect to receive $10,000 (10% of $100,000) in principal prepayments in the first year.[2] With a 6% CPR we would expect to receive $6,000 in principal prepayments in the first year; and with a 20% CPR speed we would expect to

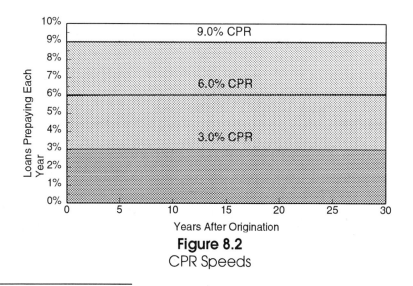

Figure 8.2
CPR Speeds

---

1 CPR is also translated as "Conditional Prepayment Rate" for the reason that the size of each anticipated prepayment is conditional on the current outstanding principal balance.
2 Total principal *payments* will in fact equal $10,615, not $10,000. This is because $683 in *scheduled* principal payments is expected in addition to the principal *prepayments*. $10,615 is received rather than $10,683 ($10,000 prepay plus $683 scheduled) because of the interrelationship between scheduled principal payments and prepayments: scheduled payments reduce principal balances and thereby reduce prepayments, while prepayments also reduce principal balances and thereby reduce scheduled payments, leading to a total that is slightly less than what might be anticipated.

receive $20,000 in prepayments. A key factor to keep in mind, however, is that a level prepayment *rate* is not the same thing as a level *dollar* amount of prepayments. Using our 10% CPR example (but removing the effects of amortization for now), if $10,000 of the $100,000 has prepaid in the first year, then only $90,000 is left for the second year. Ten percent of $90,000 is $9,000, so $9,000 in prepayments is received in the second year, leaving less principal and less prepayments for the following year and so forth, as is shown below:

Prepayment Speed Example

Year	Mortgages	CPR	Prepayments
1	$100,000	10%	$10,000
2	90,000	10%	9,000
3	81,000	10%	8,100
4	72,900	10%	7,290

(No amortization)

When we *reverse the mortgage,* this is the same thing as saying that there is a 1 out of 10 chance that any one of your neighbors will prepay their mortgage in the next year. Once you have been in the neighborhood a number of years, many of your original neighbors will have moved away, and the chances grow smaller each year that any of the remaining original neighbors will prepay. One out of every 10 in your neighborhood is still moving in each year. However, over time, more and more of the movers will be new neighbors who are there for three to seven years and then move on, rather than the other long-time residents such as yourself.

The cumulative nature of prepayments means that seemingly minor differences in prepayment rates can quickly grow over time to make a major difference in the amount of time until we as investors receive our investment principal back. The chart in Figure 8.3 illustrates when we will have received the first 25%, 50%, and 75% of our investment back under a variety of prepayment assumptions. Unlike the prepayment speed example above, this chart also includes scheduled principal amortization, once again for our familiar 9.00%, 30-year mortgage.

If we had invested $100,000 on a scheduled basis with no prepayments, we would not expect to receive our first $25,000 (25%) in *principal* back until 17 years later, as is shown on the left side of the graph in Figure 8.3. With 0% prepayments, we have not received half of our principal back until 23 years later, and $75,000 of our investment principal back until 28 years later.[3]

---

3   These figures represent return of principal only, and do not include interest income. When interest is added in, the first $25,000 is received by Year 3, the first $50,000 by Year 6, $100,000 is received by Year 11, and $289,663 is received by the end of mortgage amortization.

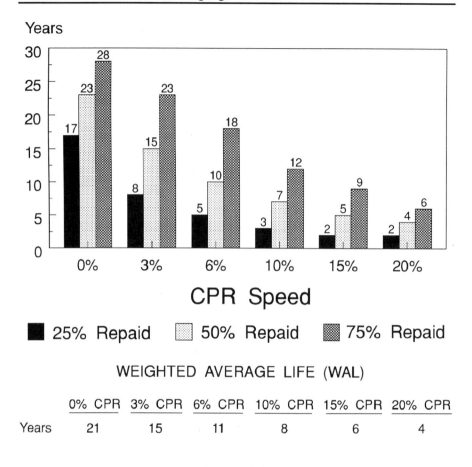

Figure 8.3
Years to Repayment of Principal

Realistically, however, prepayments will occur, and with a 10% prepayment rate we will receive the first 25% of our investment principal back within not *17* but *3* years, our first 50% back not in *23* years but in *7* years, and 75% of our original investment back within not *28* but *12* years.

The bottom line of the chart introduces a new measurement tool that is commonly used by mortgage security investors, and that is the concept of *weighted average life*. Unlike most investments, final maturity can often be almost irrelevant when comparing alternative mortgage investments. What counts is the average amount of time until the investors principal is *expected* to be returned: is it 3 years, 5 years, 10 years, or 15 years? Weighted average life

Unlocking the Mystery of Prepayments 83

(WAL) is the measure of the average amount of time until principal is returned, and is the measure most commonly used by professional investors when comparing alternative investments. This measure is not the same as the half-life measure of when 50% of our principal is received back. WAL is more accurate as it weights and includes the timing involved with each and every principal payment.[4]

CPR speed is the easiest of the prepayment speed methodologies to understand, and we should use it wherever possible, *unless* we are purchasing a mortgage-backed security that consists of mortgages that are less than two years old. Looking back to Figure 8.1, one of the most prominent features of the chart is the low but steadily rising number of prepayments during the first two to three years. This reflects a fact that most of us are aware of: most people are in their homes for two years or more, and almost everyone stays in their home for at least a year. The flat

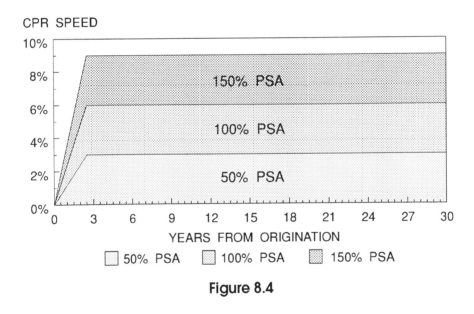

Figure 8.4

---

[4] Weighted average life (WAL) can be calculated by summing the products of the multiplication of the dollar amount of each anticipated principal payment by the years from investment until receipt of that payment, and then dividing such sum by the original principal invested. While it is the most common measure of expected "life," WAL is not the best measure. Duration, which weights the *present value* of each future *cash flow* (including interest as well as principal) is a superior measure and is often used instead of WAL by the more sophisticated segment of the institutional marketplace.

level prepayments of the CPR methodology therefore tends to overstate prepayments if applied to the first two years of a mortgage's life (the age of the underlying mortgages is however not necessarily the same as the age of the mortgage-backed security.) .[5]

The Public Securities Association (PSA) prepayment method (see Figure 8.4) was developed by the investment banking industry in order to provide a blend of the advantages of the FHA experience and CPR prepayment methodologies.

Like FHA prepayment experience charts, the PSA prepayment method assumes virtually no prepayments in the first month after mortgage origination, and then a steadily rising amount of prepayments in each month until Month 30 (2 1/2 years). As in the CPR method, from Month 30 onwards prepayments are level as a *percentage* in each year until maturity (though dollar amounts of prepayments will reduce in each year as the mortgage pool reduces in size).

A conversion is required in order to translate between PSA and CPR speeds. The base PSA speed is 100%, which is intended to correspond roughly to average historical prepayment experience for FHA loans. From Month 30 onwards a 100% PSA speed is equal to a 6% CPR speed, and we can convert PSA speeds to CPR speeds by multiplying the PSA speed times 0.06 (6%). As is shown above, doubling the PSA speed from 100% to 200% also doubles the equivalent CPR speed from 6% to 12%, and halving the PSA speed from 100% to 50% also halves the CPR speed from 6% to 3%. Converting from CPR speeds to PSA speeds after Month 30, we merely multiply times 16.7 (1/0.06). Appendix at the back of this book also allows us to quickly and easily convert from PSA speed to CPR speed, as well as from CPR speed to PSA speed.

What is the correct prepayment speed to use? That is dependent on a number of factors that we will be reviewing in the next chapter, the most important of which is the difference between the current rate at which new mortgages are being originated and the rate on the mortgages underlying our mortgage-backed security investment. If we have a "par" Ginnie Mae mortgage-backed security that corresponds to current mortgage conditions, then we would generally expect our mortgage-backed security to prepay at a 100% PSA prepayment rate (6% CPR).

---

5 The date on which a mortgage-backed security is created can mean very little, as the amortization of the security is governed by the age of the mortgages underlying the security. An approximate age can be generated by looking at the final maturity of the security and counting back 30 years, i.e., a 30-year mortgage-backed security maturing in 2017, means the loans originated 30 years earlier in 1987 (2017 - 30 = 1987), which means that the correct age in 1993 would be six years (1993 - 1987 = 6). The better method is to determine the remaining WAL or WARM (weighted average remaining maturity) of the security, as reported by the issuer (Freddie or Fannie).

Unlocking the Mystery of Prepayments 85

With a normal Fannie Mae or Freddie Mac security, we should expect a prepayment rate of 170% to 190% PSA rate (10% to 11.5% CPR). The difference between the these types of securities is that Ginnie Mae MBSs consist of pools of *assumable* FHA and VA home mortgage loans, so we do not necessarily get our principal back immediately whenever a house in one of our mortgage pools sells, as the new buyer may assume the loan. Fannie Mae MBSs and Freddie Mac PCs are comprised of *nonassumable* conventional mortgage loans, which must be prepaid in full upon sale of the home, so we are assured of getting our principal back each time a home in our mortgage pool is sold (note that there are a *few* specially designated Fannie Mae and Freddie Mac securities that are comprised of FHA and VA loans).

9
Mastering the Four Faces of Prepayments

There is a dark side to mortgage prepayments. Usually steady, predictable, and beneficial, the prepayments on mortgage-backed securities can change radically when there is a major drop in interest rates. Newspapers, magazines, and television news shows are suddenly filled with articles, programs, and advertisements advising homeowners to refinance their mortgages and save money. Prepayments of principal change from a steady flow to a torrent of cash, as homeowner after homeowner pays off the mortgage in order to refinance at the lower rates.

When we *reverse the mortgage,* we as investors have been doing quite well. Rates are lower than they were when we made our investments, and we are enjoying the benefits of owning an investment that is carrying an above-market interest rate. All of a sudden large doses of cash start arriving in our monthly checks. We are getting paid our principal back much sooner than we planned on or would like, and we must now reinvest the money at the new, lower prevailing interest rates.

Prepayment speeds also change when there is a rapid increase in interest rates. The mortgage note on that bigger house across town just became unaffordably high. The new job in another city makes less sense if the mortgage note is going to rise 50%. The steady flow of prepayments begins to slow down to a trickle.

When we *reverse the mortgage,* we are not terribly happy with the interest rate on our mortgage-backed securities. Higher interest rates are available on all sorts of alternative investments, and we can't wait for those prepayments to come in so we can reinvest our principal into higher-yielding assets. As rates continue to rise, however, the prepayments on the mortgages underlying our securities slow down more and more, and we find ourselves with steadily less money to reinvest elsewhere.

The ability to pay off debts at any time without penalty is one great advantage that individuals routinely enjoy over business borrowers. Business or municipal borrowers often face lockout periods when they cannot prepay their bonds at all for 10 years or more, and even when they can pay off these bonds, they must pay a prepayment penalty. The individual mortgage borrower can however prepay his or her mortgage at any time by repaying outstanding principal and interest. No penalties apply.

When we *reverse the mortgage,* we as investors can have our investments returned to us at any time, should the homeowners whose mortgages underlie our securities choose to exercise their right to prepay without penalty. When interest rates change, any homeowner prepayment speed changes that occur, either up or down, will be in the best interests of the homeowners and these *changes* will likely have negative implications for us as mortgage securities investors. This relationship is the reason why mortgage-backed securities generally carry the highest yield among fully government-insured investments—because of the lack of protection from prepayments.

This risk of adverse changes in prepayment speeds is in general not a desirable investment characteristic. Some mortgage-backed securities carry the risk that even a minor change in interest rates will radically decrease yields or shorten average lives. Yet other mortgage-backed securities may be scarcely affected by the same change in interest rates. Indeed, some mortgage-backed securities actually benefit from these same prepayment changes.

How do we identify which securities have the greatest *yield* risk from prepayment changes, and which have the least *yield* risk? How do we identify which securities have the greatest *average life* risk from prepayments, and which have the least *average life* risk? How do we find securities that can benefit from seemingly negative prepayment changes?

The answers to each of these questions can be found through looking at the *Four Faces of Prepayments.*

No Choice Prepayments

Sometimes you just don't have any choice at all. The transfer to Cincinnati is mandatory if you ever want a chance at another promotion. Maybe you have a two-bedroom house, and your third child is on the way. A home in your neighborhood burns to the ground, and the mortgage is paid off with the insurance money. A plant shuts its doors, the workers lose their jobs, and soon afterward many houses are being foreclosed upon. At least two million mortgages can be counted on to prepay each and every year regardless of prevailing interest rates, for the causes listed above and numerous other reasons.

This core level of prepayments is the First Face of Prepayments: *No Choice*. No matter how high mortgage rates are or what financial penalties may be associated with paying a mortgage off, there will be many homeowners who will have no choice about prepaying their mortgages, and these homeowners will provide a steady and predictable base of prepayments (see Figure 9.1).

Though *No Choice* prepayments comprise only a fraction of overall normal prepayments, this First Face provides us with surprisingly strong protection through assuring the return of our mortgage investment principal at a rate much faster than contractual mortgage amortization. As an example, let us take our sample 30-year, 9.00% mortgage, and assume that 3 years after origination mortgage rates have climbed to 14.00%. Our rate relative to the market is -5.00% (9.00% mortgage rate on our investment, 14.00% market rate), and the homeowners whose mortgages underlie our security have a strong incentive not to move. Instead of a $804.62 level monthly payment, borrowing the same amount

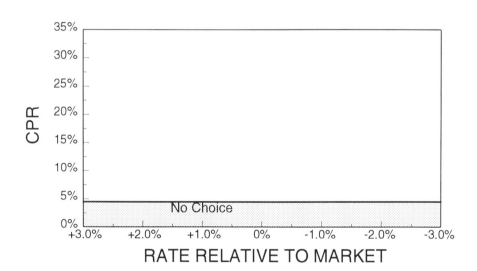

Figure 9.1
"No Choice" Prepayments

at the new mortgage rates would now cost the homeowners $1,167.68 per month. *No Choice* is the only Face of Prepayments in operation, and a low but very steady 4.5% of the mortgages are prepaying in each year (see Figure 9.2).

Looking only at scheduled payments, 30-year mortgages are a long-term investment (even after 3 years of aging), with 15 years needed to receive 25% of our principal back, 21 years needed to receive 50% back, and 25 years needed to have 75% of our principal returned. *No Choice* prepayments, however, mean that even under conditions where homeowners have a strong financial incentive NOT to prepay their mortgages, mortgage-backed securities are still primarily a medium-term investment and not a long-term investment. The real estate market never grinds to a complete halt, and when we *reverse the mortgage,* substantial cumulative prepayments will still in fact occur. We can expect to receive around one fourth of our investment back within the first 5 years, and should have half of our investment back within 12 years. Even small annual amounts of *No Choice* principal prepayments add together to give mortgage-backed securities a powerful advantage over long-term bonds in a rising interest rate environment, for this principal is available to us long before maturity so it can be reinvested in higher interest rate investments and then pull up overall earnings in our investment portfolio.

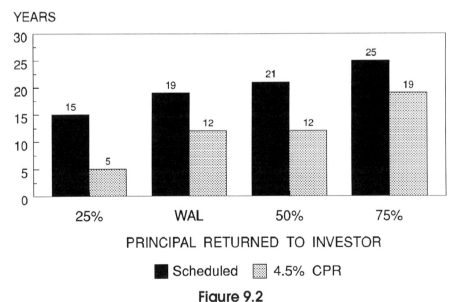

Figure 9.2
3 Year Old 9% Mortgage; High Interest Rates

Better Home Prepayments

Do you have your eye on another house? Is the kitchen in your home just too small, the bedrooms too few? Does the lawn take more time and energy than you care to put into it these days?

Whether we would like to move across town or across the country, many of us would prefer to be living somewhere different than the house we are currently living in. For most of us money plays a large role in determining when we make that move, or whether we make it at all. How much will our mortgage note increase if we buy the place we really want? Can we afford the new note? Is it worth it?

These kinds of questions comprise the Second Face of Prepayments: *Better Home.* "Better" not necessarily in the sense of larger or better-built, but just a home or location that is better for us, that we would prefer to live in. Once we as homeowners have equity in our homes, which we can then use as down payments for future purchases, then the single most important question in gauging affordability, and the ability to move, becomes the size of our new monthly payment.

Are interest rates lower than when we bought? If so, then it becomes easier for us to move. A house like the one we have now costs less per month, because of the lower interest rates. For the same note we are now paying we can afford a nicer house, and a much nicer house is becoming more affordable.

Are interest rates higher than when we bought? Then we may have to think twice about buying another house. Even buying another house at the same price we are selling our current home at would cost us more than we are currently spending, "trading up" to a much nicer house and paying a higher interest rate on a larger mortgage is becoming prohibitively expensive.

The importance of mortgage rates in *Better Home* decisions is of course highly dependent on the difference between current mortgage rates and the homeowners' existing mortgage rate. Slightly higher or lower interest rates slightly reduce or increase prepayment rates; large differences make for large differences in prepayment rates (see Figure 9.3).

When we *reverse the mortgage,* each time a homeowner makes a *Better Home* decision and sells his or her current house in order to move to another, a mortgage prepayment occurs. When current mortgage rates are lower than the rates on the mortgages underlying the mortgage-backed securities we own, then we as investors can expect to experience a significant number of prepayments which will shorten the lives of our investments. If the rates on the mortgages we own are lower than current mortgage rates, then fewer *Better Home*

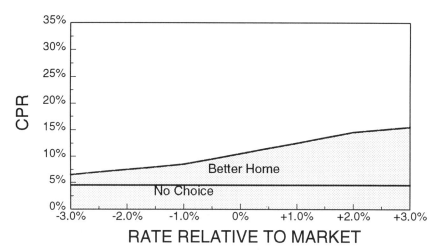

Figure 9.3
"Better Home" Prepayments

prepayments will occur, and we will receive our principal back less quickly. This relationship between interest rates and prepayment rates is illustrated in Table 9.1

A simple step-by-step study of Table 9.1 will unlock the mysteries associated with prepayments. Our first step is to determine the mortgage rate (in this case, 9.00%) on the mortgages underlying the mortgage-backed security that we own or are considering purchasing. Typically, we can assume that the mortgages are 0.50% higher than the mortgage-backed security that we are

Table 9.1
The Second Face: Better Home
(8.5% MBS; 9.0% Rate on Underlying Mortgage)

A	B	C	D	E	F
New Mtg. Rate	Diff. From 9.00%	No Choice CPR	Better Home CPR	Total CPR Speed	Weighted Average Life (WAL)
8.0%	1.0%	4.5%	9.0%	13.5%	6.1
8.5%	0.5%	4.5%	7.0%	11.5%	6.9
9.0%	0.0%	4.5%	6.0%	10.5%	7.4
9.5%	–0.5%	4.5%	5.0%	9.5%	8.0
10.0%	–1.0%	4.5%	4.0%	8.5%	8.6

Mastering the Four Faces of Prepayments

purchasing, so that an 8.00% security would be comprised of 8.50% mortgages, a 9.50% security would be backed by 10.00% mortgages, and so forth. This 0.50% difference, which pays for servicing and guarantor fees, will always be true for normal Ginnie Maes, however, Freddie Macs and Fannie Maes could be different, and you should ask your broker what the weighted average coupon of the underlying mortgages is before purchasing securities (see the Investor Checklist on page 227).

Our next step is to determine what the current rate is for new mortgages (see column A of Table 9.1). Average rates are reported in many newspapers on a weekly basis, or are often advertised at banks, thrifts, and mortgage companies.[1] When we subtract the current mortgage rate from the rate on the mortgages underlying our security, we are calculating column B in the chart, "Difference from 9.00%." This is the crucial step in determining prepayment expectations and exposure. What really matters is not whether our mortgage has a 7.00% rate, or an 8.00% rate, or a 10.00% rate, but rather how much *difference* there is between our mortgage rate and the current mortgage rate. A 7.00% mortgage when current mortgage rates are 8.00%, should prepay at about the same speed as a 10.00% mortgage does when rates are 11.00%. Using the above chart, each would be ranked as a −1.00% mortgage, and we would expect an 8.5% Constant Prepayment Rate (CPR).

We find our expected prepayment speed, our CPR rate, in column E by adding Columns C and D together. Column C is the First Face of Prepayments, *No Choice,* and is the same regardless of interest rates. Column D is the Second Face of Prepayments, *Better Home,* and changes depending on how the mortgage rate compares to the current mortgage rate:

8.5% MBS; 9.0% Rate On Underlying Mortgage

A	B	C	D	E	F
9.0%	0.0%	4.5%	6.0%	10.5%	7.4

---

1 An alternative method that is reasonably accurate is to find what mortgage-backeds are currently trading at "par," (a price of 100 cents on the dollar), and add 0.50% to determine the rate for new mortgages. If your bank originates mortgages to sell (and most do), it will likely charge a new mortgage rate of 0.50% to 1.00% above the current "par" mortgage-backed rate for their new mortgage originations, plus one to four points. The reason for this is that it is the mortgage-backed securities market that sets mortgage rates, for lenders set their rates in such a way as to create a product that can be sold at a profit.

Putting everything together:

1. We find the mortgage rate underlying our security (9.00%).
2. We find the current rate for new mortgages (9.00%).
3. We determine the difference between rates (0.00%).
4. We consider *No Choice* prepayments (4.5% CPR).
5. We look at *Better Home* prepayments based on the difference in rate (6.0% CPR).
6. We add our *No Choice* and *Better Home* prepayments together and get our total prepayments (10.5% CPR).
7. Using our 10.5% CPR, we find that the expected average time for us to get our principal back is 7.4 years (though some principal is received much earlier, and some much later).

What happens if rates then drop 1.00%? Then our new current rate is 8.00% (column A); our new rate difference is 1.00% (column B), as the rates on our mortgage loans are 1.0% above current market; our *No Choice* prepayments stay the same at 4.5% (column C); desired moves are now easier, so our *Better Home* prepayments increase to 9.0% (column D); our total prepayment speed is now 13.5% (column E); and our new expected average life is now 6.1 years. Because rates have dropped 1.0%, our *Better Home* prepayments have increased, and the expected average life of our investment has declined from 7.4 years to 6.1 years.

8.5% MBS; 9.0% Rate on Underlying Mortgage

A	B	C	D	E	F
8.0%	1.0%	4.5%	9.0%	13.5%	6.1

What happens if rates increase 1.00% instead of decreasing? Then our new current rate is 10.00% (column A); our new rate difference is −1.00% (column B); our *No Choice* prepayments stay the same at 4.5% (column C); desired moves are now more difficult, so our *Better Home* prepayments decrease to 4.0% (column D); our total prepayment speed is now 8.5% (column E); and our new expected average life is now 8.6 years. Because rates have increased 1.0% and the rates on our mortgages are now 1.0% below market rates, our *Better Home* prepayments have decreased, and the expected average life of our investment has increased from 7.4 years to 8.6 years.

8.5% MBS; 9.0% Rate on Underlying Mortgage

A	B	C	D	E	F
10.0%	−1.0%	4.5%	4.0%	8.5%	8.6

Better Rate Prepayments

Refinancing is the homeowner's dream and the mortgage investor's nightmare. For the homeowner, refinancing the mortgage is like finding someone who is willing to give money away to them. The same amount of money borrowed against the same house can now be repaid with $100 or $200 less per month, or even less. The only downsides to refinancing for the homeowner are the inconvenience of securing a new mortgage and the costs of the refinancing.

Refinancing costs generally run a minimum of 1% to 2% of the outstanding mortgage amount, and can easily total 4% to 5% if the homeowner refinances with a lower rate/higher points mortgage. These costs of refinancing mean that most homeowners do not immediately refinance for every dip in rates, or the cost of refinancing would outweigh the benefits of the lower rate. Instead homeowners generally do not begin refinancing in large numbers until current mortgage rates are at least 1.5% below their own rate,[2] with most homeowners waiting until current rates are 2.0% to 2.5% below the interest rate on their existing mortgage.

When we *reverse the mortgage,* we as investors can expect a rapid increase in prepayment rates when current mortgage rates are 1.5% to 2% lower than the rates on mortgages underlying our mortgage-backed securities, with these prepayments turning into a veritable flood when current mortgage rates reach 2% to 3% below outstanding mortgage levels (see Figure 9.4). This is the third and most powerful Face of Prepayments: *Better Rate.*

The very sharp rise in prepayments that *Better Rate* causes has a strong and *usually* adverse effect upon us as investors, *if* we bought our securities while rates were higher and prepayments were lower. A mortgage-backed security which is experiencing *Better Rate* prepayments usually has an interest rate that is well above market, and we as investors would like to receive that above

---

[2] Due to the multitude of mortgage types currently available, some homeowners are not waiting for 30-year mortgage rates to fall 1.5%, but are instead refinancing even earlier into different mortgage types, such as adjustable-rate mortgages or 15-year mortgages. The largest volume of refinancings still does not begin, however, until about the 1.5% point, and then accelerates thereafter.

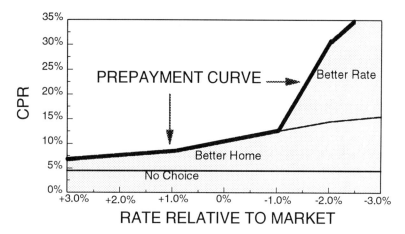

Figure 9.4
"Better Rate" Prepayments

market rate for as long as possible. The sharp increase in prepayments however has the effect of radically reducing the average life of our investment, as is shown in Table 9.2.

As Table 9.2 illustrates, once the Third Face of *Better Rate* begins triggering refinancing prepayments, then the expected life of our investment quickly falls from 6 to 8 years, down to 2 to 4 years. The largest single reason for the increase in prepayments is *Better Rates*. However, it is important to keep in mind that total prepayments is the sum of all of the first three Faces combined: *No Choice* provides the floor regardless of current mortgage rates, *Better Home* picks up

Table 9.2
The Third Face: Better Rate
8.5% MBS; 9.0% Rate on Underlying Mortgage

A	B	C	D	E	F	G
New Mtg. Rate	Diff. From 9.00%	No Choice CPR	Better Home CPR	Better Rate CPR	Total CPR Speed	Weighted Average Life (WAL)
6.0%	3.0%	4.5%	11.0%	24.0%	39.5%	2.0
7.0%	2.0%	4.5%	10.0%	16.0%	30.5%	2.7
8.0%	1.0%	4.5%	9.0%	0.0%	13.5%	6.1
9.0%	0.0%	4.5%	6.0%	0.0%	10.5%	7.4
10.0%	-1.0%	4.5%	4.0%	0.0%	8.5%	8.6

Mastering the Four Faces of Prepayments 97

the speed of prepayments as rates fall moderately, and *Better Rate* stacks on top of the first two to greatly increase speeds when current rates are substantially below the rate on our mortgages.

It is worth noting that even with current rates far below the rates on the outstanding mortgages, we still don't get all of our money back at once, as we typically would with a high-rate corporate or municipal bond once the call date is reached. Instead, we expect to receive our principal investment back over a multiyear period, with many of the mortgages not being prepaid for one year, two years, three years, or even much longer. What is happening here? Why aren't all the homeowners immediately taking advantage of the lower rates to refinance?

No Telling

One thing that can be said with certainty about the United States is that we are a nation of individuals. True, most of us react to similar situations in similar ways. If we have an opportunity to refinance and save money, most of us will do so. However, millions of us will not immediately refinance our mortgages even after rates have fallen drastically, and that is the Fourth Face of Prepayments: *No Telling*.

There are any number of reasons why homeowners do not refinance their mortgages even when it would appear to be in their best interests to do so. Some of these reasons reflect sound financial judgment on the homeowner's part, some reflect changed homeowner financial conditions, and some reflect nothing more than human nature. The first factor to keep in mind is the many timing lags between interest rate changes and mortgage prepayment changes. A typical time chart for a typical refinancing for an average homeowner we will call Fred is as follows:

Lagging Prepayments

Day	Event
1	Interest rates drop to refinancing level
30	Television news says it's time to refinance
60	Fred's friend Joe starts to refinance
75	Fred talks to friends about refinancing
90	Fred starts calling mortgage companies
120	Fred applies for new mortgage
180	Fred's new mortgage closes, he prepays remaining balance on old mortgage
200	Mortgage prepayment reaches investor

There are some homeowners who watch mortgage rates, and will jump at the first opportunity to refinance. Even these prepayments, however, take at least 60 to 90 days to reach mortgage investors because of the time needed to apply for and close on a new mortgage, as well as the time necessary for the prepayment to travel from the homeowner to the servicer to the agency to the investor. Most homeowners will take significantly longer, particularly if mortgage processors become swamped and applications are delayed. These types of lags mean that most *initial* refinancing prepayments are not received for anywhere from three months to a year.

Another common group of people who do not prepay their mortgages immediately are the "mortgage waiters".

`` 'Mortgage Waiters': –Waiting for Rates to Fall Further, –Waiting to Move.''

During times of falling interest rates, many homeowners patiently wait on the sidelines, watching as interest rates continue to drop, thinking that rates will continue to drop even further in the future, and planning on refinancing later at a still lower interest rate. Another kind of waiter is the homeowner who expects to move within the next three to five years. Refinancing generally would be an expensive mistake for those who are moving too soon, as they do not save enough money on their remaining monthly payments to recapture the up-front costs of refinancing. Each of these kinds of "waiters" will eventually prepay their mortgages, but it may take several years after rates have fallen into what would usually be considered their refinancing zone before their prepayments are passed through to investors.

`` 'The Long Timers': Adverse Financial Changes –Ignorance, –Human Nature.''

The last group who comprise *No Telling* are the long-timers who should refinance, but can't or won't, even if they have been in a refinancing range for five or more years and are paying rates 5% or more above market. Sometimes these long-timers just won't prepay, for reasons running the entire gamut of human nature: lack of knowledge, poor money common sense, procrastination,

Mastering the Four Faces of Prepayments 99

being too broke or too cheap to spend the money on refinancing costs despite the larger savings over time, or even fear or distrust of bankers and banks.

More often the long-timers have not refinanced because they cannot do so for financial reasons. A change in earnings or jobs may have lowered household income and made it impossible to qualify for a new mortgage. Property values may have declined, meaning the loan would not meet a loan-to-value test for refinancing. A recent poor credit history could be preventing a new loan. Indeed, the homeowner may be behind in his or her mortgage payments and staying only one step ahead of foreclosure. It is not uncommon for old high-interest-rate mortgage pools that should have refinanced years before to have delinquency and foreclosure rates that are many times higher than the national average, because of the concentration of homeowners with financial problems. (However, our Five Layers of Safety still provide more than ample protection for our investment.)

The *No Telling* face of prepayments represents the sum of this highly varied group of homeowner motivations: the laggers, the waiters, and the long-timers. When we *reverse the mortgage,* these different groups are strongly beneficial for us as mortgage investors, for they mean that we will continue to receive above-market interest rates long after we might otherwise have expected repayment in full. As an example, 26% of the principal amount of all 11% Ginnie Mae MBSs ever issued was still outstanding as of September 1992, despite their having amortized for an average of 8 years, and having been in a *Better Rate* refinancing range for all but a few months since February of 1986. Applying *No Telling* to our other Three Faces we can now see the entire range of prepayment expectations (see Figure 9.5).

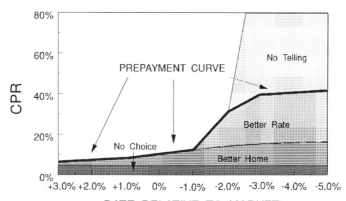

Figure 9.5
"No Telling" Prepayments

People usually act in predictable ways, and the prepayments and prepayment sensitivity associated with individual mortgage securities can be understood and successfully predicted by us if we think about how people behave. Homeowners will generally act in their own best interests, and by comparing the interest rates on the outstanding mortgages underlying the mortgage security we are examining to the current rate on new mortgages, we can gain an insight into what those homeowner interests are, and thereby predict prepayment behavior and the effect on our investments.

If the outstanding rate is 5.0%, and the new mortgage rate is 9.0% (–4.0% differential), then there is a strong incentive not to move, and most people will prepay only when they have *No Choice*; we will likely experience slow and stable prepayments if we buy a mortgage security that carries a substantially below market-interest rate. People often want to move and more people will move to a *Better Home* if they can lower their mortgage interest rate than if they have to increase their rate; therefore, a mortgage security backed by 10.0% mortgages (1.0%) will likely prepay faster than one backed by 8.0% mortgages (–1.0%).

If someone who has a 11.0% rate (2.0%) and does not want to move can save money by refinancing, then he or she will usually go ahead and get a *Better Rate*; when we buy a mortgage security whose loans are close to or within the refinancing range, we risk wide shifts in prepayment speeds, either up or down if rates move only a percent or so. Not everyone is in the same circumstances or thinks the same way, though. Some people will be procrastinating, some will be waiting for still lower rates, and some will be unable to refinance, so there is *No Telling* how long some mortgages will remain outstanding, regardless of how high their rates are compared to current mortgages. Even if prepayments move sharply against us, the actual impact on our cash flow will likely be spread out over months and years.

It is through putting together all of these very human situations and motivations that we are able to derive our prepayment curve, which represents the total likely prepayments expected for each mortgage security over time, based on their interest rate versus the current market interest rate. A historical 12-month prepayment experience curve for 30-year, fixed-rate Fannie MBSs is shown in Figure 9.6.

The historical prepayment curve appears somewhat truncated, as the long fall in mortgage interest rates had by 1992 driven mortgage rates so low that there were very few mortgage securities with interest rates low enough relative to current market to sell at a discount, let alone a steep discount. However, an

Mastering the Four Faces of Prepayments 101

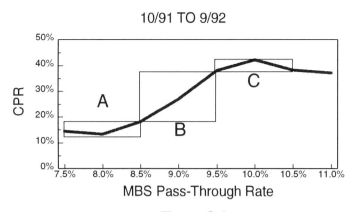

Figure 9.6
FNMA MBS Prepayments

examination of the historical curve still shows the strong influences of our Four Faces of Prepayments

Looking at Box A in Figure 9.6, we can see that the 7.5% and 8.5% Fannie Maes are separated by relatively stable and moderately rising prepayment rates, reflecting slowly rising *Better Home* prepayments stacked on top of stable *No Choice* prepayments. The same 1.0% interest rate difference between the 8.5% and 9.5% Fannies triggers a steep rise in prepayment rates in Box B, as refinancing opportunities cause *Better Rate* prepayments to climb rapidly. As our interest rates rise even further in Box C, however, we find little or no further corresponding increase in prepayments. A number of *No Telling* factors keep our prepayments from rising above a 45% Constant Prepayment Rate.

Ginnie Mae Prepayments

Our previous prepayment discussion has focused on what are called "conventional" mortgages: those mortgages that are *not* FHA or VA mortgages, are *not* assumable, and whose documentation and underwriting are such that they *are* saleable to Fannie Mae and Freddie Mac. In contrast, Ginnie Maes (and a few Fannie Maes and Freddie Macs[3] are backed by FHA and VA loans that are

---

[3] The few Fannie Mae securities that are composed of FHA and VA loans have a GL designation. The few Freddie Mac securities backed by FHA and VA loans can also be identified by special codes in their identification number.

assumable, and these loans have somewhat different prepayment characteristics.

No Choice, Better Home, Better Rate, and *No Telling* drive FHA and VA prepayments just as they do conventional loan prepayments, however the home-sale and moving-related Faces of *No Choice* and *Better Home* are modified by the effects of loan assumptions. A loan assumption by the new homeowner upon the sale of the home is commonly motivated by two different factors: the ability to borrow at a lower rate than is otherwise available, and the desire to avoid going through a loan-approval process.

Assumable loans have their greatest impact on prepayments when the current mortgage rate is higher than the assumable rate on the existing mortgage. The further that assumable rate is below the current rate for new mortgages, the greater the incentive home purchasers have to assume the mortgage, and the fewer loans will be prepayed. The *No Choice* Face of Prepayments is therefore only about 2% to 3% CPR (33% to 50% PSA) for Ginnie Mae securities, rather than the approximately 4% to 5% CPR we expect for Freddie Mac and Fannie Mae securities backed by conventional mortgages.

The other motivation for assuming someone else's home loan is to avoid going through the process of obtaining a new mortgage. Some people are unable to obtain a new mortgage to purchase a home because of their financial condition or history. They may have a poor credit history, be self-employed with an erratic earning history, or have insufficient documented income to meet bank underwriting requirements. For these and other reasons, the home-sale-driven *Better Home* Face of Prepayments is consistently lower for FHA and VA loans than for conventional loans. Assumability, however, has no effect upon refinancing; therefore, the *Better Rate* and *No Telling* Faces of Prepayments are not materially different between conventional and FHA and VA loans. Since total prepayments are based upon the sum of all the Faces, and always incorporate the effect of *No Choice* and *Better Home* prepayments, we usually find that Ginnie Mae prepayments are lower than Freddie Mac or Fannie Mae prepayments for all coupons and all parts of the prepayment curve. This is demonstrated in the comparison in Figure 9.7 of historical, seasoned Freddie Mac PC, Fannie Mae MBS and Ginnie Mae MBS prepayment curves.

Understanding prepayments and the homeowner motivations that underlie them are quite important to us as we try to judge what the effective life of our mortgage security will be, as well as how sensitive that particular security is likely to be to future changes in interest rates. There is another compelling reason for us to understand homeowner prepayments, however, and that is so that we can understand what our yield exposure is to changing interest rates and

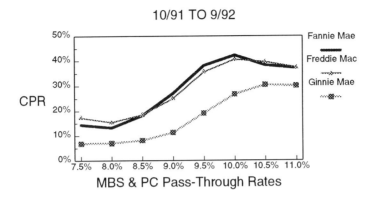

Figure 9.7
Historical Prepayments

prepayments. Not all mortgage securities react the same way to changes in prepayments. An increase in prepayments may raise the yield of one security while it lowers the yield of another, just as a decrease in prepayments can simultaneously lower some mortgage security yields while raising others. In the next chapter we will take a look at premium and discount securities, so that we will be better able to evaluate our own mortgage security investments.

10
Figuring Out Premiums and Discounts

Can we earn a 10% rate of return by purchasing a bond or mortgage that pays an 8.00% interest rate?

Is it possible that we might instead earn only a 4.00% return on that same 8.00% bond or mortgage? Even if principal and interest are paid in full?

Each of the above situations is in fact possible, as are a wide variety of other yield scenarios. Indeed, unless we purchase a security when it is originally issued and hold it until it matures, very few bonds or mortgage-backed securities will earn us a yield equal to the stated interest rate that they bear. They will instead almost always have yields that are either higher or lower than the stated interest rate. Most 6% Treasury bonds bought after their issue date will not earn us a 6% return, and even fewer 7% mortgage-backed securities return a 7% yield to us, even if we do buy them at issuance. What is happening here?

The reason for this difference between the stated interest rate on the security and the actual return realized by us is that there are four sources of yield, and the stated interest rate is only one of those sources. The four sources of yield are:
1. The PRICE we pay.
2. The INTEREST RATE we earn.
3. WHEN we get our principal back.
4. The PRICE we get when we sell.

In this chapter we will learn the relationship between interest rate changes and price changes, and what interest rate changes will cause the value of our investments to rise or fall. We will discover which investments are at the greatest risk from interest rate changes, and which investments have much less risk. We will identify the two ways in which we can lose money through investing in mortgage securities, and we will learn which kind of mortgage security holds the greatest risk for unsophisticated investors, so that we may protect ourselves from unexpected risks.

Security Prices

The value of any security is what it can be sold for, no more and no less. Just as Exxon does not set the price at which its stock trades, and the City of Seattle does not set the price at which its municipal bonds trade, so Freddie Mac, Fannie Mae, and Ginnie Mae do not set the prices at which their mortgage-backed securities trade. Rather, this price is set in the market, by finding the common price at which buyers are willing to buy and sellers are willing to sell.

> "The price of any security is what we can sell or buy it at, no more and no less."

Many factors can affect the price that someone else is willing to pay us for a security. With a stock such as Exxon, share prices are likely to rise and fall with oil prices, crises in the Middle East, tanker spills, and a myriad of other factors. With a municipal or corporate bond, changes in the creditworthiness of the borrower may have an important effect on the bond price, as investors try to judge the likelihood that contractual principal and interest payments will actually be made.

Fortunately, mortgage-backed securities and other governmental agency guaranteed securities are contractual investments of the highest credit quality, so there are fewer factors that affect their prices. The single most important factor in determining the price we can buy or sell at is the current level of interest rates. To illustrate this point, let us say that someone wishes to sell us a $10,000 bond that carries an 8.00% interest rate. If other equivalent bonds are also paying 8.00%, then we will probably be willing to pay them the $10,000 they are asking for the bond.

But what if current bond rates are not 8.00% but 9.00%? Would we pay that person $10,000 for their 8.00% bond, which will earn us $800 a year in interest, when we can earn $900 a year from buying another bond? No, we probably would not. Instead, we would pay them less than $10,000 for their bond, so that the $800 per year will be worth the market rate (9.00%) to us instead of 8.00%.

Figuring Out Premiums and Discounts

The old bond pays $800 per year. New bonds pay $900 per year, so the old bond is LESS valuable. The above example illustrates one of the *two* ways in which we can lose money through investing in agency mortgage securities. If we purchase a mortgage security, and later sell the security at a new lower price, then we *may* lose money. (If we hold the security for more than a short time then interim interest payments will likely prevent us from actually losing money.)

What if current bond rates are not 8.00% but are instead 7.00%? Other $10,000 bonds would pay us not $800 per year, but instead pay us only $700 a year. In this case we wish we could purchase the 8.00% bond for $10,000 but now the seller won't sell the bond for $10,000. He or she wants more than that. We therefore pay more than $10,000, so that our $800 interest payments will earn us the *market rate* of 7.00%. If the old bond pays $800 per year, and new bonds pay $700 per year, the old bond is MORE valuable.

Reversing positions for a moment, let us say that we bought the 8.00% bond last year for $10,000 when rates were 8.00%, and we now want to sell that bond. If rates are still 8.00%, then we can sell our bond for $10,000. If, however, rates have been *rising* above 8.00%, then the price we can sell our bond at has been *falling* to below $10,000. If, on the other hand, market rates have been *falling* below 8.00%, then the market price of our bond has been *rising* above $10,000. As we have seen in our two examples, bond (and mortgage-backed security) prices move in exactly the *opposite* direction that market interest rates do (see Figure 10.1).

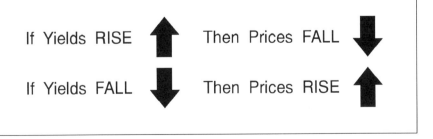

Figure 10.1
Inverse Price/Yield Relationship

How much does the price of our investment rise or fall? The answer to this question naturally depends upon how great the change in market rates has been: we would expect a much bigger price change if rates were to jump up or down 3.00% than if rates were to move up or down only 1.00%.

As a practical concern in building wealth, the exposure of our investments to changes in interest rates is a matter of no small importance. Too often, we make the assumption that interest rates in the future will be much like they are now or have been in the recent past. Over time, this is almost always a mistake, however. The graph in Figure 10.2 shows historical long-term government bond yields over the 20 years from 1970 to 1989.

Changes in rates are not the only factor in determining what our exposure to changes in price on our securities is going to be. There is another component that is just as important: the expected timing of the cash payments from that particular security. The farther away our receipt of that cash is, the greater our sensitivity to changes in interest rates. If we expect to receive our money back from a security in ten years, then that security will have a much larger exposure to price changes than would a security from which we expected to get our money back within a year.

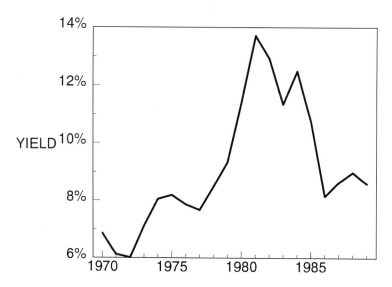

Figure 10.2
Long-Term Yields 1970 - 1989

Figuring Out Premiums and Discounts

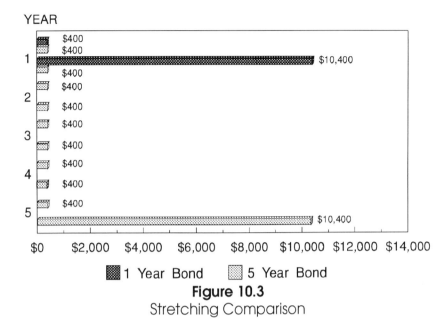

Figure 10.3
Stretching Comparison

We can better understand why this is so by taking another look at the concepts of *stretching* and *snowballing*, which we studied in Chapter 2, and applying them to a comparison of a Treasury bond that is one year away from maturity,[1] and a Treasury bond that is five years away from maturity (see Figure 10.3).

Even though both of the above have the same rate of 8.00%, the first Treasury bond only *stretches* out interest for one year, generating a total of $800 in interest earnings. The second Treasury bond *stretches* out interest for five years, generating a total of $4,000 in interest earnings (plus $10,000 in returned principal for each bond). Each and every interest payment is separately affected by any increase or decrease in yields, and because the longer-term Treasury bond has five times as many interest payments to be revalued, the change in price for that security is larger than for the shorter-term investment.

---

1   Technically, Treasury obligations issued with an *original* maturity of one year or less are called "Treasury bills" and pay interest only at maturity; issues with an *original* maturity of between 2 and 10 years are called "Treasury notes" and pay interest semiannually; and issues with an *original* maturity of greater than 10 years are called "Treasury bonds." In order to simplify our discussion and minimize the potential for terminology confusion, all U.S. Treasury obligations are referred to herein as "bonds" and are assumed to pay interest semiannually.

Mortgage Securities

The other aspect that is vitally important in determining potential price changes of securities we own is that of *snowballing*. As we learned in Chapter 2, the longer the period over which we are investing, the more important the interest on interest component that is the *snowball* becomes. As we further learned in Chapter 3, the farther out in time that we go, the more important any changes in our rate become in determining our ending value. These same principles apply to the *pricing* of bonds and mortgage-backed securities, which means that the farther out any individual cash payment is (be it principal OR interest), the greater the change in a price that a given change in market rates will cause.

Combining the *inverse* relationship between price and yield, the effect of *stretching*, and the impact of *snowballing*, we can now compare how otherwise identical investments of various maturities will change in price under different market interest rate conditions (see Figure 10.4).

In Figure 10.4, we examine how a $10,000 bond with an 8.00% interest rate is priced under various market conditions. If the market rate is 8.00%, then the bond is worth its *face* or *par* amount of $10,000 regardless of the maturity of the bond, as we can see in the middle row in Figure 10.4.

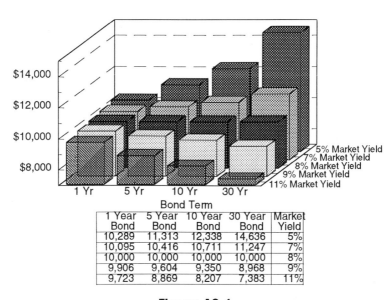

1 Year Bond	5 Year Bond	10 Year Bond	30 Year Bond	Market Yield
10,289	11,313	12,338	14,636	5%
10,095	10,416	10,711	11,247	7%
10,000	10,000	10,000	10,000	8%
9,906	9,604	9,350	8,968	9%
9,723	8,869	8,207	7,383	11%

Figure 10.4
Price Changes: $10,000, 8% Bonds

Figuring Out Premiums and Discounts   111

If, however, the current market rate is above 8.00%, then the price of the bond drops below $10,000 (*rising* rates, *falling* prices). Looking on the 9.00% market yield line, we see that a $10,000 *par* amount 8.00% bond with a one-year maturity is now worth only $9,906. Bonds (and mortgage-backed securities) that sell for less than the face amount of their principal (par) are said to trade at a *discount*, or to be *discount* securities. The amount of the discount is equal to the difference between the *par* amount of the bond, $10,000, and the price of the bond, $9,906, so that the amount of our discount is $94 (0.9%).

Though significant, this price change for the one-year-maturity bond is fairly small. A much greater price difference can be found by looking at bonds with longer maturities (the *farther away* the cash, the *bigger* the price move). Under the same 9.00% market conditions, the combined effects of *stretching* and *snowballing* mean that we experience much larger price moves with increasing maturities (see Figure 10.5).

Though the rate change has been the same, the five-year bond loses $396 in value with a 1.0% market rate rise, the ten-year bond loses $650, and the 30-year bond loses $1,032, more than ten times the $94 loss in value of the one-year maturity. Of course, the higher the market yield, the greater the discount, as is shown in Figure 10.6.

Again, the 30-year bond has almost ten times the price risk of the one-year bond. While significantly less risky than the 30-year bond, the 5- and 10-year bonds nonetheless do still have substantial exposure to price changes as a result of market rate changes. When we take into consideration that higher yields can usually be found only by investing in longer-term bonds, this is the problem

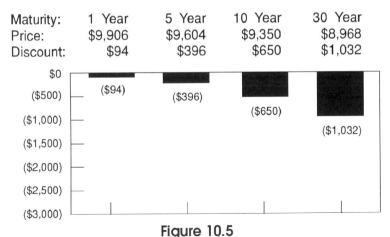

Figure 10.5
$10,000, 8.00% Bonds in a 9.00% Market

Figure 10.6
$10,000, 8.00% Bonds in an 11.00% Market

that usually confronts investors: long-term yields are higher than medium-term yields, which are higher than short-term yields. However, long-term bonds have much greater price risk than do medium-term bonds, which themselves have much greater price risk than short-term investments. Unless we invest in mortgage securities (see Chapter 13) we must risk increasingly larger price losses if we are to reach for the increasingly attractive yields that can be found by lengthening the term of our investments.

The bleak picture of dropping prices above changes entirely if rates drop below 8.00% however, (*falling* rates, *rising* prices). Because we now have an 8.00% bond in a 7.00% market, we can command a premium price for our security. Our $10,000, 8.00% bond with a one-year maturity is now saleable for $10,095. Bonds (and mortgage-backed securities) that sell for more than the face amount of their principal are said to trade at a *premium,* or to be *premium* securities. The amount of the premium is equal to the difference between the par amount of the bond, $10,000, and the price of the bond, $10,095, so that the amount of our premium is $95 (0.9%).

Just as with discount securities, the *farther away* the cash, the *bigger* the *price* move for premium securities. Looking at 7.00% market conditions, the combined effects of stretching and snowballing lead to much bigger price movements for the longer maturity 8.00% bonds (see Figure 10.7).

Should rates fall further, then still greater price appreciation is possible. If market yields fall to a 5% level, then a one-year, 8% security would gain $289 in price, and a 30-year, 8% security would command a premium of $4,636, for a total price of $14,636 (a 46% profit).

Figuring Out Premiums and Discounts

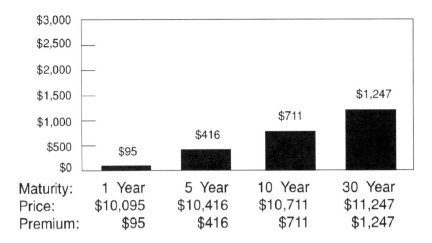

Figure 10.7
$10,000, 8.00% Bonds in a 7.00% Market

Realizing premiums from price gains on our mortgage securities when interest rates are falling is an enjoyable part of investing, but premium securities can also be the most dangerous part of investing in mortgage securities. When premiums become a hazard rather than a benefit is when we purchase securities at a price greater than the principal amount of the security, for example when we pay $11,000 for a $10,000 mortgage security. The price is likely appropriate for the above-market interest rate that the premium security is carrying, but the $1,000 premium that we are paying is neither government-guaranteed nor contractually scheduled to be *directly* repaid in any way. Instead it is expected that we will earn back our extra $1,000 payment through higher interest payments: we would expect to pay a premium for a 10% mortgage security when the market is 8%, with the extra 2% (10% −8%) in coupon paying us another $200 per year in interest payments (prior to prepayments and amortization).

Our risk is that mortgages can prepay at any time, and if a very large amount of principal prepayments come in a short period of time, we may not have enough principal left to generate sufficient interest payments to pay for our purchase of the premium, leaving us with a loss. This potential loss of our premium purchase price is the second of the two ways we can lose money, and it is more dangerous than the first. If we do not sell a mortgage security that has experienced a market value loss as a result of rising interest rates, the passage of time will eventually recover the value of our investment for us through interest payments and the full repayment of principal at par (100 cents on the dollar). With rapid prepayments on premium mortgage securities however, we do not eventually get the premium back, but risk a real and permanent economic loss.

"Caution Is Required When Purchasing Premium Mortgage Securities"

Not all premium mortgage securities are bad or especially risky investments. Some are excellent investments offering significant enhancements for minimal risk. Telling good premium mortgage securities from dangerous premium securities requires an evaluation of the amount of the premium and of the particular prepayment risk carried by that security. In the next chapter we will integrate what we have learned about prices and prepayments so that we will be able to distinguish good investment opportunities from poor speculations.

11
Same Prepayments, Opposite Results: Discounts, Premiums, and Rate Changes

The most important difference between the pricing of bonds, which we examined in the last chapter, and the pricing of mortgage-backed securities lies in the area of prepayments. Of particular pricing importance to us as investors is the distribution of cash flows over the life of the mortgage caused by expected prepayments, and the effect on prepayments of changes in interest rates.

In the pages ahead, combining our knowledge of the Four Faces of Prepayments with what we have just learned of discounts and premiums, we will examine the unique but simple ways in which interest rate changes and prepayment changes together determine price changes for mortgage securities. We will learn the very different manners in which premium and discount mortgage securities react to the same changes in interest rates and prepayments. This critically important knowledge will complete our understanding of the basic principles of mortgage-backed securities investing.

Underlying the rest of the prepayment curve is our First Face of Prepayments: *No Choice*. (See Figure 11.1.) Marriages and divorces, promotions and layoffs, births and deaths; there are many reasons why we can be confident that a goodly number of mortgages must and will prepay in every year, regardless of current interest rate conditions. These *No Choice* prepayments provide us as investors with a stable floor of principal returns from our investments. This floor is usually overshadowed by the other, more prominent Faces, but *No Choice*

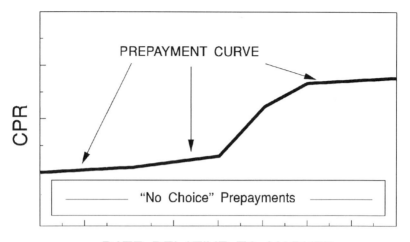

Figure 11.1
Prepayment Curve

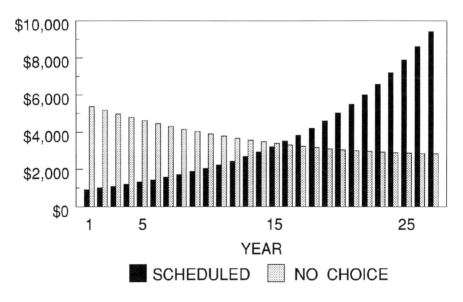

Figure 11.2
Scheduled & "No Choice"
Annual Principal Payments

prepayments are sufficient by themselves to change the nature of our investment, to add sizzle to our discount securities, and to exact an unavoidable toll on our premium securities.

Without the benefit of principal prepayments, mortgage securities are long-term investments. Starting with their first payment, homeowners do pay back at least a few dollars of principal every month, and *reversing the mortgage,* we as investors begin receiving our investment principal back commencing with the first payment we receive. However, it takes a number of years before *stretching* and *stacking* increase to the point where significant amounts of principal are being paid each month, as is shown in Figure 11.2.

When we include the effect of mandatory *No Choice* prepayments, the nature of our investment shifts entirely. Using a 4.5% Constant Prepayment Rate (CPR) for *No Choice* prepayments as is shown in Figure 11.2, we now get our largest principal payments in the early years of our investment and the smallest payments in the final years, a complete reversal of our scheduled mortgage amortization. Despite the long-term maturity of the mortgage security, *No Choice* prepayments mean that in practice we are purchasing a security that has short-term, medium-term, and long-term components all combined into one.

Discount Securities

The addition of these short- and medium-term principal components is a great help to us when we purchase mortgage securities at a discount. To see how *No Choice* prepayments add sizzle to our yields, let us look at an example $10,000 discount security. Let us assume that this security bears a below-market interest rate of 7.50%, and that because of this low interest rate we can purchase it for 90 cents on the dollar ($9,000). What will our yield be from this investment?

$$\text{Current Yield} = \$750 / \$9,000 = 8.33\%$$

If we compare our annual interest earning of $750 to our investment of $9,000, then we find that we are earning an 8.33% return on our investment. This calculation of annual interest earnings compared to cash invested is called a *current yield.* While this is useful to know, current yield does not take into consideration the $1,000 discount at which we bought the security. We paid $9,000, we are getting $10,000 back (plus interest), and we need to include the extra $1,000 in our evaluation of the desirability of the security.

$$\text{Yield to Maturity} = 8.45\%$$

If we received our principal back as we would with a bond investment of equal maturity (27 years), we would receive no principal until final maturity, and then we would receive our $9,000 investment back plus our extra $1,000 in principal. Adding in our $1,000 extra profit at maturity results in a yield to maturity of 8.45%, a relatively modest increase of 0.12% over our current yield. Unlike bonds however, mortgages *amortize* and we receive principal payments continuously over the life of our investment.

Yield to Amortization = 8.67%

Including even small amounts of principal payments in our early years is a significant yield enhancement, for this represents the return of money to us at one dollar for which we only paid 90 cents. The amortization of principal considerably increases the yields which we can realize by purchasing mortgage securities, particularly when compared to bonds of equal maturity purchased at equivalent discounts.

Few people pay their mortgages on a contractual basis all the way to maturity, however. Most prepay their mortgages long before maturity. Remembering how much more principal we received in early years when we include *No Choice* prepayments, we would expect a still greater yield enhancement when we include these minimum prepayments, and that is exactly what happens.

"No Choice" Yield = Prepayment Yield = 9.10%

No Choice prepayments are a welcome protection when we purchase discount mortgage securities. With other types of investments, call or prepayment options are rarely exercised when the security is selling at a discount. Corporate or municipal investors don't want to give up the advantages of what are then below-market financing rates. Normal lifecycle changes among homeowners assure us as mortgage security investors that we will receive full value prepayments purchased at a discounted price regardless of interest rate changes. These *No Choice* prepayments provide us a "floor" yield that is significantly better than we would receive purely from scheduled mortgage amortization payments, and are a reliable means of increasing our income.

Premium Securities

No Choice prepayments have an opposite effect when we purchase premium mortgage securities instead of discount mortgage securities. With a premium security *No Choice* prepayments act as a ceiling that inevitably lowers the income we realize, rather than a floor that raises our minimum yields. To see how our apparent earnings are dragged down with premium securities, let us

Same Prepayments, Opposite Results   119

go to our previous example and assume that we now have a $10,000, above-market 9.50% security, for which we pay a premium price of $11,000 (110 cents on the dollar). Dividing interest paid ($950) by price paid ($11,000) we find our current yield:

Current Yield = $950 / $11,000 = 8.64%

Looking just at interest compared to price paid, we find a relatively attractive 8.64% *current yield* on our premium mortgage security. Unfortunately, we know that we cannot receive that yield indefinitely, for we must have our principal returned to us. We know we will be getting only $10,000 in *principal* back for the $11,000 we invested, and we must recognize that there will be a real loss of $1,000, which will inevitably lower the actual yield that we realize.

Premium Security

Yield to Maturity	= 8.55%
Yield to Amortization	= 8.39%
"No Choice" Yield = Prepayment Yield	= 8.03%

Adding the return at final maturity 27 years from now of our principal at a $1,000 loss (as we would with a long-term bond) has a fairly small effect on yield. We would only lose 0.09% from our current yield. Contractual mortgage amortization now has a negative effect on our investment as principal is returned early to us at a loss, dropping our yield to 8.39%. When we include even minimal *No Choice* prepayments, our yield drops quite a bit further to 8.03%, a decline of 0.61% from our apparently attractive current yield.

It is important for our own protection as investors that we recognize that we *cannot* achieve our current yield with premium mortgage securities, for principal *will* be returned to us, and the return of that principal at a loss *will* lower our actual yields. Through their role in bringing the recognition of these principal losses forward into the early years of our investment, *No Choice* prepayments can be counted on to inevitably lower the yields that we will receive as investors from premium mortgage securities.

''NEVER Use Current Yield as The Primary Basis for Making Mortgage Security Investment Decisions.''

Some investment salesmen will use the sensible-sounding approach of current yield in selling premium mortgage securities, and a comparison of our examples above shows why we should never use current yield to make our mortgage investment decisions. Our discount security had a current yield of 8.33%, but the real minimum yield rose to 9.10% when we took into account the profitable returns of principal from mortgage amortization payments and *No Choice* principal prepayments. The premium security had an apparently more attractive 8.64% current yield, but the real maximum yield was only 8.03% after taking into account the certain return of scheduled and *No Choice* investment principal at a loss. As we will see in the next few pages, our real loss in yield from current yield on premium securities is in fact likely to be much larger than that after we take into account the more powerful prepayment effects of *Better Home* and *Better Rate* prepayments.

Underlying Simplicity

When evaluating the potential profits or losses we may realize from our investments, we must take into account not only the direct changes in price that result from interest rate changes, but also the changes in prepayments caused by these interest changes, which themselves change the pricing of the security. *No Choice* prepayments don't change with changes in interest rates, which makes their effect upon us as investors quite straightforward. However, *Better Home* and *Better Rate* prepayments do change with changes in interest rates, and in doing so they alter the speed with which our principal is returned to us. Further complicating matters is the problem that par, discount, and premium securities each have their own differing price responses to changes in interest and prepayment rates.

At first glance, this may seem hopelessly complicated, and a good reason for leaving mortgage securities to the professionals. This need not be the case at all, however, for underlying this seeming complexity are a few simple-to-understand principles which we can all easily understand.

Mortgage securities are the most personal of investments. There is no need for us to understand double-entry accounting, how changes in the balance of trade interrelate to currency fluctuations, or the implications of an increase in the Federal Reserve discount rate upon the valuation of growth stocks. In order to understand the profit and loss potential of differing mortgage securities all we have to do is understand that people act in their own self-interest: *Acting In Our Own Self-interest HOMEOWNERS want to pay LESS money and INVESTORS want to get MORE money*

Homeowners will consistently act in their own self-interest to pay less money on their mortgages as often as possible, and investors will consistently act in their own self-interest to always earn as much money as they can. Merely considering how we ourselves try to minimize expenses and maximize income will give us the knowledge we need to understand every aspect of how par,

Same Prepayments, Opposite Results   121

discount, and premium mortgage securities change in price with rising and falling interest rates. This personal understanding will empower us to act in our own self-interest and select for ourselves the mortgage securities most suited to our own individual needs.

Par Mortgage Securities

Better Home prepayments decline when interest rates rise and it becomes relatively more expensive for homeowners to move to a more desirable location; for homeowners act in their own self-interest and move less often. *Better Home* prepayments rise when interest rates decline and it becomes relatively less expensive for homeowners to move to their dream home or city. (See Figure 11.3.) These prepayment changes have a direct effect on the profits and losses we realize with our mortgage-backed securities under conditions of falling or rising interest rates.

Let us first take a look at falling rates. With falling interest rates our mortgage-backed security becomes more attractive to other investors, since it has a higher interest rate than new investments have. Because of this higher rate, the value of our security to other investors rises, and we can now sell our investment at a profit compared to the price we originally paid.

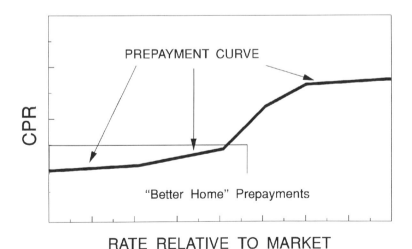

Figure 11.3
"Better Home" Prepayments

At the same time, the *Better Home* Face of Prepayments tells us that the homeowners whose mortgages comprise our mortgage-backed security are more likely to move elsewhere and prepay their mortgages, since the decline in rates has reduced the cost to the homeowners of moving. This increase in prepayment rates means that we get more cash sooner, and less cash later, which shortens the average life of our investment.

Combining these two effects, the decline in interest rates does definitely increase the value of our investment, as it now bears an above-market interest rate, which makes it more attractive to other investors. However, this decline in interest rates shortens the life of our investment at the same time because of increasing *Better Home* prepayments. Since the increase in price is less for shorter-term investments than for longer-term investments (the *closer* the cash, the *smaller* the price move), this means that the increase in value of our investment to other investors is less than it otherwise would have been.

Below is an example of a framework we can use when we wish to determine how different mortgage securities change in price with different changes in interest rates:

Par Securities, Falling Interest Rates

1. Homeowners take advantage of lower interest rates by moving more often.

2. Investors are willing to pay more for our security, because it now yields more than new mortgage securities.

3. The increase in homeowner moves means that we have more *close-in cash,* and less *faraway cash*, as more mortgages are more rapidly prepaid.

4. *Close-in cash* means smaller price swings, as investors desire short-term, above-market securities less than long-term, above-market securities.

5. We realize a profit in our securities, but it is reduced by the increased homeowner prepayments, which make the security less valuable to investors than it would have been without a change in prepayments.

This relationship is clearly not advantageous to us as investors. What happens if rates are rising instead of falling?

Par Securities, Rising Interest Rates

1. Homeowners save their money during times of higher interest rates by moving less often.

Same Prepayments, Opposite Results 123

2. Investors will pay us less for our security, because it now yields less than new mortgage securities.

3. The decrease in homeowner moves means that we have less *close-in cash*, and more *faraway cash*, as mortgages are less rapidly prepaid.

4. *Faraway cash* means bigger price swings, as investors *penalize* long-term, below-market securities more than short-term, below-market securities.

5. We realize a price *loss* in our securities, and it is *increased* by the decreased homeowner prepayments, which make the security less valuable to investors than it would have been without a change in prepayments.

The way in which the *Better Home* Face of Prepayments reacts to interest rate changes, always either reducing our profits or increasing our losses, is clearly unattractive for us as investors. Just how bad is the effect of changes in *Better Home* prepayments upon our mortgage securities investments? Let us first take a look at what happens to the price of an 8.50% mortgage-backed security in markets that move up or down 1.00%, with no prepayment changes. Please note that our prepayment rate is no longer the worst-case 4.5% CPR, but a more realistic 10.5%, which is about right for a Fannie Mae or Freddie Mac that has a rate that is close to current market:

Price Changes With No Prepayment Changes

Market Yield	MBS Rate	CPR Prepay	Average Life	Market Value
7.50%	8.50%	10.5%	7.4	$10,494
8.50%	8.50%	10.5%	7.4	$10,000
9.50%	8.50%	10.5%	7.4	$ 9,548

With no prepayment changes, a *fall* in rates of 1.0% means that price *rises* by $494. A *rise* in rates of 1.0% means that price *falls* by $452 (10,000 – 9,548 = 452).

"Better Home" Prepayment Price Changes

Market Yield	MBS Rate	CPR Prepay	Average Life	Market Value
7.50%	8.50%	16.0%	5.2	$10,381
8.50%	8.50%	10.5%	7.4	$10,000
9.50%	8.50%	9.0%	8.3	$ 9,514

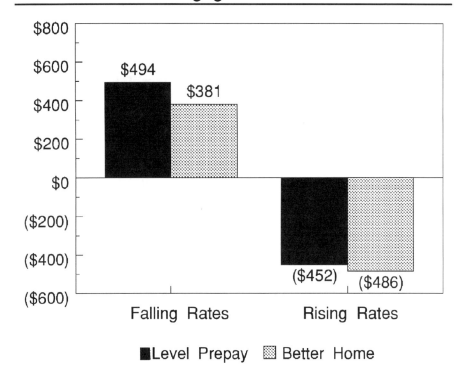

Figure 11.4
Better Home Prepayment Changes Price Effect

Our picture changes significantly once we include the effects of changes in *Better Home* prepayments caused by the change in market rates. *Falling* rates still mean *rising* prices, but they also mean increased prepayments as homeowners find it less expensive to move. These increased prepayments mean a shorter average life, and as *closer-in cash* means *smaller* price moves, we gain only $381 in price instead of $494.

Rising rates still mean *falling* prices, but they also mean decreased prepayments as homeowners find it more expensive to move. These decreased prepayments mean a longer average life, and as *farther-away cash* means *bigger* price moves, we now lose $486 in price instead of $452 (see Figure 11.4).

The impact of *Better Home* prepayments upon price changes is negative, and is significant but not to an overwhelming degree. We see our profits decreased by a little more than 1% in the example above, and our losses increased by about 0.33%.

Discount Securities

Better Home prepayments are also an important consideration when we purchase either discount or premium mortgage securities. Unless we are purchasing a security that is composed of mortgages with deeply below-market interest rates, *Better Home* prepayments will be having a strong influence on our return of principal. If we have purchased discount mortgage securities, then *Better Home* prepayments speed the return of full value principal to us, which we bought at a discounted price, enhancing our yield:

Discount Security

Current Yield = $750 / $9,000	= 8.33%
Mortgage Yield = Yield to Amortization	= 8.67%
"No Choice" Yield = 4.5% CPR Yield	= 9.10%
"Better Home" Yield = 9% CPR Yield	= 9.58%

In addition to raising the yields that we can realize through purchasing discount mortgage securities, *Better Home* prepayments also play an important role in determining price changes. When rates fall, *Better Home* prepayments speed up, as more and more homeowners who would like to be able to move find it economically easier to do so. Principal dollars are expected to come in sooner and sooner as more mortgages prepay, and the price assigned to each of these principal payments is increasing because rates are falling. Working together, these two factors give our discount mortgage securities a significant increase in both yield and price as rates fall:

Discount Securities, Falling Interest Rates

1. Homeowners take advantage of lower interest rates by moving more often.

2. Investors are willing to pay more for our security, because it now yields more than new mortgage securities.

3. The increase in homeowner moves means that we have more *close-in cash,* and less *faraway cash,* as more mortgages are more rapidly prepaid.

4. *Close-in cash* means smaller price swings, as investors penalize short-term, below-market securities less than long-term, below-market securities.

5. Faster prepayments leading to *close-in cash* also means that we are getting the profit back from our discount sooner, which increases our yield and the amount of money that other investors are willing to pay us for the security.

6. We realize an enhanced profit on our securities, as the boost in yield we enjoy from the accelerated return of our discounted principal to us increases the yield advantage that our security holds over new securities, thereby making our security more valuable to other investors than it would have been without a change in prepayments.

If, however, market rates rise, then homeowner discretionary moves decrease because of higher new mortgage rates. This reduction of *Better Home* prepayments means that we do not get the profits from the return of our discounted principal until later than anticipated, thereby reducing our yield. The rise in rates makes our mortgage securities less valuable, and as our cash moves farther away, our price loss is even increasing (*faraway cash* means big price moves). Both factors, prepayment changes and yield changes, are working in conjunction to magnify price changes. However, this time they are both working to reduce price:

Discount Securities, Rising Interest Rates

1. Homeowners save their money during times of higher interest rates by moving *less* often.

2. Investors will pay us less for our security, because it now yields less than new mortgage securities.

3. The decrease in homeowner moves means that we have less *close-in cash,* and more *faraway cash,* as mortgages are less rapidly prepaid.

4. *Faraway cash* means bigger price swings, as investors penalize long-term, below-market securities more than short-term, below-market securities.

5. Slower prepayments leading to *faraway cash* also means that we are getting the profit back from our discount later than expected, which decreases our yield and the amount of money that other investors are willing to pay us for the security.

6. We realize an enhanced price *loss* in our securities, and it is *increased* by the decreased homeowner prepayments, which extends the life and slows down the discount recapture by our security, making it less valuable to investors than it would have been without a change in prepayments.

Same Prepayments, Opposite Results   127

"Better Home" prepayments Increase the magnitude of
Discount security profits and losses.

Better Home prepayments fortunately work to enhance our market value profits from discount mortgage securities when rates fall, but unfortunately those same factors also work to increase the level of our market value losses when rates rise (though such profits or losses need not be recognized unless we sell our investments).

As we can see in Figure 11.5, for our example $10,000 discount, 7.50% security selling at 90, adding in changes in prepayments has the effect of increasing profits by 0.1% with a half percent fall in rates, and of increasing losses by 0.4% with a 0.5% rise in rates. With steeper discounts, we will see increased magnitude of profits or loss swings, with smaller discounts, we see a pricing relationship that is closer to that of par securities.

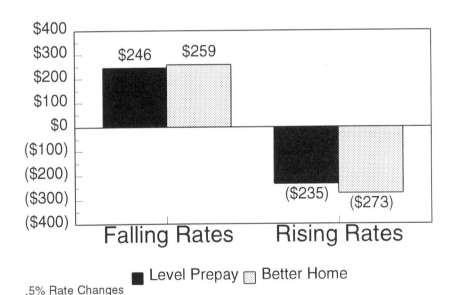

Figure 11.5
Better Home Prepayment Changes Price Effect

Premium Securities

The speedier return of principal attributable to *Better Home* prepayments has a strongly positive impact on our realized yield when we purchase discount mortgage securities. This same speed increase in the return of our principal has the opposite effect however when our principal is coming back to us at a loss rather than a profit:

Premium Security

Current Yield = $950 / $11,000	= 8.64%
Mortgage Yield = Yield to Amortization	= 8.39%
"No Choice" Yield = 4.5% CPR Yield	= 8.03%
"Better Home" Yield = 9% CPR Yield	= 6.95%

Each time that we add a level of realism to our evaluation of premium mortgage securities, our realized yield drops farther beneath our current yield or yield to scheduled amortization. This is not to say that premium securities will yield less than discount securities. In many cases premium securities will carry higher expected yields than discount securities even after realistically adjusting for full expected prepayments. The important conclusion that we should draw from this is that as dollars spent on purchasing premiums are our only mortgage security investment dollars that we are not certain of getting back, we should exercise caution in purchasing premium securities. This is particularly true when we are considering purchasing securities priced at 104 cents on the dollar or higher. Such securities should only be purchased by individuals who are thoroughly familiar with and comfortable in evaluating prepayments; otherwise, expectations can become illusions as tantalizing yields turn into disappointing losses. Please note that this a problem with premium securities only, and that we can easily avoid this problem by not purchasing securities at more than slight premiums.

The same factors that cause *Better Home* prepayments to magnify discount security price changes have an opposite effect upon premium securities. Let us consider what happens to premium security prices when rates fall, and prices rise. These same falling rates allow more homeowners to take advantage of lower potential mortgage rates and payments by moving to new locations, thereby increasing *Better Home* prepayments. The increase in early cash resulting from *Better Home* prepayments reduces our price gain (*close-in cash* means *smaller* price moves). The same prepayments also reduce our collection of above-market interest rates because our principal is being repaid earlier

Same Prepayments, Opposite Results   129

than we expected at a loss to us of our premium, thereby decreasing our yield further. Adding all these factors together, our price still increases, but by a smaller amount than we might expect, because the negative price effects of *Better Home* prepayments are working in opposition to the positive price effects of the decrease in market rates:

Premium Securities, Falling Interest Rates

1. Homeowners take advantage of lower interest rates by moving more often.

2. Investors are willing to pay more for our security, because it now yields more than new mortgage securities.

3. The increase in homeowner moves means that we have more *close-in cash*, and less *faraway cash*, as more mortgages are more rapidly prepaid.

4. *Close-in cash* means smaller price swings, as investors desire short-term, above-market securities less than long-term, above-market securities.

5. Faster prepayments leading to *close-in cash* also means that we are forced to recognize the loss of the money we paid in premium sooner, which decreases our yield and the amount of money that other investors are willing to pay us for the security.

6. We realize a reduced profit on our securities, as the loss in yield we face from the accelerated write-off of our premium reduces the yield advantage that our security holds over new securities, thereby making our security less valuable to other investors than it would have been without a change in prepayments.

The same factors that limit our gains when rates fall also reduce our losses when *rising* rates cause security prices to *fall*. Increases in mortgage rates make it more difficult for homeowners to afford discretionary moves, and *Better Home* prepayments fall. The decrease in prepayments increases the value of our above-market interest rates, as we are receiving them for a longer time now, and also defers the recognition of our losses from the return of principal at par for which we paid a premium. Adding all these factors together, our investment is losing value, but by a smaller amount than we might expect, because now it is the positive price effects of *Better Home* prepayments that are working in opposition to the negative price effects of the decrease in market rates.

Premium Securities, Rising Interest Rates

1. Homeowners save their money during times of higher interest rates by moving less often.
2. Investors will pay us less for our security, because it now yields less than new mortgage securities.
3. The decrease in homeowner moves means that we have less *close-in cash,* and more *faraway cash*, as mortgages are less rapidly prepaid.
4. *Faraway cash* is more valuable as investors desire long-term, above-market securities more than short-term, above-market securities.
5. Slower prepayments leading to *faraway cash* also means that we are realizing the loss back from our premium later than expected, which increases our yield and the amount of money that other investors are willing to pay us for the security.
6. We realize a reduced price loss on our securities, as decreased homeowner prepayments extend the life and slow down the premium loss recognition by our security, making our loss less than it would have been without a change in prepayments.

When we purchase mortgage securities at a premium, then, we have an opposite pricing effect from when we purchase them at a discount, for instead of magnifying price swings, changes in prepayment speeds now *reduce* the magnitude of price swings.

Better Home prepayments decrease the magnitude of premium security profits and losses. Instead of larger profits and losses, we now have smaller profits when rates rise, and lower losses when rates fall. It is also worth noting that because premium securities are usually made up of higher-coupon mortgages that are experiencing relatively high prepayment levels, their *close-in cash* means that they are generally less exposed to price risk than discount or par securities (see Figure 11.6).

Prepayments are clearly a most important factor in determining the future value of our investment, or what yield discount or premium investments will actually generate for us. *No Choice* and *Better Home* prepayments work together to keep our investments within certain bounds of yield, life, and price, though their effect may differ widely depending on whether we are purchasing discount or premium mortgage securities.

Same Prepayments, Opposite Results 131

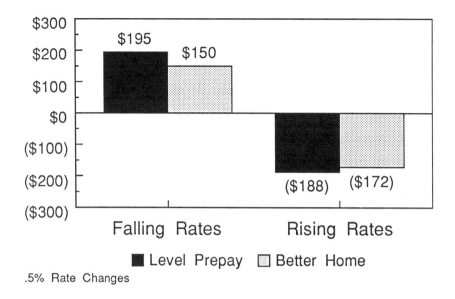

Figure 11.6
Premium Securities & Better Home Prepayments

In the next chapter we will expand our exploration of prepayments to include *Better Rate* and *No Telling* prepayments, completing our understanding of these simple but important relationships.

12
The Pitfalls and Pleasures of Topping The Prepayment Curve

The most powerful Face of Prepayments, and the face that is sometimes the most damaging to us as mortgage investors, is *Better Rate*. When new mortgage rates drop to the point that refinancings become advantageous to homeowners, then large numbers of those homeowners begin to prepay their mortgages. The lower that new mortgage rates go, the greater the advantage to refinancing, and the more mortgages that prepay.

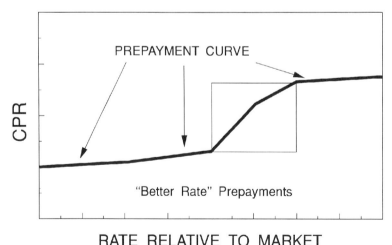

Figure 12.1
Prepayment Curve

When we *reverse the mortgage,* this means that just as large declines in interest rates should be making our high-rate, mortgage-backed security extremely valuable (BIG interest rate changes = BIG price moves), prepayments are speeding up drastically (see Figure 12.1). If rates continue to fall, thereby making the high rate on our security even more valuable, prepayments just continue to accelerate as more and more homeowners refinance their mortgages. Unfortunately, the shorter the amount of time we have to receive above-market interest rates, the less valuable those interest rates are, so that *Better Home* prepayments keep us from realizing the large profits that we otherwise would during times of sharply falling market interest rates.

This is the same relationship that we saw with *Better Home* prepayments, except that refinancing prepayments can grow much more rapidly than moving-related prepayments. There are many more people who will refinance their existing homes in order to take advantage of lower mortgage rates than would consider going through the inconvenience and expense of selling their existing home and moving to another. The effect of all these refinancing-induced *Better Rate* prepayments is to drastically reduce the expected average life of our investment. As an example, let us take a look at our 27-year, 8.50% mortgage-backed security again, and observe the changes in price and average life as market yields drop from 1% below our security to 2% below, and then to 3% below, sending *Better Rate* prepayments soaring as homeowners rush to refinance:

"Better Rate" Prepayment Price Changes

Market Yield	MBS Rate	CPR Prepay	Average Life	Market Value
5.50%	8.50%	35.0%	2.3	$10,614
6.50%	8.50%	27.0%	3.1	$10,517
7.50%	8.50%	16.0%	5.2	$10,381

Our 8.50% mortgage security is poised above the refinancing range when market yields are 7.50%, with *Better Home* prepayments having pushed our prepayment level up to a 16% CPR. A further 1% drop in market yields has the effect of making our securities (and the underlying mortgages) a full 2% above the current rate, a level that triggers a surge of *Better Rate* prepayments as homeowners lower their monthly payments through refinancings. This has the effect of lowering the average life of our investment from 5.2 years to 3.1 years, a decline of 40%. A further 1% drop in market yields brings in still more *Better Rate* refinancing prepayments, cutting the expected life of our investment another 25% to just over two years.

Topping the Prepayment Curve

The value of our investment is continuing to rise with falling market yields, however *Better Rate* prepayments are reducing the benefits to us of the drop in interest rates, as the value of our investments increases by a smaller margin with each decrease in rates. *Better Rate* prepayments are exacting an increasing penalty compared to what our price gains would have been if it were not for prepayments (see Figure 12.2).

If our prepayments had stayed level as yields dropped, we would have realized several times more in profits than we do with *Better Rate* prepayments. Unfortunately, *Better Rate* prepayments bring the timing of our principal payments forward and our profits down.

Better Rate Pricing
Closer-in Cash = Smaller Price Moves
Offsets
BIG Interest Change = BIG Price Move
Leaving
Very Small Price Move

The loss of most of our upside profit potential does not come without corresponding benefits to us, however. If we own a mortgage security that is experiencing *Better Rate* refinancing prepayments, and interest rates rise, then the time over which we are receiving above-market interest payments, and amortizing our premium loss, extends dramatically. The impact for us as investors is that the decrease in refinancing prepayments can offset nearly all

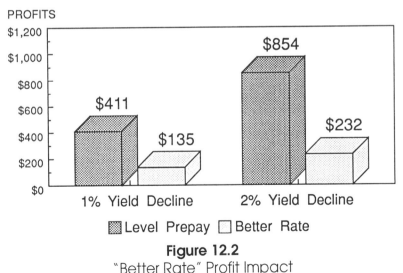

Figure 12.2
"Better Rate" Profit Impact

of the losses that we would otherwise experience from the rise in rates, leaving us with a very small price loss (see Figure 12.3).

Another way of stating reduced exposure to profits and losses is to say *reduced price risk*, and this is in fact a powerful advantage of investing in mortgage securities that are *already* well into the *Better Rate* refinancing range (if we are just below the refinancing range, then we have small profit potential and significant loss potential). With the corresponding shifts in *Better Rate* prepayments offsetting most of the negative or positive effects of a change in market interest rates, our net price risk is a small fraction of what it would be with other mortgage securities, let alone long-term bonds. However, it should be noted that these premium securities do not have the full protections we find went with par or discount securities: the recovery of our premium is in no way guaranteed, purchase prepayment speeds are easily manipulated, and changes in anticipated prepayments can have a powerful effect on realized yield. For these reasons, mortgage securities selling at significant premiums (prices of 104 or above) should only be purchased by individuals who are thoroughly comfortable with prepayments and who know what is entailed in premium pricing and yields, and the various parts of the prepayment curve.

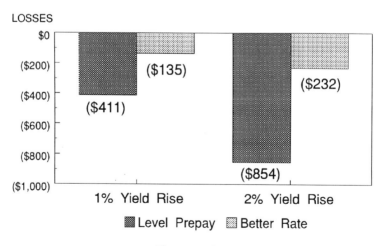

Figure 12.3
"Better Rate" Loss Impact

No Telling

The *No Telling* Face of Prepayments is the moderating influence that prevents the *Better Rate* Face from prepaying all outstanding high-rate mortgages in full as soon as refinancing becomes advantageous. If every homeowner in the country were to act as one when mortgage rates reached a refinancing point, then every 11.00% mortgage would have paid off within a few months of when mortgage rates first reached 9.00%, just as every 10.00% mortgage would have paid off shortly after rates first reached 8.00%. Not everyone knows about the rate reductions or wants to or can prepay at one time, however, and so the accelerated level of mortgage prepayments continues at a high percentage level for a number of years.

The effects of constant *Better Rate* prepayments moderated by the *No Telling* lack of prepayments to a level of a 35% CPR are shown in Figure 12.4. While our prepayment rate is remaining constant, nearly all of our cash flow occurs in the first few years. Over time, our high-rate mortgages do almost completely prepay. Within 4 or 5 years after the economy enters a lower interest rate period, which makes refinancing advantageous, the great majority of high interest rate mortgages from the preceding higher interest rate period will have paid off.

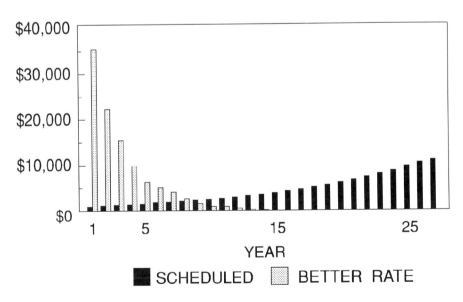

Figure 12.4
Scheduled & "Better Rate" Annual Principal Payments

No Telling does not then permanently stop the effects of the *Better Rate* Face of Prepayments. By slowing down the prepayments of principal and *stretching* out the receipts of above-market interest rate payments, *No Telling* does, however, allow us as mortgage-backed securities investors to still substantially profit from falling interest rates, albeit not as much as we would have without prepayments. Combined, the *Better Rate* and *No Telling* Faces of Prepayments create an effective cap on the prices of mortgage-backed securities in the range of 110% to 120% of par (see Figure 12.5). This means that a $100,000 mortgage-backed security is unlikely ever to trade significantly above $115,000, as rising prepayments cancel out the effects of further decreases in interest rates (though a few high-premium securities that have been in a refinancing range for years and have "burned out" their *Better Rate* prepayments will trade at higher prices, due to a relative decline in their prepayment rates).

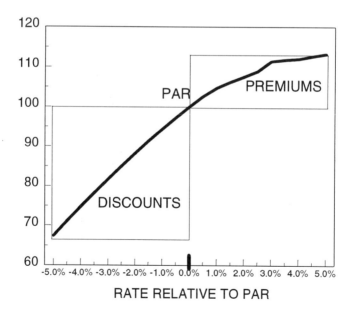

Figure 12.5
Mortgage Security Price Curve

Better Rate Prepayments And Discount Securities

All of our discussion so far of *Better Home* and *No Telling* prepayments has revolved around premium mortgage securities. This is appropriate, because with few exceptions,[1] any mortgage security that is experiencing *Better Rate* prepayments is doing so for the reason that the underlying mortgages are carrying rates significantly above market. While we generally cannot buy a discount or par mortgage security that is experiencing *Better Rate* prepayments at the time of purchase, we may own a security that we bought at par or a discount at an earlier time when market rates were higher.

Our price movements for such securities during a time of *Better Rate* refinancing prepayments will be much the same as if we had purchased them as premiums. We will be carrying substantial profits in these securities relative to our original purchase price. However, our future price movements during a long fall in interest rates will be governed by the cap on mortgage security prices, with steadily reducing price gains per unit of interest rate change, until we bump up against our ceiling price.

Our realized yields from such securities will be strongly affected by *Better Rate* prepayments if we purchased our security at a discount (yields on par securities do not change with prepayment changes unless we sell the security prior to maturity). With discount securities we have already seen that we experience substantial increases in yield with decreasing market rates, as the principal that we purchased at 90 cents on the dollar is returned to us at full value. The rapid rise in prepayments triggered by *Better Rate* refinancings causes a sharp rise in yield for securities that we purchased at discount (see Figure 12.6).

While it is worthwhile to note that *Better Rate* prepayments can actually benefit mortgage security yields, we should also note it would take a steep and fast decline in interest rates to achieve results like those shown above, so that the actual likelihood of achieving such results is quite low (though this is precisely what happened during much of the 1980s).

---

[1] There are some derivative mortgage securities that do allow us to pay discount prices for securities whose underlying mortgages are in or near the *Better Rate* refinancing range. Examples include principal-only securities (POs) and some low-coupon tranches of collateralized mortgage obligations (CMOs).

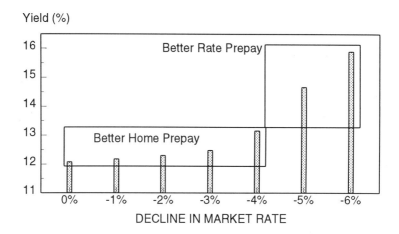

Figure 12.6
10% MBS Purchased at 90

A No-Win Proposition?

Looking only at the *Better Home* and *Better Rate* aspects of prepayments, we might be tempted to stay away from mortgage-backed securities altogether. With very few exceptions, it seems to be a no-win proposition. Every time rates go up and we want our money back so we can invest our money at higher rates, prepayments slow down and we get our money back more slowly. Every time rates go down and we don't want our money back because we would be forced to reinvest it at lower interest rates, prepayments speed up and we get our money back sooner than planned. If we should be lucky enough to buy when rates are high but heading much lower, then the *Better Rate* Face of Prepayments means that most of our money is quickly returned to us, before we can fully benefit from high rates in a low-rate market.

> "Rates Up, Prepayments Down, We Lose.
> Rates Down, Prepayments Up, We Lose."

Before we give up entirely on mortgage-backed securities, however, there are several other points we may want to take into consideration:

1. We get our money back.
2. There are two sides to every coin.
3. The pros are usually not stupid.

Topping the Prepayment Curve 141

1. We get our money back.

A single unexpected negative earnings report can send a growth stock plunging 30%, 40%, even 50% or more in a matter of days or weeks. A bankruptcy filing can leave the corporate bond holder or municipal revenue bond owner waiting years as a court determines how many pennies on the dollar they will receive back. Bad guesses and unexpected market moves can leave the futures or options investor losing his or her entire investment portfolio (and more) in a matter of days. With a mortgage-backed security, we get all of our *principal* investment back, plus interest in full (premium is not guaranteed, but we can avoid high-premium securities). Though they are very important, market moves and changes in price directly affect us only if we sell our security; otherwise they are "paper" losses and gains. Even if we do sell before maturity, so long as we have held our investment for at least three to five years, it is almost certain that the total principal and interest we will have received in combination with even a deeply discounted sale price will exceed our initial investment. The level of our return is at risk if we sell prior to maturity, but at least we can count on its being positive over a multiyear period, something that cannot be said about most investments.

2. There are two sides to every coin.

When rates rise, discount mortgage-backed securities do drop especially fast in price because of declining prepayments. When rates fall, premium mortgage-backed securities do rise especially slowly in price because of accelerating prepayments. While each of these relationships are undesirable, there is a flip side to each of them. If we buy a discount mortgage-backed security and rates fall, the increase in prepayments means that our security *increases* in price and yield extra fast! If we buy a premium mortgage-backed security and rates rise, the decrease in prepayments gives us a security that falls extra *slowly* in price, compared to other securities.

Decreases and increases in interest rates and prepayments can have a widely varying impact on our mortgage-backed securities investments, depending on the interest rates on the underlying mortgages and how those rates compare to current market rates, as well as what the price is at which we purchase the security. By selecting whether our security purchase will be a discount, premium, or near-par, and where on the prepayment curve the underlying mortgages are (see Figure 12.7), we can control the relative chances we are taking with regard to prepayment risk, yield risk, and price risk. There are always *at least* two sides to prepayment changes, and while we do not have the ability to change the reasons homeowners make prepayments, or how the market will value our securities, we do have the ability to individually position ourselves based upon our own investment goals, situation, and risk tolerance.

142 Mortgage Securities

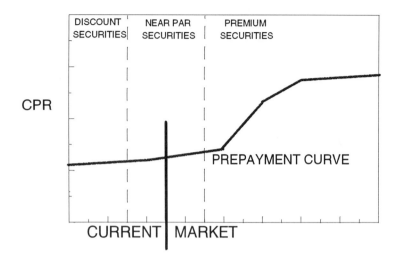

Figure 12.7

3. The pros are usually not stupid.

The professional investors who collectively manage the trillions of dollars held in our pension funds, insurance companies, and banking institutions are not stupid people. They are sometimes prone to fads and trends and some of them do make costly mistakes (as with junk bonds and commercial real estate lending in the late 1980s), but if a product turns out to be riskier than expected, they desert it en masse.

After 22 years of investing in mortgage-backed securities and several trips up and down the prepayment curve, professional investors have not deserted the mortgage-backed security marketplace. Quite the reverse. The market is eagerly continuing to purchase as many mortgage-backed securities as possible. Even after experiencing floods of *Better Rate* refinancing prepayments in recent years, the professional investor's market continues to drive the yields on mortgages lower and lower. Why?

The surprisingly positive answers to this question will be found in the next few chapters.

13
The Surprising Truth about Price Risk

To be able to see the future is an age-old desire of mankind. In olden days soothsayers cast bones, shamans pulled out the entrails of animals, and astrologers charted the positions of the planets and the stars as people searched for the patterns that would allow them to predict the future. Today, economists study leading indicators and unemployment figures; market technicians chart heads, shoulders, waves, and cycles; journalists track hemlines and baseball teams; and we continue our elusive search for a way to peer into the future.

The investment stakes are high, as the most important information to us in selecting an investment strategy is not what different strategies have yielded in the past, for while this is useful to know, the past rarely repeats itself in a predictable manner. Nor is the current yield of an investment strategy the most important information to us, for both yields and relative values change in changing markets. The most important information we need to know is what our investments *will* yield over the time that we own them, and how this will compare to our investment needs. The number-one yield question is not "What HAS it yielded?" or "What IS it yielding?" but "What WILL it yield?"

There are some who are quick to provide the answers to this question. Rates are going up, so we must invest short-term. Rates are going down, so we must invest long-term. Unfortunately, however, the technicians and chartists of modern financial markets are by and large no more accurate or reliable than the shamans or astrologers of times past. Numerous credentialed economic and financial experts are willing to offer up well-thought-out and supported predictions, but how do we know which expert to believe? This leaves us as investors in a perpetual state of uncertainty as to what the markets will be doing next. Are rates going up or down? Is the market going up or down? How can we invest if we do not know the answers to these questions?

144 Mortgage Securities

This is the heart of the investor's dilemma. In order to do what we would really like to do, which is to consistently make large profits without ever taking losses, we need to know what we cannot know, which is the future. There is no absolute way around this dilemma. However, there are investment tools that we can use to help reduce our risks and increase our gains in an uncertain future.

Looking at Many Futures

An effective investment management tool used by many professional investors involves considering a number of likely possible market scenarios for the future. For instance, interest rates may moderately rise or fall, they may sharply rise or fall, or they may stay level. Instead of selecting one scenario (rising rates) as being more likely than the others and investing for that market (thereby taking on the notoriously difficult task of predicting the market), we accept that we do not know the future and we examine how each of several investment alternatives performs under different possible future markets. Based upon the overall performance of each of our alternative investments under a variety of market conditions, we are then able to sort out which investments carry more risk than we are willing to take, which investments are usually unsatisfactory, and which investments offer us superior performance under a diversity of possible future markets.

Professional investors like this conservative methodology because it is a better way to achieve superior results over the long term than market speculation. We too can use this methodology to carefully control our risk exposure while achieving our own superior investment results over the long term, without our being forced to gamble our savings on someone's ability to try to predict the vagaries of the markets. It is through using this methodology that we will discover why mortgage securities are such a favorite of professional investors, who must face the task of making investment decisions every day while knowing that the sum of their decisions will be precisely judged in the future. We will learn how mortgage securities "beat the market" with a superior combination of increased yields and reduced risks for an uncertain future, and how we can use this unique risk/return combination to solve a thorny investment problem that faces most individual investors.

Table 13.1 applies the tool of multiple-scenario analysis. It may at first glance appear to be an impenetrable maze of numbers, but if we remember the basic price relationships we learned in earlier chapters, it is not only easily understandable but highly useful. Within the table is a guide to the exact relationship between yields we receive versus the price risks we take in different

Table 13.1
Assessing Investment Price Risk

	Interest Rate Change Scenario			
	2.0%	1.0%	−1.0%	−2.0%
1-year 4.50% bond	-1.9%	-1.0%	1.0%	2.0%
3-year 6.00% bond	-5.2%	-2.7%	2.8%	5.6%
4-year 6.50% bond	-6.7%	-3.4%	3.5%	7.2%
27-year 8.50% MBS	-9.8%	-4.9%	3.8%	5.2%
6-year 7.25% bond	-9.1%	-4.7%	4.9%	10.2%
10-year 7.75% bond	-12.6%	-6.6%	7.2%	15.1%
20-year 8.00% bond	-17.2%	-9.2%	10.7%	23.1%
30-year 8.25% bond	-18.5%	-10.1%	12.2%	26.9%

markets with bonds of various maturities, and the key to how we can consistently "beat the market" with above-market returns and below-market risk. Let us take a step-by-step look at how to use the table as an investment tool for uncertain markets.

The investments are all examples of U.S. Treasury obligations, with the exception of the 27-year, 9% MBS, which is an agency mortgage-backed security. What we are examining are the changes in prices we would experience for each security under each of the four possible future interest-rate scenarios that we are looking at: rates rising 2%, rates rising 1%, rates falling 1%, and rates falling 2%.

	1.0%	-1.0%
3-year 6.00% bond	-2.7%	2.8%

Rising rates mean *falling prices*, and *falling rates* mean *rising prices*. If we look at our example 6.00% bond with a 3-year maturity, we see that if rates *rise* 1.0%, the new bond rate is now 7.00%, and the value of our old, less-desirable 6.00% bond *falls* by 2.7% (from $1,000 to $973). Conversely, if rates *fall* 1.0%, the new bond rate is now 5.00%, and the value which we can sell our old, more-desirable 6.00% bond for *rises* by 2.8% (from $1,000 to $1,028).

	-1.0%	-2.0%
6-year 7.25% bond	4.9%	10.2%

Big rate changes mean *big* price moves, and *small* rate changes mean *small* price moves. Looking at our example 7.25% bond with a 6-year maturity, we can see that a *big* fall in rates of 2.0% means a *big* 10.2% rise in price; and that a *smaller* fall in rates of 1.0% means a *smaller* 4.9% rise in price:

	2.0%
1-year 4.5% bond	-1.9%
6-year 7.25% bond	-9.1%
30-year 8.25% bond	-18.5%

Faraway cash means a *big* price move and *close-in cash* means a *smaller* price move. If we own a 4.50% bond with a *one*-year maturity and rates rise 2.0%, then the price of our bond falls an unpleasant but manageable 1.9%. If, however, we own a *six*-year, 7.25% bond, and rates rise the same 2.0%, the *farther away cash* means that we have a much bigger price drop: 9.1%. If we instead own a *thirty*-year, 8.25% bond where the cash is even *farther away*, then our fall in price increases to 18.5%, almost ten times the loss we would have incurred with a one-year bond.

What our table of different interest-rate scenarios provides us with is a quick, accurate guide to the degree of *price* risk that we take in purchasing bonds of different maturities. The two right-hand columns of Table 13.1 show us our potential profits with large (1.0%) and very large (2.0%) drops in market interest rates. The two left-hand columns demonstrate our potential losses with large (1.0%) and very large (2.0%) increases in market interest rates. Reading down the table, we see that with increasing maturities on our investments, we have increasing amounts of risk: the 3-year bond has more risk than the 1-year bond, the 4-year bond has more risk than the 3-year bond, and so forth. The fluctuations between possible losses and profits steadily increase all the way from the 1-year bond to the 30-year bond, and with each increase in maturity we get an increase in interest rate to compensate for the increased price risk we are taking.

The Exception to the Rule

There is one exception to this tradeoff of higher price risk for higher yield, and that is the high-yielding 8.50%, 27-year mortgage-backed security, which for some reason is positioned on our price-risk scale not between the 20- and 30-year bonds, but rather between the *4*- and *6*-year bonds. Is this a mistake?

Farther away cash does after all *mean bigger* price moves, and the mortgage-backed security has almost 30 years remaining to maturity. Add to this the bad habit that mortgage portfolios have of decreasing prepayments when

The Surprising Truth about Price Risk 147

interest rates rise, thereby magnifying price decreases, and we might expect the 27-year mortgage-backed security to have a greater price fall than the 30-year bond if rates rise. Why isn't this so?

The surprising truth is that seasoned 30-year mortgage-backed securities carry no more price risk than do medium-term 3- to 7-year Treasury bonds, even after incorporating the negative effects of changing prepayments:

	1.0%	-1.0%
27-year 8.50% MBS	-4.9%	3.8%
6-year 7.25% bond	-4.7%	4.9%
30-year 8.25% bond	-10.1%	12.2%

The reason for this seeming contradiction lies in the composition of the mortgage security cash flows (see Table 13.2).

Table 13.2 shows the cash paid to investors for several of the securities that are included in our interest-rate scenario table: the 6-year, 7.25% Treasury; the 27-year, 8.50% mortgage-backed security; the 30-year, 8.25% Treasury; and off to the right the same 27-year, 8.50% mortgage-backed security with the prepayment changes resulting from 1.0% increases and decreases in market rates. No need to read or understand every number and every line, the reason why long-term mortgage securities have far less price risk than long-term bonds can be seen with a quick summary scan.

Look at each column, and remember as you look: *close-in cash* means *small* price changes, *faraway cash* means *big* price changes. Look at the 6-year bond, which provides moderate amounts of cash for 5 years, and then a large sum of cash in Year 6 (*close-in cash, small* price change). The 30-year bond has moderate amounts of cash for 29 years, and then a large sum in Year 30 (*faraway cash, big* price change).

The mortgage-backed security does have cash payments extending out through Year 27, but look at how small those latter payments are. As can be quickly seen, most of the mortgage-backed security cash is received in the first ten years, indeed the MBS receives about twice as much cash ($77,773) in the first 5 years as do any of the bonds, as can be seen in Figure 13.1. The largest dollar amounts of cash payments are all close in, and because *close-in cash* means *small* price moves, this means that the mortgage-backed security is much less sensitive to interest rate movements than other long-term securities.

Table 13.2
Annual Cash Flows: $100,000 Investment

Year	Level Rates 6-Year 7.25% Bond	Level Rates 27-Year 8.50% MBS	Level Rates 30-Year 8.25% Bond	Rising Rates 27-Year 8.50% MBS	Falling Rates 27-Year 8.50% MBS
1	$7,250	$19,369	$8,250	$17,943	$24,594
2	7,250	17,249	8,250	16,253	20,534
3	7,250	15,353	8,250	14,716	17,133
4	7,250	13,659	8,250	13,318	14,286
5	7,250	12,144	8,250	12,046	11,903
6	107,250	10,790	8,250	10,889	9,910
7		9,579	8,250	9,836	8,242
8		8,498	8,250	8,879	6,848
9		7,531	8,250	8,007	5,683
10		6,668	8,250	7,215	4,710
11		5,896	8,250	6,494	3,898
12		5,208	8,250	5,839	3,221
13		4,593	8,250	5,242	2,656
14		4,044	8,250	4,700	2,186
15		3,554	8,250	4,207	1,794
16		3,117	8,250	3,759	1,469
17		2,727	8,250	3,351	1,199
18		2,379	8,250	2,980	975
19		2,069	8,250	2,643	789
20		1,793	8,250	2,337	636
21		1,548	8,250	2,058	509
22		1,329	8,250	1,805	404
23		1,134	8,250	1,575	319
24		961	8,250	1,366	248
25		807	8,250	1,176	191
26		671	8,250	1,004	144
27		550	8,250	847	106
28		0	8,250	0	0
29		0	8,250	0	0
30		0	108,250	0	0
Total	$143,500	$163,219	$347,500	$170,489	$144,585
1-5	36,250	77,773	41,250	74,277	88,450
1-10	143,500	120,839	82,500	119,103	123,843
11-20	0	35,380	82,500	41,553	18,822
21-30	0	7,000	182,500	9,833	1,920
CPR:		10.50%		9.00%	16.00%
WAL	6.0	7.4	30.0	8.3	5.2
Duration	4.9	4.8	10.7	4.9	3.8

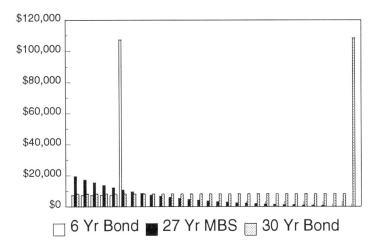

Figure 13.1
Annual Investment Cash Flow

While there are substantial cash-flow changes with changes in prepayments, this relationship remains the same with both rising and falling prepayments. Even with the wide differences caused by prepayment differences, *close-in* cash flows are remarkably similar for the first 10 years:

8.50% MBS Cash Payments Over 10 Years
Falling rates (16.0% CPR) $123,843
Level rates (10.5% CPR) $120,839
Rising rates (9.0% CPR) $119,103

Too often perceived as inordinately risky because of their long maturities and shifting prepayments, mortgage-backed securities are in fact the *least* risky way for investors to access the higher yields available with longer-term securities. Mortgage-backed securities allow the investor to "beat the market"[1] through combining the lower price risk usually associated with shorter-term securities, with the high yields generally associated with longer-term securities (see Figure 13.2).

---

1   Assuming the positive yield curve which usually prevails in the market; in which long-term securities have higher yields than medium-term securities which have higher yields than short-term securities.

Mortgage Securities

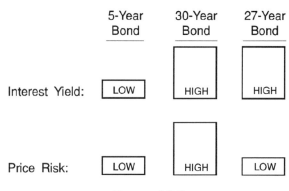

Figure 13.2
"Beating the Market"

The idea that even 25- to 30-year mortgage-backed securities actually have *less* price risk than much shorter-term bonds may be a difficult concept for many experienced investors to accept. These mortgage securities are, after all, long-term investments. Whether interest rates are rising or falling, every time prepayments are mentioned in the financial newspapers it is because of the harmful changes in *Better Home* and *Better Rate* prepayments that are taking place as a result of market-rate changes. It only stands to reason that those poor mortgage-backed security investors *must* be taking it on the chin, again and again, as adverse prepayment changes whipsaw the prices of these long-term investments back and forth.

As logical as that may sound, that is *not* how mortgage-backed security prices actually change. While mortgage securities are created from 30-year loans, the overall effect of prepayments is to shorten the effective term of our investment, and give mortgage securities the price risk of short- to intermediate-term bonds, while maintaining a yield equal to or exceeding those of the longest-term bonds. For the skeptic, independent confirmation of this can easily be found merely by comparing prices among various mortgage-backed securities and Treasury bonds. Take the following test.

1. Look at the prices[2] of several MBSs with different coupons; i.e., Freddie Mac 7s, 8s, 9s, and 10s. Compare the interest rate (coupon) difference

---

[2] Sources where price information can be found include financial newspapers, electronic databases, and brokerage houses. The *Wall Street Journal* carries a listing of a number of GNMA MBS prices in the "Government Agency and Similar Issues" section.

The Surprising Truth about Price Risk   151

with the price difference. You will find that for discount and par MBSs, each 1.0% difference in interest rate means about[3] a 4% to 5% difference in price, and that for premium mortgage securities, each 1.0% difference in rate means about a 1%-3% difference in price, depending on how great the premium is.

2. Look at the prices of a range of Treasury obligations of different maturities, and look at the price differences for a given change in interest rate. You are likely to find that the five- to six-year Treasuries have a price change per 1.0% interest rate change that is about equal to the price changes for the par and discount MBSs, and the one- to four-year Treasuries have price changes per 1.0% interest change that are about equal to the price changes for premium MBSs. You have just established for yourself that par and discount MBSs have about the same price risk as five- to six-year Treasuries, and that premium MBSs have about the same price risk as one- to four-year Treasuries.

3. Compare the yields on the Treasuries you just looked at to the yields on MBSs.[4] Notice how much higher the MBS yields are than the yields for Treasuries of equivalent price risk.

Congratulations! You have just finished the test and established for yourself that *Mortgage securities really do "beat the market" with Short-term price risk and Long-term yields.*

This is not to say that prepayment risk no longer exists, or that the effects of prepayments are unimportant with regard to price risk. The negative effect upon investors of the *Better Home* Face of Prepayments is in fact prominently visible in Figure 13.2, which shows a graphical representation of the price relationships we found in our previous interest-rate scenario table.

Note that for each of the *bonds* in Figure 13.3 the profit produced by a 1.0% decline in rates is slightly larger than the loss caused by a 1.0% rise in market rates, and that the profit produced by a 2.0% decline in rates is significantly larger than the loss caused by a 2.0% rise in rates. For example, the 4-year bond gains 3.5% but only loses 3.4% with a 1.0% decrease/increase in rates, and the

---

[3] Numerous factors including coupon, market yield, prepayments and callability determine the exact price range, and these "rules of thumb" should not be used for actual trading purposes, they are however reasonably accurate enough for demonstration generic pricing.

[4] The "Test" works well except in those rare cases where the yield curve is inverted, and long-term yields are lower than short-term yields.

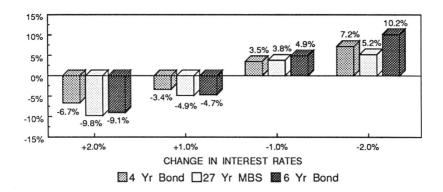

Figure 13.3
Price Risk

same bond gains 7.2% but only loses 6.7% with a 2.0% increase/decrease in rates. This property of bonds, which is that they rise in price slightly faster than they fall in price, is called *positive convexity*, and is desirable for investors.

When we look at the mortgage-backed security, however, we see a different picture. Here the price rises only 3.8% when rates decline by 1.0%, and the price declines by a full 4.9% when rates rise by 1.0%. This relationship gets worse with larger interest rate swings; prices rise by only 5.2% with a 2.0% rate decline, but fall by 9.1% with a 2.0% rate increase. This is called *negative convexity*[5] when prices fall in price faster than they rise in price, and it is caused by the *Better Home* and *Better Rate* Faces of prepayments: homeowners acting in their own financial interests, which in turn reduces our profits and increases our losses.

Good and Bad Applications

It is clear that there are two significantly different conclusions to be drawn about the price risk to be found in mortgage-backed securities. We know that these securities represent a way to increase yield without increasing price risk. We also know that the negative effects of prepayment changes mean that these securities lose value faster than they gain value. So, are they a good investment or a bad investment?

---

5   For those who are mathematically inclined, duration is the first derivative of price, and convexity is the first derivative of duration, meaning that convexity is the second derivative of price. Duration then measures the rate of change in price as interest rates change, and convexity measures the rate of change in duration as interest rates change.

The Surprising Truth about Price Risk

Our answer depends on why we are buying the mortgage-backed securities. If we are trying to make a quick profit by attempting to predict interest rate changes and move rapidly in and out of the market with purchases and sales, then mortgage securities are a poor choice.

> "Mortgage-backed securities are a lousy way to speculate, or 'play the market.'"

Interest rate speculation is dangerous for even the most knowledgeable and well capitalized of the professionals who have real-time market information and little or no transaction costs; for the small investor who has to pay higher commissions on numerous transactions it is almost always a losing game. Add to this the factor of changing prepayments increasing our losses and decreasing our gains, and it is clear that mortgage-backed securities should be avoided by short-term market speculators who are frequently buying and selling.

If, however, we are an *investor* and are buying securities to hold rather than to trade, then the yield/price risk characteristics of mortgage-backed securities are highly attractive to us. Mortgage-backed securities are an excellent way to *increase yields* while *reducing price risk*.

Mortgage-backed securities give us the ability to substantially increase our rate of return on our investment portfolio, while minimizing the chances of a devastating loss if the market changes rapidly and we have to unexpectedly sell our investment portfolio. Ordinarily we must face a choice between increasing yields or reducing risk. Mortgage-backed securities represent a unique way to achieve the best of both.

This is not to say that mortgage-backed securities and MBS funds should be used in lieu of a money-market fund for temporarily parking cash that is expected to be needed in the near future. Though much less risky than long-term bonds, the value of mortgage-backed securities does fluctuate, and quick 2%, 5%, and higher gains and losses can and do occur when overall market interest rates are changing rapidly.

MBS Suitability by Investment Horizon
Less than six months   POOR
More than one year   GOOD

If, however, we are investing for at least a one-year period, but are concerned about the possibility that we may unexpectedly need significant cash sooner, then mortgage-backed securities represent an excellent choice. Unlike mutual funds and short-term CDs, mortgage-backed securities will generate a yield that has an excellent chance of being sufficient to beat inflation. Unlike stocks and many other investments, the chances of taking a sudden 20%, 30%, or even greater loss if we unexpectedly need our money back sooner than planned are minutely small.

Mortgage securities do offer an attractive solution to a thorny problem faced by many of us: what to do with our emergency savings? Most financial planners recommend building a reserve of at least three to six months' salary as a first step in implementing a personal financial management plan. The purpose of the savings is to have a ready reserve available for situations such as unemployment, medical emergencies, or family crises. To ensure ready availability, investment of our emergency savings into safe assets such as money-market funds is usually recommended. Unfortunately, this prudent financial strategy means that for many of us, most or all of our investments will be stuck in low-yielding assets that may not even be able to keep up with inflation on an after-tax basis; we are unable to use our savings to get ahead. Through utilizing mortgage securities, we are able to maintain the highest level of safety, have ready liquidity, reduce our price risk compared to long-term investments, and keep an attractive yield that will allow us to build wealth over time.

While an important consideration, the short-term price changes that we have looked at in this chapter are not the most important criteria for selecting a medium- or long-term investment strategy. What will matter to us is the total performance of our portfolio, which will include interim interest payments as well as the eventual sale price of our investments. A thorough examination of how mortgage-backed securities perform over different time horizons and through different market conditions will be the subject of the next two chapters. This information will be invaluable to us in selecting the best investment strategy to meet our personal investment needs and goals.

14
Minimizing Yield Risk: The Real Story

A little knowledge can be a dangerous thing. In our case, judging investment performance solely on the difference between the purchase price and the sale price of our investments can lead to some potentially expensive misunderstandings, as we will see below.

Five years ago George and Pattie Smith purchased a three-bedroom home in the suburbs for $120,000. They just sold their home for $140,000. The Smiths know they didn't do as well as their parents did in the 1970s, but $20,000 is the biggest profit they have ever made on anything, and they are happy with their investment.

The Smiths
Purchase their house for	$120,000
Sell their house for	$140,000
Making a profit of	$ 20,000

Carl and Tonya Jackson decided to take a chance, and make some real money by buying 2,000 shares of a growth stock, Stellar Electronics, at $50 a share for a total investment of $100,000. Five years later they decided to sell their investment at a price of $60 a share, for a total of $120,000. The Jacksons are disappointed that Stellar Electronics didn't double in value like their broker thought it would, but they still made a hefty profit of 20%, and they are happy with their investment decision.

The Jacksons
Purchase Stellar stock for	$100,000
Sell Stellar stock for	$120,000
Making a profit of	$ 20,000

Andrew and Elizabeth McGowan were more cautious than the Jacksons. They decided to buy a government-guaranteed 6.50%, 10-year Treasury bond for $100,000. Five years later, when they needed access to their funds, interest rates had risen by 1.0%, and the most that they could sell their now 5-year bond for was $95,894. Disappointed and unhappy with their $4,106 loss, the McGowans resolved to stay away from risky investments like long-term bonds in the future.

The McGowans

Purchase a 6.50% bond for	$100,000
Sell the 6.50% bond for	$ 95,894
Taking a loss of	($4,106)

So the Smiths made $20,000 profit on their home, the Jacksons realized a 20% profit on their stock investment, and the McGowans lost more than $4,000 on their bond investment. Or did they?

While the difference between the price we purchase something at and the price we sell it at is certainly important, concentrating exclusively on price change as we just did is a poor way to make financial decisions, and can easily lead to some bad investment decisions. Let us take another look at each couple's investment, and this time let's include factors other than just the purchase price and sale price.

The Smiths paid for their house by taking out a $105,000, 30-year, 10% mortgage and making a $15,000 down payment. They paid 1% in closing costs on the house ($1,200), and paid 2 points on their mortgage ($2,100). Their monthly principal and interest payment during the five years they were at the house was $921, and their taxes and insurance escrow payments were $250 a month, for a total monthly payment of $1,171. The Smiths painted their house, put in some new carpeting, and added a fence and a back deck while they were in their home, for a total of $10,000. The Smiths paid a 7% real estate commission and 2% in closing costs when they sold their house, and still had $101,403 to pay on their mortgage when they sold. Adding all those up, we find the Smiths may not have done as well as they thought:

The Smiths

Home purchase costs	($3,300)
Monthly payments	($70,260)
Upkeep and improvements	($10,000)
Selling costs	($12,600)
Mortgage principal reduction	$3,597
Home price gain	$20,000
TOTAL LOSS	($72,563)

Minimizing Yield Risk: The Real Story 157

Rather than walking away with a $20,000 profit, the Smiths are actually out a net of more than $70,000 over the five years they are in their home. There is of course much more than just cash at issue here. The Smiths have enjoyed a nice home and quality of life for five years, and have received some tax benefits as well. Even after tax benefits, however, they are still on a net basis paying out more than $50,000 in cash, rather than taking in the $20,000 that the simple comparison of purchase price to sale price would suggest.

In contrast to the Smiths, the Jacksons are genuinely profiting from their stock investment. However, their "20%" profit represents another of the hazards of judging investment performance merely on the difference between the purchase price and the sale price. The missing factor with the Jacksons is the *time* that it took for them to earn their profit of 20%, which is 5 years. Simple division of 20% by 5 years would indicate an annual return of only 4%. If we account for the compounding of earnings (*snowballing*) that could have occurred in the meantime as well, we find that the real annual rate of return[1] realized by the Jacksons is as follows:

The Jacksons
Purchase price	$100,000
Investment period	5 years
Sale price	$120,000
REAL rate of return	3.7%

Despite their apparently attractive 20% return then, the Jacksons in actuality did no better with their risky investment in Stellar Electronics stock than they would have if they had purchased federally insured bank CDs.

Finally, let us take another look at the "bad" investment in bonds made by the McGowans. During the five years they owned their bond, they received a total of 10 semiannual interest payments at a rate of 6.50%, which means they got a check for $3,250 every six months. The total amount of money they received from their bond investment is therefore $32,500 in interest payments, plus $95,894 in ending sale price, for a total cash return of $128,394. In addition, they began receiving the interest payments six months after making their investment, so that they could reinvest that money elsewhere and earn still more money. Building in interest payments between purchase and sale, as well as the time value of those payments, an entirely different picture of the McGowan's investment emerges:

The McGowans
Purchase price	$100,000
Interest payments	$32,500
Sale price	$95,894

Total cash received	$128,394
Investment period	5 years
REAL rate of return	5.8%

Taking into account other factors besides purchase price and sale price turns our results upside down. We find the Smiths paid out a lot of money; the Jacksons earned only a 3.7% *real* return; and despite selling their bond for less than they paid for it, the McGowans actually had the best investment results of anyone, with a *real* return of 5.8%. In evaluating any investment, we cannot look only at the difference in sale and purchase prices. We must also take into account the *time* between purchase and sale, and any *cash* we received or paid out in the time between purchase and sale.

These are the same four sources of yield that were introduced in Chapter 10:
1. The PRICE we pay
2. The INTEREST RATE we earn
3. WHEN we get our principal back
4. The PRICE we get when we sell

To fully understand how relatively safe or unsafe the yields are that we may receive from our mortgage security investment, we then need to bring all four of these yield factors together under our scenarios representing the different possible futures of rising, falling, and level interest rate conditions. Indeed, because high *monthly* interest payments and *monthly* repayments and prepayments of principal at par are attractive components of mortgage securities that distinguish them from alternative investments, we must consider all four sources of yield if we are to fairly assess mortgage securities investment performance. By comparing the yields that we realize with the yields that we could otherwise have realized through investing in more traditional securities, we can then judge for ourselves which investment is the safest way of meeting our investment needs in an uncertain future.

Falling Interest Rates

Falling interest rates mean rising prices, and mortgage-backed securities do well in falling interest rate environments, as do almost all bonds and most stocks. Figure 14.1 shows a summary of how our different example investments perform *over time* if rates fall 1.0% immediately after we purchase our security.[1]

---

[1] For purposes of simplicity, an immediate change in rates with an immediate resulting change in prepayments is assumed for these examples. In practice, interest rate shifts take place over time, and as is discussed in Chapter 9, prepayment shifts then lag those rate changes. In general, this prepayment lag reduces the negative impact of prepayment changes and improves mortgage-backed security performance.

Minimizing Yield Risk: The Real Story

HOLDING PERIOD RETURNS   1% RATE DECLINE

Years Owned	1 Year 4.50% Bond	5 Year 7.00% Bond	27 Year 8.50% MBS	10 Year 7.75% Bond	30 Year 8.25% Bond
1	4.50%	10.42%	12.03%	14.19%	19.73%
2		8.27%	10.10%	10.57%	13.63%
3		7.56%	9.48%	9.38%	11.64%
4		7.21%	9.18%	8.79%	10.66%
5		7.00%	9.01%	8.44%	10.07%
7			8.83%	8.04%	9.41%
10			8.72%	7.75%	8.92%
15			8.66%		8.56%

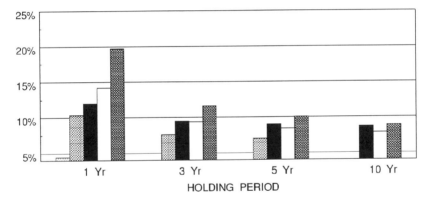

☐ 1 Yr Bond ▧ 5 Yr Bond ■ 27 Yr MBS ☐ 10 Yr Bond ▨ 30 Yr Bond

Figure 14.1
Holding Period Returns

Again, the chart in Figure 14.1 may at first seem to be an incomprehensible mass of numbers, but if we take a step-by-step approach, utilizing what we have already learned, the chart will quickly become both easy to understand and a highly useful guide that will illuminate much of the appeal that mortgage securities have for professional investors, as well as why we as individual investors should be purchasing them as well.

What the chart shows us is the yield we will realize if we buy the security listed in the top row, hold it for the amount of time listed in left-hand column, and then sell it at a rate 1.0% lower than the rate we bought it at.

	5-year, 7% bond
2-year	8.27%

If we buy a 5-year bond for $100,000 (Yield Source #1: purchase price), receive a 7.00% interest rate (Yield Source #2: interest rate) for two years (Yield Source #3: time) and then sell the 7.00% bond in a 6.00% market for a price of $102,709 (Yield Source #4: sale price), we will realize a yield of 8.27%. A "holding period return" is the total return we realize from all four yield sources when we hold an investment for a given period of time and then sell it, and is the same as "realized yield."

	5-year, 7% bond
1-year	10.42%
2-year	8.27%
3-year	7.56%

Our realized yield varies significantly depending on when we sell our investment. If we sell our example bond in one year, then with four years remaining to maturity on our bond, the sale price is particularly high (*Faraway cash = big* price moves), our one year's worth of interest is not as important, and we receive a yield of 10.42%, which is substantially higher than the 7% bond interest rate. If we sell our example five-year bond in three years, then with two years remaining to maturity, our price is not as high *(close-in cash = small* price moves), the three years' worth of interest at 7.00% is becoming quite important, and we realize a yield of 7.56%, much closer to the bond interest rate. Should the bond have time to mature within our holding period, then our realized yield is of course equal to our purchase yield of 7%, as we see in the five-year holding period.

This relationship holds true across all of the example investments. The shorter the amount of time we own our investment, the more important price moves are, the less important interest earnings are, and the more variation we see in our yields. The longer our investment period, the less important price moves are, the more important interest earnings are, and the less variation we see in our yields.

What this tells us as investors is that the amount of risk that we are taking by investing in any particular security is directly dependent on the amount of time that we own that security. Yields over holding periods are a good evaluation method for those of us who are using our portfolios to generate current earnings in order to support or supplement our standard of living, or who are investing toward medium-term investment goals such as accumulating a down payment

Minimizing Yield Risk: The Real Story

for a house, or saving the money to start a business. If we are certain that we will not need our principal for a long time, then interest rate and price fluctuations are less important to us, and the annual interest payments from our investment are what matter the most. If we think we are likely to need access to our cash in the next month or six months, then the price risk of investments that we looked at in the previous chapter is of paramount importance. If, however, we are concerned that we may need to sell our investments within the next several years, or if we are using a combination of interest earnings and gradual principal sales to support ourselves, then holding period yields with their combination of price and interest rate are the best way for us to evaluate potential investments.

It is worthwhile to note that while we are increasing the sophistication of the way in which we look at mortgage securities, the securities themselves are remaining as simple as ever. If you can understand a home mortgage, you understand the key elements of mortgage securities. What we are doing herein is comparing relative attractiveness with other investment alternatives, and in order to do so we must incorporate both interest rate and price. Mastery of holding period yields is however by no means necessary in order to invest in these securities (although it helps).

The yields that we realize can vary substantially for a given holding period and possible future interest rate scenario, depending on the maturity and interest rate of the investment (see Figure 14.2).

Faraway cash still means big price moves, and *close-in* cash still means small price moves. (Note that previously we were discussing the amount of time owned for the security, here we are talking about the cash payments on the security.) When this larger price move is combined with the rate advantage that longer-term bonds can provide, we find that during times of falling interest rates

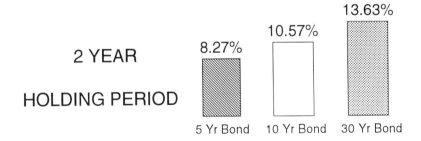

Figure 14.2

Mortgage Securities

we can realize much higher yields if we are holding longer-term bonds rather than shorter-term maturities (see Figure 14.3).

How do mortgage-backed securities fit into this yield picture? Over the short term, mortgage-backed yields are heavily influenced by price changes, much like bond yields. The mortgage security in Figure 14.3 is changing in price somewhat more than the 5-year bond, and much less than the 10-year bond. The reason that the mortgage security yield is almost 2.0% greater than that of the 5-year bond, and almost as great as the 10-year bond is because of the higher interest rate carried by the mortgage security. Because its closer-in cash flows (*close-in cash* means *small* price moves) reduce its price gains, the mortgage security does not perform as well as either the 10- or 30-year bonds over short-term holding periods, despite its higher interest rate.

This difference has been accentuated by the effect of changes in *Better Home* prepayments. Had homeowners not been taking advantage of lower mortgage rates by increasing their discretionary residence changes, then we would have realized a 10.42% yield rather than the 10.1% yield shown.

When we hold our investments for longer periods of time without selling them, the relative attractiveness of our different alternatives changes (see Figure 14.4). If we hold our investment for five years, then the five-year bond matures at its par amount, and we receive the stated 7% yield on our investment. The 10-year bond is still worth substantially more than we paid for it, but now we have been holding it for five years while it yielded 7.75% annually. The five years receipts increases the importance of the interest payments, and the same five-year delay substantially reduces the size and importance of our price gain; the resulting 8.44% real total yield on our 10-year bond investment is much closer to its 7.75% interest rate than the initial price appreciation. This same principle of increased importance of annual interest earnings and decreased importance of price changes also decreases the *percentage* yield that we receive

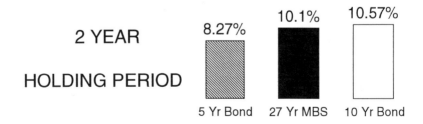

Figure 14.3

Minimizing Yield Risk: The Real Story 163

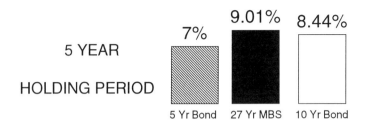

Figure 14.4

as mortgage securities investors. However, relative to how we would have done with other investments, the passage of time works to increase the advantages to us of investing in mortgage securities rather than bonds. The 9.01% mortgage security yield realized over a 5-year investment period is higher than either the 5- or 10-year bond alternatives, though it still lags behind the 30-year bond yield.

Putting a complete picture together then, *mortgage-backed securities substantially outperform short-term investments such as one-year or two-year bonds in moderately falling interest rate environments because of the dual advantage of larger price gains and higher interest rate earnings.* Mortgage securities have comparable price gains with five-year bonds, but their higher rates give them a strong performance advantage. Long-term bonds do significantly outperform mortgage securities over short holding periods during times of falling interest rates because of their much larger price gains and the negative effects of increased prepayments upon mortgage pricing, but the long-term bonds lose much of that yield advantage when we hold our investments for longer time periods.

Rising Rates

Rising interest rates mean falling prices, and like almost all other securities bearing a fixed interest rate, mortgage-backed security yields are lower if we sell our security at a price loss prior to maturity in such an environment (see Figure 14.5).

Our relationships between purchase price, interest rate, time, and sale price remain the same with rising interest rates as they did with falling interest rates, except our movement in price is a negative factor, with losses pulling our yield down. The farther away the cash, the bigger the price loss, and the worse off

164 Mortgage Securities

Years Owned	1 Year 4.50% Bond	5 Year 7.00% Bond	27 Year 8.50% MBS	10 Year 7.75% Bond	30 Year 8.25% Bond
1	4.50%	3.66%	4.06%	1.63%	-1.82%
2		5.74%	6.58%	5.02%	3.40%
3		6.44%	7.42%	6.16%	5.17%
4		6.79%	7.83%	6.73%	6.05%
5		7.00%	8.07%	7.07%	6.58%
7			8.34%	7.46%	7.19%
10			8.51%	7.75%	7.63%
15			8.61%		7.96%

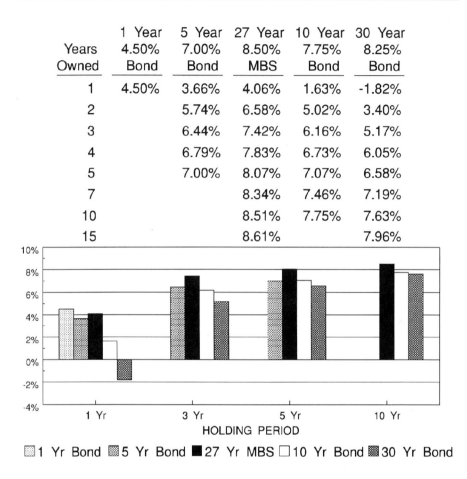

Figure 14.5
Holding Period Returns

we are. Indeed, if we bought the example 30-year bond we would have a negative total first-year return even after earning 8.25% in interest in the first year, due to the 10% decline in the value of our bond (see Figure 14.6).

Minimizing Yield Risk: The Real Story

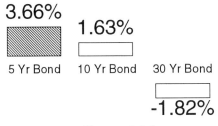

Figure 14.6
1 Year Holding Period

As another result of falling prices for our investments during times of rising interest rates, the relationship between the amount of time that we own our security and our annual realized yield has reversed as well:

	30-year, 8.25% bond
1-year	−1.82%
2-year	3.40%
3-year	5.17%

Now we are carrying a loss in the security, and the sooner we sell the security, the more important price is, the less important rate is, and the lower our yield. If, however, we hold on to our security, then *rate* becomes more important as we collect more interest payments, price becomes less important, and our yield rises.

[*Note: Holding-period yield is an excellent way to judge risk and return before making security purchase decisions, it is however a poor way to make sale decisions. Selling at lower rates allows us to recognize our profit now, but we must reinvest our proceeds at lower rates. Selling at higher market rates forces us to recognize a loss now, but allows us to reinvest at higher rates.*]

The performance of mortgage-backed securities with a moderate rise in interest rates is simple to describe: they have the *best or near best expected performance in every holding period* examined. With the exception of the one-year bond in the one-year holding period (which experiences no price loss), mortgage securities should outperform all medium- and long-term bonds, regardless of whether we are looking at a 1-year or 15-year holding period:

Years Owned	5-Year 7.00% Bond	27-Year 8.50% MBS	30-Year 8.25% Bond
1	3.66%	4.06%	−1.82%
3	6.44%	7.42%	5.17%
10		8.51%	7.63%

166 Mortgage Securities

This superior performance results from the characteristics of what we have learned about mortgage-backed securities in the previous chapters. Their unique combination of short-term price risk and long-term yields means that for the short holding periods, reduced price losses working in combination with their higher long-term interest rates allow mortgage securities to outperform the short-term securities. If we invest for a short period of time in other securities that carry high long-term yields, large price losses with rising interest rates may generate a real loss for us. With increased time and the receipt of more of their higher-rate interest payments, the longer-term securities begin to outperform the shorter-term securities. Because the mortgage securities carry a higher rate than the long-term securities, however, the long-term securities can never catch up, and we earn the best returns by investing in mortgage securities for all holding periods.

If interest rates rise in the future, we *do* lose yield if we sell our mortgage security prior to maturity, as that sale would necessarily be at a loss compared to our purchase price. Changes in *Better Home* prepayments *will* accentuate our losses as homeowners respond to higher mortgage rates by reducing their residence changes: our one-year holding period yield would have been 4.43% instead of 4.06% if it had not been for the slowdown in prepayments and resulting increase in price loss. The performance of mortgage securities *relative* to other investments is however quite positive.

Level Interest Rates

With no interest-rate-caused price changes to be concerned with, we receive the yield we purchased:

Holding Period Returns

Years Owned	1-Year 4.50% Bond	5-Year 7.00% Bond	27-Year 8.50% MBS	10-Year 7.75% Bond	30-Year 8.25% Bond
1	4.50%	7.00%	8.65%	7.75%	8.25%

Our conclusion is again quite simple with level interest rates: because mortgage-backed securities generally carry the highest rates, they generate the highest yields across any holding period in which interest rates are level (note that all the yields are "bond equivalent," and an 8.50% monthly-pay mortgage yield is equivalent to an 8.65% semiannual-pay bond yield for the reasons discussed in Chapter 4).

Minimizing Yield Risk: The Real Story 167

Comparisons

To complete our look at yield risk, we will combine what we learned about yield changes under different possible future market conditions, and see how much yield risk lies within each investment. In Figure 14.7, looking at a three-year holding period, and ranking our results from best to worst, we find the following (please note that we have expanded our interest-rate scenarios to include more-extreme 2.0% and 3.0% increases and decreases).

How to interpret the table in Figure 14.7 depends on our own investment philosophy. If we like to speculate, enjoy gambling, or believe that we have a special insight that allows us to accurately predict interest rate moves, then we should determine (guess) whether rates are going up or down, decide (guess) whether the interest rate change will be sharp or moderate, find which investment does best under our projection (guess), and then purchase that investment.

If, however, we do not want to gamble with our savings, if we feel no special ability to outguess the market on the future direction of interest rates, and if we want to minimize the chances of poor investment performance in an uncertain future, then we should look at the table in an entirely different way. We need to start at the bottom, the worst yield performance, and try to figure out how to avoid getting stuck with those worst results. Then, once we have avoided the worst returns, we try to find the best way to maximize our yield performance. This is easier said than done.

Rates Fall 3%	Rates Fall 2%	Rates Fall 1%	Level Rates	Rates Rise 1%	Rates Rise 2%	Rates Rise 3%
19.48% 30 Yr	15.37% 30 Yr	11.64% 30 Yr	8.65% MBS	7.42% MBS	6.09% MBS	5.34% 5 Yr
12.77% 10 Yr	11.06% 10 Yr	9.48% MBS	8.25% 30 Yr	6.44% 5 Yr	5.89% 5 Yr	4.52% MBS
9.49% MBS	9.53% MBS	9.38% 10 Yr	7.75% 10 Yr	6.16% 10 Yr	4.61% 10 Yr	3.10% 10 Yr
8.71% 5 Yr	8.13% 5 Yr	7.56% 5 Yr	7.00% 5 Yr	5.17% 30 Yr	2.36% 30 Yr	-0.20% 30 Yr

Figure 14.7
Three-Year Holding Period

168 Mortgage Securities

As we can see in Figure 14.8, if rates fall, then the large price gains that the 30-year bond experiences (*faraway cash* means *big* price move) substantially raise our yields and make this investment highly attractive. However, if rates rise, then the big price move turns into a big loss, and we have a very poor yield performance.

If rates rise sharply, then our best protection is to buy a shorter-term security like the five-year bond, which will experience smaller price changes (*close-in cash* means *smaller* price moves) and avoid the large losses that long-term bonds experience with rising rates. However, as we can see in Figure 14.9, if rates don't rise, the lower yields of the shorter-term securities give us the worst yield performance.

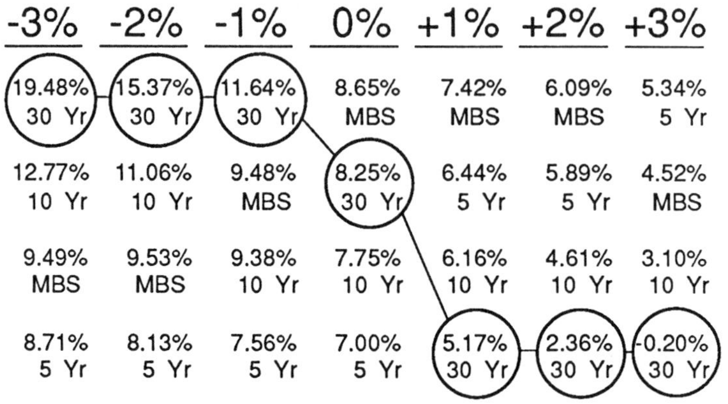

-3%	-2%	-1%	0%	+1%	+2%	+3%
19.48% 30 Yr	15.37% 30 Yr	11.64% 30 Yr	8.65% MBS	7.42% MBS	6.09% MBS	5.34% 5 Yr
12.77% 10 Yr	11.06% 10 Yr	9.48% MBS	8.25% 30 Yr	6.44% 5 Yr	5.89% 5 Yr	4.52% MBS
9.49% MBS	9.53% MBS	9.38% 10 Yr	7.75% 10 Yr	6.16% 10 Yr	4.61% 10 Yr	3.10% 10 Yr
8.71% 5 Yr	8.13% 5 Yr	7.56% 5 Yr	7.00% 5 Yr	5.17% 30 Yr	2.36% 30 Yr	-0.20% 30 Yr

Figure 14.8

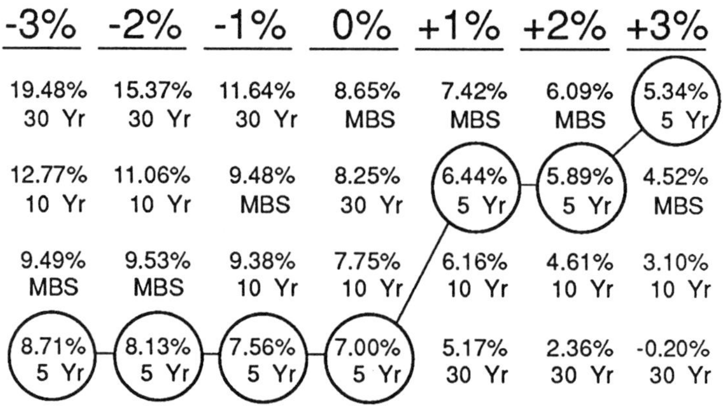

-3%	-2%	-1%	0%	+1%	+2%	+3%
19.48% 30 Yr	15.37% 30 Yr	11.64% 30 Yr	8.65% MBS	7.42% MBS	6.09% MBS	5.34% 5 Yr
12.77% 10 Yr	11.06% 10 Yr	9.48% MBS	8.25% 30 Yr	6.44% 5 Yr	5.89% 5 Yr	4.52% MBS
9.49% MBS	9.53% MBS	9.38% 10 Yr	7.75% 10 Yr	6.16% 10 Yr	4.61% 10 Yr	3.10% 10 Yr
8.71% 5 Yr	8.13% 5 Yr	7.56% 5 Yr	7.00% 5 Yr	5.17% 30 Yr	2.36% 30 Yr	-0.20% 30 Yr

Figure 14.9

Minimizing Yield Risk: The Real Story

-3%	-2%	-1%	0%	+1%	+2%	+3%
19.48% 30 Yr	15.37% 30 Yr	11.64% 30 Yr	8.65% MBS	7.42% MBS	6.09% MBS	5.34% 5 Yr
12.77% 10 Yr	11.06% 10 Yr	9.48% MBS	8.25% 30 Yr	6.44% 5 Yr	5.89% 5 Yr	4.52% MBS
9.49% MBS	9.53% MBS	9.38% 10 Yr	7.75% 10 Yr	6.16% 10 Yr	4.61% 10 Yr	3.10% 10 Yr
8.71% 5 Yr	8.13% 5 Yr	7.56% 5 Yr	7.00% 5 Yr	5.17% 30 Yr	2.36% 30 Yr	-0.20% 30 Yr

Figure 14.10

Clearly, going to the extremes of shortest- and longest-term securities offers us no protection from poor yield performance. To reach for the superior yields that these investments offer us in sharply up or down markets, we must take the chance of the worst yields if the market goes in the opposite direction. Not an attractive option for the investor who wishes to enjoy a steady return without worry or fear.

The traditional way to avoid these extremes is to invest in the middle, to buy intermediate-term securities that have average price risk and mediocre yields. These securities do indeed shelter us from the worst of the yield swings, but as we can see in Figure 14.10, in reaching that shelter we give up any chances of achieving a top return as well. The other price to be paid for mediocrity is that it is difficult to beat inflation over the long term on an after-tax basis with the intermediate-term securities, meaning that we may just be locking in a very gradual real loss.

Mortgage-backed securities offer a way out of this trap of choosing between risking very bad performance and accepting mediocre performance. The table that we saw in Figure 14.7 demonstrates that the "market-beating" characteristics of short- to medium-term price risk and long-term yield that we discussed in the last chapter do carry over into superior yield performance as well. Looking first at the bottom row of the table, we find that our mortgage security investment never yields the worst return, as it does not experience the extreme price losses of long-term bonds during rising interest rates; the long-term yield means that it does not have the lowest returns when rates are level or falling. If our definition of risk is the chance of our choosing the wrong investments and getting the worst yields, then:

Mortgage-backed securities have the LEAST YIELD RISK.

Avoiding this risk does not condemn us to mediocre returns, however. Mortgage securities do usually carry the highest current interest rate, and this means that we have the highest yield of all the alternatives if interest rates remain approximately level. Should interest rates fall, increasing prepayments do keep us from reaping the full benefits of long-term bond price gains such as those experienced by the 30-year bond. However, we still enjoy the benefits of a significantly enhanced yield.

Perhaps the best *relative* yield performance feature of the mortgage securities has to do with their performance when interest rates rise. Despite their long-term maturities, our example mortgage securities actually have the best yield of the alternatives that we have examined if rates rise a moderate 1.0%, or even with a more substantial 2.0% increase in market rates. With a more severe 3.0% rise in market rates, our mortgage-backed security drops to slightly below the five-year alternative, but its yield advantage continues increasing over the thirty-year bonds.

With market-beating yield performance in level and rising interest rate environments, and good (though not great) yields in falling interest rate environments, mortgage-backed securities are indeed the best way to increase potential yields without risking disastrous losses.

An important factor to keep in mind as well is the importance of the length of time that we own our investment. As we discussed earlier, *short* ownership periods can lead to *big* yield fluctuations because of the exaggerated importance of price swings. If we are likely to own our investment for only a year or two, then mortgage securities do grow comparatively more risky, as shown in Figure 14.11.

With short holding periods and large rate fluctuations in interest rates, mortgage securities may be outperformed in both rising and falling rate environments by intermediate-term securities due to the adverse pricing changes caused by *Better Home* and *Better Rate* prepayments. It should be noted that even in these short holding periods mortgage securities still do not experience the worst performance, as the extremes are always occupied by the very short- and long-term securities. With the passage of time and the increasing importance of interest payments, the relative performance of mortgage securities both smooths out and improves relative to other investment alternatives.

Long ownership periods *reduce* our yield fluctuations because of the increasing importance of interest payments compared to price changes. The longer the time for which we hold our investments, the better mortgage-backed securities perform relative to our alternatives due to the increasing importance of interest rate and the decreasing importance of price fluctuations.

Minimizing Yield Risk: The Real Story

Rates Fall 3%	Rates Fall 2%	Rates Fall 1%	Level Rates	Rates Rise 1%	Rates Rise 2%	Rates Rise 3%
47.93% 30 Yr	32.86% 30 Yr	19.73% 30 Yr	8.65% MBS	4.50% 1 Yr	4.50% 1 Yr	4.50% 1 Yr
28.09% 10 Yr	20.96% 10 Yr	14.19% 10 Yr	8.25% 30 Yr	4.06% MBS	0.41% 5 Yr	-2.76% 5 Yr
17.53% 5 Yr	13.93% 5 Yr	12.03% MBS	7.75% 10 Yr	3.66% 5 Yr	-0.73% MBS	-6.15% MBS
13.34% MBS	12.88% MBS	10.42% 5 Yr	7.00% 5 Yr	1.63% 10 Yr	-4.18% 10 Yr	-9.71% 10 Yr
4.50% 1 Yr	4.50% 1 Yr	4.50% 1 Yr	4.50% 1 Yr	-1.82% 30 Yr	-10.69% 30 Yr	-18.54% 30 Yr

Figure 14.11
One-Year Holding Period

Our one-year holding period can then be seen as almost a worse case, for what happens if we have to sell our investments earlier than planned. As we increase our investment periods, our mortgage security yield risk grows steadily smaller, and our risk minimization advantages get steadily larger.

"The longer we own our investments, the more advantageous mortgages become."

As we lengthen our investment horizon, however, our analysis of any one investment grows steadily less important. Instead, it is the *snowballing* (compounding) of our portfolio that becomes increasingly important, as more and more of our earnings come from reinvestments rather than just the original investment. In planning a savings strategy, then, what is required is not so much selecting a single investment, but rather selecting an investment strategy. This brings us to our next chapter, where we will combine everything we have learned so far in order to take a look at the performance of a long-term strategy of investing in mortgage-backed securities.

15
Accumulating Wealth the Safe Way

Once there were twin brothers named Theodore and Jack. On their thirtieth birthday the brothers decided that they would each start putting $200 a month into their individual retirement accounts (IRAs), so that they could retire together. Theodore and Jack agreed to meet for a celebratory dinner on their sixtieth birthday, when they would eat lobster, drink champagne, and toast their retirement.

Theodore diligently saved $200 a month, each and every month for the next 30 years. He invested his money in a mutual fund that purchased low-risk, one-year Treasury securities at a 4.5% yield.[1] As his interest and principal came back from the securities, he reinvested the money in the fund, which then purchased more 4.5% securities.

> Theodore saves $200 monthly for 30 years.
> Theodore invests and reinvests at 4.5%.

Jack diligently saved $200 a month as well, except that he put his money into a mutual fund that purchased 8.5% mortgage securities. As his interest and principal payments came back to him, Jack reinvested the money with the fund, which then purchased more 8.5% mortgage securities.

---

1 We are ignoring for now the management fees and other expenses charged by the funds. For simplicity, we are using an equal monthly compounding frequency for each investment for the story as well.

However, Jack did not save for 30 years. Instead, he had a mid-life crisis when he turned forty. Jack stopped sending money to his mutual fund account, and used the $200 a month to help make payments on a red sports car. Later he used the money to help pay for ski trips, Caribbean cruises, and other pleasures. Though Jack never did contribute any new money to his retirement account again after he turned forty, he did continue to reinvest the money from his retirement savings back into the 8.5% mortgage securities.

>Jack saves $200 monthly for 10 years.
>Jack doesn't save anything for the next 20 years.
>Jack invests and reinvests at 8.5%.

As the time for their retirement dinner drew near, Theodore found that he had mixed feelings about the dinner. His 30 years of self-discipline and thrift had paid off, his latest fund statement showed that his $200 a month over 30 years had compounded to $151,877, a tidy sum that would help to ensure a comfortable retirement. Theodore felt bad for his brother, though. Jack's years of frivolity must mean that he would be retiring with little savings. Theodore decided that he would buy dinner, as he was unsure whether Jack could afford lobster and champagne.

Theodore was surprised when Jack insisted on picking up the tab for their dinner. When Theodore protested, a smiling Jack pulled out his retirement fund statement, and showed his brother the balance of $204,741. Theodore was dumbfounded. How could his irresponsible brother have $53,000 more than Theodore did, when Jack hadn't saved a dime in 20 years?

>Theodore's retirement fund $151,877
>Jack's retirement fund $204,741

The moral of this story is not that we should go out and buy a sports car and stop saving as soon as we turn forty. What our story illustrates is that when we are building savings over a long period of time, whether it is for our retirement, college for the kids, or any other reason, our future *reinvestment* rates will be the most important factor in determining our actual ending amount of wealth.

Jack did not save more money than Theodore did, Jack saved only $24,000 to Theodore's $72,000. Though Jack did earn a higher interest rate, the *stretching* and *stacking* over 30 years of the 8.5% interest earned on his $24,000 in monthly payments totals only $51,085, compared to the $48,735 of *stretching* and *stacking* of 4.5% interest payments on Theodore's savings. The real difference is that Jack realized $129,656 in interest earnings from the *reinvestment* at 8.5% of his interest earnings, while Theodore only realized $31,142 in interest earnings on the *reinvestment* at 4.5% of his interest earnings (see Figure 15.1).

Accumulating Wealth the Safe Way 175

Snowballing (or compounding) as interest builds on interest, which builds on interest, is of vital importance if we are to accumulate wealth. Our example of buying back our mortgage in Chapter 2 showed that with a level monthly purchase earning 9.0%, our interest on interest component is purchasing more than our direct payments are by the end of Year 7, and this is exactly what happened with Jack. By the end of Year 10, when Jack stopped contributing new savings to his retirement account, the 8.5% interest on the $37,628 he had accumulated was already adding $267 per month to his account, and this amount just continued to compound over the next 20 years. Even though Jack was not saving anymore, his money was steadily working for him in his last 20 years before retirement. As we discussed in Chapter 3, the speed with which our investments *snowball* varies radically with our interest rate, and the difference in speed between 4.5% and 8.5% investments was the reason that Theodore's reinvestment earnings were so much less, despite his greater contributions.

Many of us do not have the ability to save $100,000 or $200,000 toward retirement when our primary source of money is *us working for our money*. Even if we diligently clip coupons, buy generic brands, and defer purchases to save $200 out of our monthly income every month for 30 years, we will still have "only" $72,000 in savings. The key to accumulating long-term wealth, as we saw with our example of Jack and Theodore, is to get *our money working for us* as quickly and as effectively as possible. If we combined Theodore's diligence of saving $200 every month for 30 years with Jack's effectively putting his money to work for him at 8.5%, then our ending wealth would be $330,141, with 78% of that ending wealth coming from our money working for us, and only 22% ($72,000) from direct savings. Mortgage securities are a powerful and safe way to make our money work for us, as we will find in this chapter.

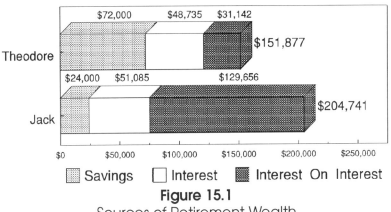

Figure 15.1
Sources of Retirement Wealth

Reinvestments and reinvestment earnings are the critical consideration for us in evaluating any long-term investment strategy. Note that when discussing strategies we are no longer confining ourselves to the evaluation of any one particular investment or investment decision. Instead, we are considering the cumulative and interrelated effects of a whole series of investment purchases, with the cash produced by the sum of a series of previous investments determining how many dollars we have available to purchase new investments in each year. Unfortunately, what future reinvestment rates and opportunities are likely to be in another 10, 20, or 30 years is much more uncertain than what they will be in another 1, 2, or 5 years.

When the future is likely to be something entirely unexpected, our examination of different possible scenarios to learn the flexibility, resilience, strengths, and weaknesses of different investment strategies becomes more important than ever. Let us take another look at our rising, falling, and level interest scenarios, and this time let's include the critically important factor of reinvestments, so that we can see how price changes, cash flows, and reinvestment changes all work together. For as Theodore found out, it is our reinvestments that will determine how much wealth we will actually accumulate.

Level Yields

Mortgage-backed securities clearly have an advantage over bonds when it comes to yield. This difference in yield, enhanced by the difference in snowballing speed, should offer the mortgage security investor a significant wealth accumulation advantage. As we saw in Chapter 4, a 9.0% mortgage-backed security will compound to a 55% advantage over an 8.0% bond over a 30-year period, so long as rates remain level.

This *snowballing* advantage of mortgage-backed securities, where interest piles on interest, which piles on interest, faster and faster over time, is an advantage held over all Treasury bonds, as is illustrated in Figure 15.2.

As the chart in Figure 15.2 demonstrates, for a $1,000 initial investment, if we invest, and then more importantly reinvest, at our original investment rates, the mortgage-backed securities will significantly outperform our other federally guaranteed alternatives. Mortgage securities do generally have a yield advantage over longer-term bonds, and the longer we hold our investments, the more important that advantage becomes in our accumulation of wealth. The most dramatic difference is the advantage that mortgage securities hold over short- and intermediate-term securities. As Theodore found out, 8.50% investments do *snowball* in value much faster than 4.50% investments, and if we compare

Accumulating Wealth the Safe Way 177

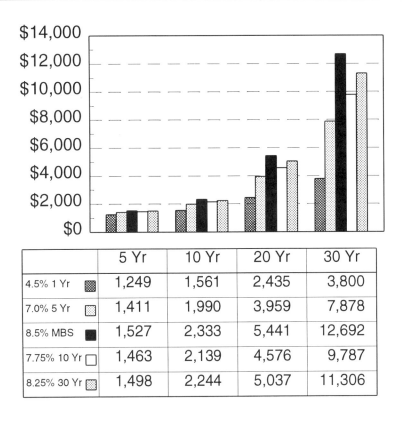

Figure 15.2
Level Interest Rates

them on equal terms over a 30-year period, then we find that we accumulate more than three times as much wealth through purchasing the higher-yield investment.

Our problem, however, is that rates do change, and it is highly unlikely that we will be able to steadily compound our earnings at our initial 8.5% rate. Worse, with any rate changes, we are likely to have prepayment *changes* that will be working directly against us. When rates rise and we would like to reinvest more of our money in the new higher-rate mortgages, *Better Home* prepayments slow down and we have less money to invest. When rates fall and we would rather keep our money invested at 8.5% instead of reinvesting in the new lower-rate mortgages, *Better Home* and possibly even *Better Rate* prepayments rise rapidly, and we have more money to invest at a time when we would rather

178 Mortgage Securities

not. When we are looking at investment strategies, then these negative prepayment changes snowball against us, just as favorable yield advantages are snowballing in our favor:

Yield advantages snowball *for* us.
Prepayment changes snowball *against* us.

Do the rewards of higher yields build fast enough to outstrip the compounding problems of adverse prepayment changes? To answer this important question, let us continue our look at how the strategy of investing in mortgage-backed securities compares to various bond investment strategies when interest rates are falling.

Falling Interest Rates

Let us say that market rates fall 1.0% a year after we purchase our investments, fall another 1.0% the next year, and then fall another 1.0% the year after that. This gradual change in interest rates is representative of the way rates often move, which is in long cycles:

Scenario: Falling Interest Rates

	1-Year Bond	10-Year Bond	27-Year MBS	30-Year Bond
Year 1	4.50%	7.75%	8.50%	8.25%
Year 2	3.50%	6.75%	7.50%	7.25%
Year 3	2.50%	5.75%	6.50%	6.25%
Years 4-30	1.50%	4.75%	5.50%	5.25%

Under this scenario, we would expect to have increasing difficulties with *Better Home* prepayments. As rates fall progressively lower, it becomes increasingly easy for homeowners to afford voluntary moves, and therefore prepayments increase in each year. Cash as it comes in is reinvested in the new, lower interest rate mortgages, which are all that are available, but those mortgages as well are then subject to rising prepayments as rates continue to fall.[2]

Soon we reach the point where refinancings become advantageous for homeowners, and *Better Rate* prepayments quickly become our most important

---

[2] For the sake of simplicity in these illustrations, we assume a once-a-year purchase of the new lower-rate mortgages, and we continue our uniform assumptions that they are purchased at par with 27 years remaining to maturity. Under these circumstances, 27-year mortgage-backed securities priced at par might or might not be available.

Table 15.1
Falling Interest Rates, Rising Prepayments

Year	1	2	3	4-30
Market MBS Rate	8.5%	7.5%	6.5%	5.5%
8.5% MBS prepayments	10.5%	16.0%	27.0%	35.0%
7.5% MBS prepayments		10.5%	16.0%	27.0%
6.5% MBS prepayments			10.5%	16.0%
5.5% MBS prepayments				10.5%

All prepayment speeds are CPR.

concern. Cash is pouring in, and it must now be reinvested at the new lower rates. The mortgage principal that has not yet prepaid is worth substantially more than we paid for it, but there is less and less of this principal remaining each month as rapid prepayments continue.

Table 15.1 shows how changes in rates affect the prepayment rates on the mortgage securities which we purchase in each year.

Our initial investment is in 8.5% mortgage securities, which we expected to prepay at a steady 10.5% Constant Prepayment Rate (CPR) per year. However, at the beginning of our second year rates fall, *Better Home* prepayments speed up to 16%, and our cash flow increases. Market rates have dropped, so all we can reinvest our money in is the 7.5% mortgage securities, which we expect to prepay at a 10.5% rate since they are now at market. During our third year, rates drop again, however, our original 8.5% securities experience a 27% prepayment rate as *Better Rate* prepayments kick in, our 7.5% securities are experiencing *Better Home* problems as prepayments increase to 16% CPR, and our new reinvestment rate for all this unexpected cash is now only 6.5%.

Our wealth-accumulation strategy is clearly not going as planned. We are getting our 8.5% and 7.5% investments back sooner than wanted, and the most we can reinvest the money at is 6.5% in Year 3, and then 5.5% in Year 4 and thereafter. How bad is the damage to our plans, and how much better or worse would we have done if we had invested in bonds instead? Let us see how each of the different types of investments that we have been examining compare to mortgage-backed securities under a strategy of reinvesting cash into like securities (1-year bond cash is reinvested into 1-year bonds; mortgage security cash is reinvested into mortgage securities, and so forth):

Strategy Yield with Reinvestments
Falling Interest Rates

	1-Yr Bond	27-Yr MBS	10-Yr Bond	30-Yr Bond
Year 3	3.50%	9.60%	12.67%	19.31%
Year 5	2.70%	7.98%	9.47%	13.57%
Year 7	2.35%	7.28%	8.11%	11.16%
Year 10	2.10%	6.77%	7.09%	9.37%

Taking a look at prices first, *falling* rates means *rising* prices, and the yields on all of our investments (except the one-year bond) substantially benefit from rising prices. As we saw before, the shorter our holding period, the more important price moves are, and the bigger our yield change. As the time we own our investments extends, however, not only do our original interest earnings become more important than price moves, but our reinvestment earnings rate becomes increasingly important. This means that our yields decline faster and farther than they did in the previous chapter, when we looked at return on a single security only.

This puts us in a situation where our strategy or portfolio return drops below our original investment rate, as our new lower rate reinvestments gradually replace our original investment. Adding reinvestments over long periods of time reverses our earlier results from when we looked at price changes only or single-security yield changes only. Whereas market rate declines do *increase* single-security prices and holding period yields, over time rate declines will *decrease* portfolio returns, as lower-yielding reinvestments become increasingly important. In our example, our mortgage securities investment strategy has an aggregate yield of less than 8.5% by Year 5, despite the price gains in our original 8.5% security.

This is a scenario that many of us who took advantage of the new tax laws and established IRAs in the 1980s are uncomfortably familiar with. At the time, we looked at projections of compounded cash flows at the then current rates of 10%, 11%, and 12% and perhaps thought we could retire as millionaires without ever leaving the security of government-guaranteed securities. The future was not like the past, however, and the lower interest rates of the early 1990s are compounding our nascent wealth much slower than we might have expected. (Even under this worst-case scenario, however, mortgage security investors did surprisingly well in the 1980s, as we will see in the next chapter.)

This point is reinforced by taking a look at our total accumulated wealth in each of our holding periods, and comparing it to our level interest rate scenario (see Figure 15.3).

Accumulating Wealth the Safe Way

Despite the initial price gains that we experience as rates drop, in comparison to level interest rates, our total wealth accumulation has declined for all of our investments by the end of Year 10, except for the 30-year bond. Two points in particular are worth noting about the mortgage security results.

Declining interest rates and long-term investing:
1. Mortgages outperform short-term bonds.
2. Long-term bonds outperform mortgages.

The combination of price gains and higher yields for the principal that has not yet prepaid increases the performance advantage that mortgage securities hold over short- and intermediate-term securities in a declining interest rate environment. However, we also find that the negative snowballing of adverse changes in *Better Home* and *Better Rate* prepayments is such that it outweighs

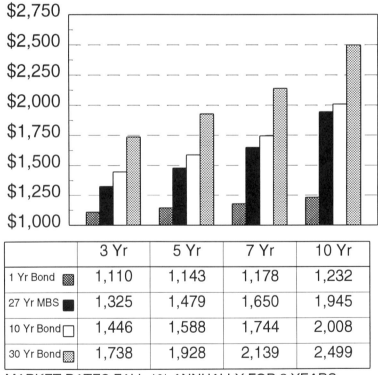

	3 Yr	5 Yr	7 Yr	10 Yr
1 Yr Bond	1,110	1,143	1,178	1,232
27 Yr MBS	1,325	1,479	1,650	1,945
10 Yr Bond	1,446	1,588	1,744	2,008
30 Yr Bond	1,738	1,928	2,139	2,499

MARKET RATES FALL 1% ANNUALLY FOR 3 YEARS

Figure 15.3
Falling Interest Rates

the positive snowballing of the yield advantages associated with mortgages securities. This means that the mortgage securities are slightly outperformed by the 10-year bonds, and substantially outperformed by the 30-year bonds, which are still earning an 8.25% rate long after our other investment strategies have had their returns driven down by lower-yielding reinvestments.

Rising Interest Rates

What if the future holds rising interest rates? Let us say that instead of falling, market rates rise 1.0% a year after we purchase our investments, rise another 1.0% the next year, and then rise another 1.0% the year after that:

Scenario: Rising Interest Rates

	1-Yr Bond	10-Yr Bond	27-Yr MBS	30-Yr Bond
Year 1	4.50%	7.75%	8.50%	8.25%
Year 2	5.50%	8.75%	9.50%	9.25%
Year 3	6.50%	9.75%	10.50%	10.25%
Years 4-30	7.50%	10.75%	11.50%	11.25%

Under this scenario, we would expect to have growing difficulties with *Better Home* prepayments. As rates steadily climb higher, it becomes increasingly difficult for homeowners to afford voluntary moves, and therefore prepayments decrease in each year. Reinvestment rates for current market mortgage securities are growing continually more attractive with what cash we do receive, but those mortgages as well are then subject to declining prepayments as rates continue to rise (see Table 15.2).

Combining our rising interest rates with our declining prepayments, we find the following results for our different investment strategies:

Table 15.2
Rising Interest Rates, Falling Prepayments

Year	1	2	3	4-30
Market MBS Rate	8.5%	9.5%	10.5%	11.5%
8.5% MBS prepayments	10.5%	9.0%	8.0%	6.5%
9.5% MBS prepayments		10.5%	9.0%	8.0%
10.5% MBS prepayments			10.5%	9.0%
11.5% MBS prepayments				10.5%

All prepayment speeds are CPR.

Strategy Yield with Reinvestments
Rising Interest Rates

	1-Yr Bond	27-Yr MBS	10-Yr Bond	30-Yr Bond
Year 3	5.50%	5.48%	3.27%	0.13%
Year 5	6.30%	7.98%	6.23%	4.51%
Year 7	6.64%	9.06%	7.51%	6.41%
Year 10	6.90%	9.87%	8.48%	7.85%

Rising rates means *falling* prices, and the initial yields on all of our investment strategies (except the one-year bond) are hurt by falling prices. However, we have higher reinvestment rates pushing yields in the opposite directions from price changes, and the longer the investment period we are looking at, the more important the reinvestment rate. What we see then is just the reverse of what we saw with falling rates: *single*-security price and yield changes are *negative,* and if we just focus on the security we originally purchased, we are likely to be disappointed; however, when we include reinvestments at the new higher market rates, our strategy returns over time climb past what our original yields were.

Add the cumulative, *snowballing* effect of these reinvestment yield changes to our reduction in prepayments caused by declining *Better Home* prepayments, and we find the wealth accumulation totals shown in Figure 15.4.

Looking at the dollar totals, it is clear that in a rising interest rate environment, the net effect of the combination of yield snowballing and prepayment snowballing is in fact substantially positive.[3] Indeed, the advantage enjoyed by mortgage-securities increases *rather than decreases* when we take reinvested cash flows into account. The reason for this is that as we discussed earlier, while prepayment *changes* are almost always negative, prepayments themselves are generally positive. While fewer mortgages are being prepaid, the remaining prepayments, interest payments, and scheduled principal payments on the mortgage securities are still sufficient to generate about twice as much cash in early years as is generated by the long-term bonds, as is shown in Figure 15.5, which shows cumulative principal and interest receipts for two years from investing in mortgage securities compared to those received from investing in long-term bonds.

---

3   Note that the market value table and the previous total strategy return table are identical, except that one displays results in compounded dollars, and the other displays results in yield. A percentage point or two difference in yield, compounded over several years, truly does make a major difference in ending wealth.

184 Mortgage Securities

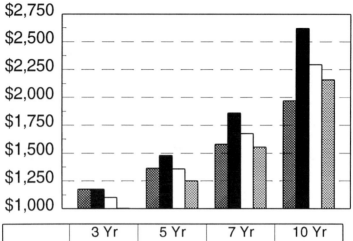

	3 Yr	5 Yr	7 Yr	10 Yr
1 Yr Bond	1,177	1,363	1,580	1,970
27 Yr MBS	1,176	1,479	1,859	2,620
10 Yr Bond	1,102	1,359	1,675	2,294
30 Yr Bond	1,004	1,250	1,555	2,160

MARKET RATES RISE 1% ANNUALLY FOR 3 YEARS

Figure 15.4
Rising Interest Rates

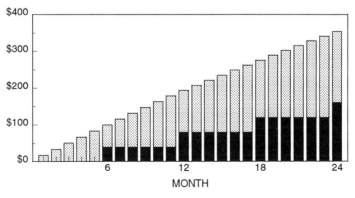

Figure 15.5
Cumulative Cash Payments

Accumulating Wealth the Safe Way 185

The monthly payments of mortgage securities give us cash to reinvest months earlier than we get from bonds, and the receipt of principal prepayments gives us a powerful increase in early cash flow. It is these sometimes maligned factors of monthly payments and principal prepayments that account for the remarkably resilient performance of mortgage securities portfolios during times of rising interest rates. We do face a loss in price on the remaining principal balance of our original investment, but high monthly interest payments and principal prepayments combine to quickly make our original investment less important than our reinvestments. Using our earlier example of interest rates rising 1% per year for three years, we can see a quick rise in the percentage of our mortgage security portfolio that is comprised of reinvestments (see Figure 15.6).

By the end of Year 3, our reinvestments already account for 45% of the total market value of our portfolio, and by the end of Year 5 our original par mortgage security (which is trading at a price of 86 cents on the dollar) accounts for only 35% of the total market value of our portfolio. The most important result for us to consider is not the 14% loss on what remains of original security (after prepayments), but the 65% of the portfolio that is invested in new, higher-rate securities. It is this rapid ability to respond to changing rates that gives mortgage securities such a major performance advantage in rising interest rate environments.

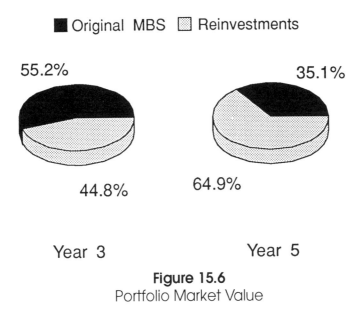

Figure 15.6
Portfolio Market Value

Rising interest rates, long-term investing:
1. Mortgages have the best performance.
2. Mortgage performance improves with time.

In the last three chapters we have learned a great deal about what mortgage-backed securities can do for us as investors. We have *not* learned the exact yields that we are likely to earn with our mortgage security or bond investments. Markets do not change in the precise and neat manner that we have been using. In practice market rates change every day and every hour, not every year. Prepayments are never *wholly* predictable for individual securities, and their monthly fluctuations are mostly but not entirely caused by interest rate changes. Relationships between interest rates (the yield curve) continually fluctuate as the gap between short- and long-term interest rates widens, narrows, and sometimes even inverts.

The lessons that we have been learning are crucial nonetheless, for the three building blocks we have learned here will apply to our actual future investment performance, and understanding these building blocks will allow us to knowledgeably select the investments that are likely to earn us the best returns in an uncertain future without exposing us to unacceptable risks.

In summary, the three building blocks are:

1. **Moderate price risk.**
   Our first building block is that long-term mortgage-backed securities have the moderate *price risk* that is associated with a four- to seven-year Treasury note or bond, not the high price risk that is associated with long-term bonds. This moderate price risk means that we shouldn't temporarily park cash in mortgage securities that we know we are likely to need in the near future, as we would place funds in a money-market fund or interest-bearing checking account. It does mean, however, that we can likely access our savings if we unexpectedly need them with much less risk than we would have with long-term bonds or stocks.

2. **High interest yields.**
   Our second building block is that of high yield: mortgage securities usually carry the highest yields available among the highest-credit-grade securities. These high yields become increasingly important over time, and they minimize the chance of subpar performance for any mortgage securities held more than a year or two, even in rising interest rate environments. High yields mean that mortgage securities do well in both level and falling interest rate environments.

Accumulating Wealth the Safe Way 187

3. **High reinvestment sensitivity.**
   Our third building block is that of high sensitivity to reinvestment rate changes. This building block comes from the relatively large cash flows that mortgage securities experience in their first few years after purchase. While this building block does drag down strategy performance with falling interest rates, when combined with the first two building blocks it means that mortgage-backed securities have exceptional relative performance in rising interest rate environments.

The combined effect of these three building blocks is to give mortgage-backed securities a unique niche in the investment world. *Moderate price risk* combined with *high interest yields* means that mortgage securities never have the worst yield or price performance. *High interest yields* means that mortgage securities outperform all others in level interest rate environments. *High reinvestment sensitivity,* combined with *moderate price risk* and *high interest yields,* means that a strategy of purchasing long-term mortgage securities can work surprisingly well even in a rising interest rate environment.

With superior performance in level and rising interest rate environments, and attractive though moderate performance in falling interest rate environments, mortgage-backed securities offer a unique way for us to put our money to work for us in accumulating wealth, without taking many of the risks usually needed to achieve top-notch returns.

16
A Hidden History of Success

In the preceding chapters we have learned a great deal about how mortgage security prices and yields change in reaction to rising and falling interest rate environments, as well as how this performance compares to the likely performance of other investments under these same scenarios. As useful as our multiple scenarios are to us in evaluating the relative risks and rewards of investing in different security types, and in aiding our understanding of why those performance differences exist, these simplified models cannot fully prepare us for the complexities of the real world of investing.

Interest rate levels do not suddenly change in even 1% increments once per year in the real world, instead they are continually changing in an unpredictable fashion. Not all interest rates change in the same way. Short-term rates may rise while long-term rates fall, or long-term rates may rise while short-term rates fall. Not all of the changes in mortgage security yields will be tied exactly to changes in the yields on Treasury obligations. Prepayments will not crisply change in exact and even increments simultaneously with changes in interest rates. Instead, prepayment changes will lag behind interest rate changes, and will rise and fall with the seasons of the year and the slow and busy seasons of the real estate market. Refinancing prepayments will eventually burn out and slow down as all those who can refinance will have refinanced.

Mortgage-backed securities do not all respond in the same way to changes in market interest rate levels. As we saw in Chapters 11 and 12, discount and premium mortgage securities sometimes have opposite reactions to the same changes in interest rates and prepayments. Long-term changes in market conditions may also have a profound effect upon the overall availability of discount and premium securities. Prolonged increases in interest rates sharply reduce the supply of available premium securities as former premium securities turn into discount securities, and sustained declines in interest rates decrease the availability of discount mortgage securities as former discount securities turn into premium securities.

A History of Building Wealth

While some major brokerage houses have in-house indexes that track mortgage security performance, there is no recognized standard for evaluating overall mortgage security performance that has an equivalent role to those served by the Dow Jones Industrial Average or the Standard & Poor's 500 indexes in evaluating overall performance in the stock market. A useful proxy that we can use in tracking mortgage security performance is to look at the overall performance of mutual funds that invest primarily in mortgage securities. This approach does have potential methodology problems to the extent that mutual fund managers may collectively make investment decisions that separate their portfolio performance from the average of the overall mortgage security market. Most individual investors do, however, purchase their mortgage securities through mutual funds, and mutual fund performance is affected by the relative availability of premium and discount securities. From a practical standpoint, mutual fund performance may then be an excellent way for us as individual investors to gauge the historical performance of mortgage securities.

The chart and table in Figure 16.1 are a historical version of the same type of analysis that we looked at in Chapter 14: one-year realized yields from investing in mortgage securities under a variety of interest rate scenarios. The total return that mortgage security mutual funds realized in each year, as measured by Morningstar,[1] is shown as bars in the graph and in the top row of the table. The change in long-term treasury yields[2] from the beginning of the year to the end of the year is the line on the graph and the second row of the

---

[1] Total return data compiled by Morningstar, Inc., and adjusted by adding expenses back to reported total yield. Average fund expenses in each year ranged from a high of 1.21% in 1981, to a low of 0.77% in 1986.

[2] Annual changes in Standard & Poor's year-end closing weekly indexes of long-term U.S. government bond yields.

A Hidden History of Success

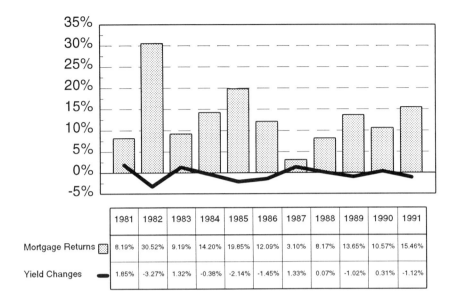

Figure 16.1
Total Mortgage Security Returns And
Changes In Long-Term Treasury Yields

table. What we see in the table has a strong correlation with what we learned about mortgage security holding period yields.

Looking to the far left at 1981, we can see that interest rates rose by 1.85%, and that our total return was 8.19%. In 1982 rates *fell* by 3.27%, and our total return *rose* to 30.52%. Indeed, during each of the years when rates *fell*, we experienced particularly *high* total returns, as we can see by looking additionally at 1984, 1985, 1986, 1989, and 1991. Our lowest relative yields were experienced in the years when interest rates were *rising*, and prices were *falling*, as we can see by looking at 1981, 1983, 1987, 1988, and 1990. In each case, the wider the change in interest rates, the greater the relative change in realized yield, just as we would expect based on our study of the building blocks that underlie mortgage security performance.

Two of our other building blocks can also be seen by examining historical performance. Had we invested in mortgage securities at the start of 1981, and reinvested those earnings in each year thereafter, we would have accumulated a significant amount of wealth by the end of 1991. The increase in wealth that we would have realized if we had started with a $10,000 investment on December 31, 1980, is illustrated in Figure 16.2.

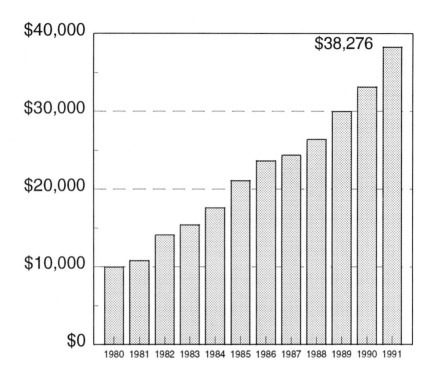

Figure 16.2
Mortgage Security Wealth Accumulation: 1981 - 1991

Our mortgage securities investment would have grown at a 13.0% average annual rate, with an almost four-to-one pre-tax increase in wealth over the 11-year period (if we had actually invested in those mutual funds and paid their expenses, then our wealth accumulation rate would have been 12.0% and our ending wealth would have been a still attractive $34,921).

Of equal importance to many of us would have been another building block, the steady increase in ending wealth in each and every year. We learned earlier that the unique mortgage security combination of long-term yields and moderate price risk allow us as investors to "beat the market" with the wealth-compounding benefits of high yields and the safety benefits of reduced price movements. This is precisely what mortgage security investors have been experiencing over the long term: while long-term yields rose in five of the eleven years we examined, in each case our high interest income received was still sufficient to offset our price losses and leave us with a net gain by year end.[3] When these lower though still positive yields are combined with the attractive yields achieved by mortgage securities during years of falling interest rates when we had both price gains and high interest rates, we find ourselves with a highly effective, reduced-risk means for building wealth over the long term, as well as of safely enhancing returns over the shorter term.

> "Mortgage securities:
> Highest Credit Safety
> + High Interest Yields
> + Moderate Price Risk
> = The Safest Way to Build Real Wealth"

Overcoming Adversity

What makes this historical performance particularly impressive is that it was achieved during a period when we were repeatedly experiencing the negative effects of the most powerful Face of Prepayments: *Better Rates*.

As we can see in Figure 16.3, new mortgages purchased[4] in 1980 were within a refinancing range in two years, and mortgages purchased in 1981 were within a refinancing range within one year, as the plunge in interest rates of 1982 triggered *Better Rate* prepayments. As unwanted principal payments came pouring in during 1982, 1983, and 1984, investors were forced to reinvest their money into new lower-yielding securities. Then in 1985 interest rates tumbled again. Homeowners rushed again to lower their mortgage payments, and investors were forced to reinvest their cash yet again over the next few years into still-lower-yielding new mortgage securities. Even these securities themselves then experienced the damaging effects of *Better Rate* prepayments as mortgage yields plummeted yet another time during 1991, and homeowners rushed to lock in the first 30-year mortgages with fixed rates below 9% since the 1970s.

---

3   Mortgage securities can and do incur real annual losses: mortgage funds lost 1.88% (pre-expense) during 1980, a year in which long-term bond rates rose 1.69%. This was, however, a much smaller loss than those experienced by long-term bond investors in 1980.

4   Mortgage purchase yields shown are Freddie Mac year-end 30-year, fixed rate, 30-day-cash-program purchase yields.

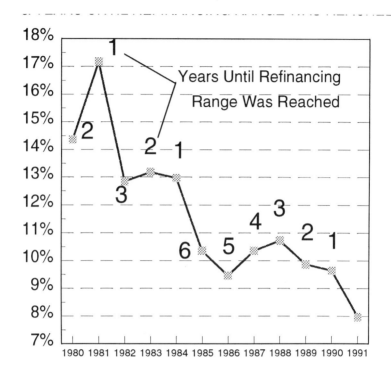

Figure 16.3
Mortgage Purchase Yields
and Years Until Refinancing Range Was Reached

The repeated drastic falls in interest rates between 1982 and 1991 were a boon to all of us who were able to purchase our homes with increasingly affordable monthly payments, and then later lower our payments even further through refinancing. When we *reversed the mortgage*, these years constituted a worst-case scenario far tougher than any that we examined in our scenario analyses, as rates fell more than 6.0% over the 11-year period. Three major waves of *Better Rate* prepayments removed most (but *not* all) of our high-yielding mortgages from our portfolios, and drove our yields downward.

The bottom line result for mortgage investors was a good but not great performance, which is exactly what we expect from our scenario modeling of prior chapters. With 20/20 hindsight, we now know we would have been better off if we had invested in long-term bonds at prevailing yields of 14% and higher in 1981, so that we could have benefited from huge price gains and high yields on our full investment, undiluted by prepayments. We would have been even better off if we had known that the long bear market in stocks was ending, and we had purchased a broad-based portfolio of common stocks in 1981 when the Dow Jones Industrial Average was below 900.

"The price of Better Rate prepayments is good, but not great performance"

If we wish to make our investment decisions by watching the rear-view mirror and limiting our review to those investments that have had the absolute best recent historical performance, then we would not select mortgage securities to be our investment strategy for the future. Instead, we would buy the longest-term government bonds available and wait for interest rates to repeat their record-breaking fall. Or if we didn't need the safety of government bonds, we would purchase common stocks and wait for the stock market to duplicate its record-setting decade-long bull market.

If however we are uncertain about what the future holds, and we are investing for that uncertainty, then we can draw some dramatically different conclusions from our historical review. A strategy of investing in mortgage securities experiences its worst *long-term* relative yield performance during a sustained bull market in bonds[5] when rates fall significantly, yet even with a 6.0%+ long-term fall in rates, such a strategy would still have substantially outperformed short-term treasuries, money-market funds, and short-term certificates of deposit. Even after *Better Rate* prepayments forced mortgage securities investors to take most of their principal and reinvest it at lower rates not once but three times, mortgage securities still outperformed gold, silver, junk bonds, and commercial real estate by wide margins. Just as the most accurate gauge of a person's character can often be found in his or her behavior under trying circumstances, the truest test for the long-term suitability of an investment strategy can be found by evaluating its performance during adverse market cycles rather than under more favorable conditions. Judged by this standard, the real wealth-building performance of

---

5 The point that a long-term basis a strategy of investing in mortgage securities performs its poorest in a major bull market (falling interest rates) may at first seem nonsensical, but this is the case. Individual mortgage security yields are enhanced by falling rates and rising prices, as are short-term results. As we saw in Chapter 15, long-term portfolio performance suffers, however, as high-coupon mortgages rapidly prepay at par and the money must be reinvested at lower interest rates.

mortgage securities is impressive indeed, when we consider it was achieved during a decade when the advantage of moderate price sensitivity became a major drawback, and when the worst aspects of changing prepayments were maximized time and again.

Looking Ahead

Looking to the future, we can be comfortable that if the past repeats itself, and rates fall further, then we would continue to earn a good yield (albeit much less than 13%) compared to many other investments. But mortgage securities would likely continue to be outperformed by long-term Treasury bonds, and to be significantly outperformed by the stock market. In assuming that the recent past repeats itself, we must also assume that two record bull markets, one in the bond market and one in the stock market, also each repeat themselves. The long-term results of stacking two such record-breaking markets upon each other would necessitate 30-year Treasury bond yields below 2% by 2004, and a Dow Jones Industrial Average exceeding 12,000 that same year.

The Markets in 2004?
30-Year Bond Rates	1.25% ?
Dow Jones Industrial Average	12,600 ?

We certainly cannot discount the possibility that the stock and bond markets might just not only meet but exceed the targets listed above; the financial markets have a long history of major moves in generally unexpected directions. However, it might also be prudent to remove our gaze from the rear-view mirror for a moment, and consider that there may be some good reasons to believe that the investment road may be entirely different from that just traveled.

If we believe that the road ahead consists of basically level markets, then a strategy of investing in high-yielding mortgage securities will likely slightly outperform a strategy of high interest rate long-term bonds, and will likely widely outperform low interest rate short-term Treasury securities and CDs, money-market funds, and low-dividend-yielding common stocks. If we believe that the road ahead consists of rising interest rates, then a strategy of investing in mortgage securities will lead to reduced yields or even losses over the short term as moderate price losses pull down performance, followed by a long-term increase in yields and wealth as our significant monthly principal and interest payments are rolled over into new high-yielding mortgages, thereby strongly outperforming the high interest rates but large loss performance experienced by

A Hidden History of Success 197

long-term bonds, and drastically outperforming the low dividend yields and very large loss performance that common stocks realize in bear markets.

It is when we say that we do not know what the future holds that mortgage securities assume their greatest appeal, as we saw in Chapter 15. Level rates? Over the long term we do quite well, if not great. Rising rates? Over the long term we do quite well, if not great. Falling rates? As we saw during the last decade, over the long term we do reasonably well, if not great. It is this relatively stable combination of good (though rarely spectacular), long-term real wealth-building performances across level, rising, and falling interest rate environments that gives mortgage securities their uniquely appealing position in the world of investments.

17
Buying Mortgage Securities

As with most other types of investments, there are two basic ways of investing in mortgage securities: directly and through mutual funds. Those of us who have the time, resources, and inclination to purchase securities directly from securities brokers will enjoy the full benefits of undiluted high mortgage-backed securities yields through direct purchases. There are also substantial benefits to be gained through the purchase of shares in mutual funds that invest in mortgage securities: professional management, convenience, diversification, and ease of reinvestment. In the pages that follow we will take a look at some of the unique issues involved with mortgage securities investing, so that we can determine for ourselves whether we should be purchasing these securities directly or through a mutual fund. These issues include:

- Ways of gathering information
- Determining fair prices
- Evaluating fair prepayment speeds
- The safest and simplest security to buy
- Other flavors and varieties of mortgage securities
- How CMOs and Remics rearrange risk
- How pool sizes affect our investments
- Tax calculation considerations for mortgage securities
- Investing in mortgage security mutual funds

Gathering Information

The amount of information that we need in order to keep up with a particular security or portfolio of securities is much less for agency mortgage securities than we might prudently need to invest in stocks, corporate bonds, or municipal bonds. Because of the high credit quality of mortgage securities, we don't need to worry about quarterly earnings reports, or rating-agency credit watches. We don't have to concern ourselves with analysts downgrading the future earnings potential of our stocks, or with unpleasant company announcements that would decrease the value of our investments.

We would like to find out information regarding what market conditions are like for mortgage securities in general as well as for specific mortgage securities that we own or might be considering purchasing. Copious quantities of information about the $1.2-trillion-dollar market as a whole is available at the touch of a finger regarding bid-ask prices, expected yields, expected prepayments, historical prepayments, and price volatility, through electronic data services, including Bloomberg and Telerate. Online information bases are also provided by Freddie Mac and Fannie Mae on a pool-specific basis. Using either a touch-phone telephone or a computer modem, we can quickly find the most recent factor for a pool (percentage of original balance still outstanding), or learn the original and current Weighted Average Remaining Maturities and Weighted Average Coupons of the underlying mortgage loans in that pool.

"Individual investors may find obtaining information to be inconvenient."

Unfortunately, much of this information, which is readily available to large investors, can be inconvenient for the individual investor to obtain. The plentiful sources of electronic information that are available, if you can afford to pay a steep monthly connect fee for professional-quality data services, dry up when you go to the printed media or popular consumer financial databases. National financial newspapers such as *The Wall Street Journal* and *Barron's* do carry limited information on some mortgage securities prices and yields, as well as occasional commentaries regarding changes in prepayment rates. While the information provided has been growing recently and is helpful for keeping abreast of the mortgage security market in the broadest of terms, its scope is still too limited to provide the basis for many actual investment analysis and purchase decisions. These same limitations are also true of at least some of the individual-investor-oriented computer databases; for apparent reasons of tradition, as of the writing of this book it is easier for individual investors to track the price moves of tiny, thinly held over-the-counter stocks that may trade a couple of thousand shares a day, than it is to track the prices of a mortgage security class such as Freddie Mac 8.5% PCs, which has tens of billions of dollars in securities outstanding.

Determining Prices

Hopefully, the financial media will be correcting this situation in the near future. In the meantime, our best option is to make use of our brokers for our information sources. Some brokerage firms make available terminals in their lobbies that can access the mortgage security databases. If you are uncomfortable using a terminal or if your brokerage firm does not offer this option, then ask your broker to print out and mail to you at least two pages for each security that you are considering purchasing: a price page, which includes the generic bid-ask prices for the particular coupon and type of mortgage security (i.e., 7.50% FNMA MBSs) you are interested in, as well as a prepayment page, which consists of brokerage house estimates of future prepayment speeds for the coupon and type of mortgage security you are considering. If your broker is unable or unwilling to do so, then you should use a different broker for your mortgage security purchases.

Use caution—check prices and prepayments. Our reason for caution in checking prices is that while the mortgage security marketplace is extraordinarily large and efficient, it does not use a central exchange structure like a stock exchange; instead, it is a negotiated marketplace. Current market bids and asking prices that are precise down to 1/32 of 1% are continually available for each mortgage security type and coupon, but that does not mean that all mortgage securities trade to those prices. Instead, the price you get is whatever price you and the seller (your broker) agree to, with the difference between market price and the price you pay going to the broker as his commission. Securities regulations provide you with a limited amount of protection against excessive mark-ups. However, your broker's trading desk has reasonable discretion in deciding the price it makes the security available to your broker at (and thereby their profits in the trade), and your individual broker likely also has reasonable discretion in deciding how much personal profit he or she wants to make from the sale. We do have to pay a reasonable price for the broker's services, but we need to be careful that we have an idea what that price is, as the broker may have an entirely different perception of an appropriate profit.

Institutional investors often deal with this problem by getting quotes from several brokers when they purchase mortgage securities, a situation which makes for highly competitive bids from the brokers. Maintaining multiple brokerage accounts is not convenient for most individual investors, and we are not likely to get the same price on a $20,000 trade as Aetna or Prudential will on a $20 million trade in any case. Seeking comparable price information before purchasing is a prudent practice that has little downside, indeed just asking for and obtaining current market information may substantially lessen the chances of our ever being offered a security at too high of price in the first place.

Comparing Prepayment Speeds

Prepayment estimates are of importance to us in determining the expected life and yield of our mortgage security, at least under current market conditions. Indeed, we should never purchase a mortgage security on the basis of expected yield alone without having investigated the reasonableness of the prepayment speed, for it is too easy to control expected yields through the selection of an advantageous prepayment speed.

> "Expected yields can be manipulated through prepayment speed selection."

Prepayment speeds are estimated by the major Wall Street brokerage houses and made available through the professional information services. Each house has their own reasons for selecting what they believe to be the most appropriate prepayment speeds for each security, based on a number of factors that their in-house experts take into consideration. Our problem is that as with many other economic and investment forecasts, the experts are rarely in agreement as to what the future holds. Most prepayment estimates for a particular type and coupon of mortgage security are reasonably close, but usually there are also estimates that are significantly higher or lower: it is not uncommon for there to be a 100% to 150% PSA (6% to 9% CPR) variation between the high and low Wall Street projected prepayment speeds for discount and par mortgage securities, and 300+% PSA (18% CPR) variations in prepayment speeds for high-coupon mortgage securities that trade at substantial premiums are not unusual.

To illustrate the problems that relying upon individual brokerage house prepayment estimates can cause us, let us take a look at three example mortgage securities: one selling at a significant discount, one selling near par (100 cents on the dollar), and one selling at a significant premium. In Figure 17.1, we will look

	Discount	Near Par	Premium
Price	88	99	105
Coupon	6.00%	8.00%	10.00%
Broker A			
Prepayment Projection	4.0%	6.0%	20.0%
Yield Projection	7.89%	8.31%	8.57%
Wall Street Average			
Prepayment Projection	8.0%	10.0%	27.0%
Yield Projection	8.42%	8.35%	8.14%
Broker B			
Prepayment Projection	12.0%	14.0%	34.0%
Yield Projection	9.00%	8.39%	7.66%

Figure 17.1
Expected Yields

at our expected yields using three different prepayment estimates: Broker A, who has low prepayment expectations; Broker B, who has high prepayment expectations; and using an average of the different Wall Street brokerage house estimates.

If we look at our example discount security, a 6.00% mortgage security selling at a price of 88 cents on the dollar, we can see that on average Wall Street expects it to experience an 8% Constant Prepayment Rate and an 8.42% yield. Brokerage House A is projecting low 4% CPR prepayments and a lower 7.89% yield, and Brokerage House B is projecting high 12% CPR prepayments and a much higher 9.00% yield. These varying yields are for the identical security, at the identical price, which will in practice generate an identical *actual* yield regardless of who we buy it from; all of our *projected* yield differences lie in the prepayment projections.[1] Besides the confusion this generates in comparing

---

1 The wide variation in prepayment projections for discount and near-par securities is caused not so by much disagreements over what prepayments are likely to be as by disagreements over the future direction of interest rates, which some firms base their prepayment projections upon. This practice unfortunately turns those brokerage houses' projections from being prepayment projections to being long-term interest rate forecasts, a dubious proposition at best, given the lack of proof that any firm can accurately project the direction of interest rates on a long-term basis.

yields from different brokers, this also potentially leaves us open to less-than-ethical Broker C, who marks the price up to 90 (putting the extra 2 points in his pocket), and shows us an "above market" yield of 8.46% based upon the widely respected Broker B's prepayment projections. This is why we need to compare prices first, prepayments second, and projected yields last.

> "Compare Price,
> Compare Prepayments,
> Then Talk Yield."

We face an opposite problem if we look at our example premium security, a 10.00% security selling at a price of 105 cents on the principal dollar. As we see in Figure 17.1, Broker B's fast prepayment projections now have the effect of decreasing our yield from the market expectation of 8.14% down to only 7.66%; while Broker A's slow prepayment projection calls for the identical security to earn a yield of 8.57%. In this situation, less-than-ethical Broker C shifts his source of prepayment projections to respectable Broker A's slow expected prepayments, and offers us the above-market yield of 8.26% based on a 20% CPR and a price of 106 (putting the extra 1 point in his pocket).

An even bigger danger when looking at mortgage securities that sell at substantial premiums is truly slimy Broker D, who does not worry about technical things like prepayments, maturities, or amortizations. Because he is your "friend," Broker D will sell you that 10% security at the low price of 110 for an enticing 9.09% *current yield* (10%/110%), and put 5 extra points in his pocket. For the reasons discussed in Chapter 10, it is literally impossible for us to earn the current yield on a premium security if we hold that security to maturity. "*Never* buy solely on current yield!"

It is important to remember that having to keep an eye out for potentially undesirable sales practices is not a problem that is unique to mortgage securities, persons of that ethical persuasion (or lack thereof) can be found in just about any part of the investment world. Indeed, if we are concerned about the possibility of becoming the victim of sharp trade practices, mortgage securities offer a couple of advantages over most other investments:

1. **We get our money back.**
   In most areas of the investment world, whether we are looking at limited partnerships, penny stocks, futures trading schemes, or pyramid cons, if we fall prey to an unethical operator, we as victims tend to lose every penny, or at the least most of our investment principal. With agency

pass-through mortgage securities we still have Ginnie Mae, Fannie Mae, and Freddie Mac paying us principal and interest, which even at a premium price of 110 or 115 should nearly always at least equal our purchase price. The "price" that we pay is loss in yield, which is certainly undesirable but still better than being wiped out.

2. **Simplicity provides protection.**
   We have relatively few factors to concern ourselves with because of the uniformity, simplicity, and high credit quality of agency mortgage securities. Checking that price and prepayment assumptions are reasonable, and understanding our potential yield and average life exposure to shifts in prepayments are generally sufficient by themselves to prevent gross mistakes.

A Simple And Safe Selection

If we are concerned about our yields fluctuating with changing prepayments, or if we are apprehensive about our ability to gauge the reasonableness of the prepayment assumptions and yields being shown to us, there is a simple way for us to minimize our exposure to potential yield fluctuations and prepayment manipulation. The closer our price is to par (100 cents on the dollar), the lower our exposure to yield fluctuations. If we can buy a security exactly at par, and we hold it to maturity, then we do not have to worry about the effect of prepayments on yields at all[2] for we will receive our stated interest rate.

"Buy near par' to minimize yield fluctuations."

It is, however, uncommon to be able to buy a mortgage security exactly at par, so we will usually have to make our purchases at "near par," that is slightly above or below par (see Figure 17.2) An example of buying a near-par security was included in Figure 17.1, where we examined the purchase of an 8.0% mortgage security at a price of 99 cents on the dollar. With our discount and premium securities, shifting from Broker A's slow prepayment projections to Broker B's fast projections was sufficient to cause about a 1% variation in yield; our near-par security, however, experienced only about 1/12 of the yield risk, with the yield differential totaling a mere 0.08%.

---

2 While the purchase of par securities protects us from yield fluctuations, it does not protect us from prepayment risk in general. Our prepayments will still slow down with rising rates and speed up with falling rates.

96   (99) | 102   104
           Par

Figure 17.2
The Discount Security Closest to Par is Often the Best Bet

There is no single correct answer as to whether we should buy the near-par security that trades at a slight premium, or a slight discount, it all depends on the price and how close each is to par. Some professional investors do as a matter of practice try to avoid purchasing any sort of premium securities whatsoever, instead they prefer to purchase discount securities whenever possible, as prepayments have more room to move up than down, and prepayment increases will increase their yields. This is not a bad policy for us either, if we want to select a stable investment for ourselves that has minimal *yield* exposure to prepayment uncertainties, and slightly more upside yield potential than downside yield risk if prepayments do fluctuate.

Buying the discount security closest to par is not always the best choice for all of us. Sometimes we are better off purchasing deeper-discount securities or even premium securities, depending on market conditions, our particular investment needs, and our own tolerances for yield risk, price risk, and prepayment risk. If we do not know what we really want, however, and are uncomfortable with what is involved in evaluating shifting prepayments, yields, and prices, then near-par discount securities are easy to evaluate (just check price), conservative investments that are most unlikely to get us in trouble in the future.

Flavors and Varieties

Underlying all of our discussion so far has been one common assumption, that we are purchasing one of the three most common types of mortgage securities:
- Government National Mortgage Association Mortgage Backed Securities (Ginnie Mae MBSs)
- Federal Home Loan Mortgage Corporation Participation Certificates (Freddie Mac PCs)
- Federal National Mortgage Association Mortgage Backed Securities (Fannie Mae MBSs)

Buying Mortgage Securities

To keep our approach as simple as possible in this introductory volume, our example mortgage securities were all pass-through securities with underlying mortgage pools comprised of fixed-rate mortgages with 30-year maturities. These types of securities issued by one of the three agencies are the most common of mortgage securities. However, they are far from being the only type of security available.

Virtually every type of mortgage or housing loan we can think of has been securitized and turned into mortgage securities at one time or another. Apartment complexes and mobile homes are each commonly financed by loans that are later turned into mortgage securities. Low-income-housing loans, both for apartments and single-family homes, are often converted into mortgage securities, which are then used to secure tax-exempt revenue bond issues, giving us an attractive blend of high safety, higher yields, and tax-free income.

There are a wide variety of maturities, amortization types, and interest types that can be purchased as well. Some securities are backed by 15-year loans, while others are backed by 5- and 7-year "balloon" loans, which mature with a large final payment. Still other mortgage securities change their interest rate every 1, 3, or 5 years along with the adjustable-rate loans of which they are comprised.

Caution and Knowledge

We should approach the wide array of alternative mortgage securities with caution, and make purchase decisions only when we are knowledgeable about the specific characteristics of the security we are considering purchasing. The reason for our caution is not safety fears (a Freddie Mac is a Freddie Mac for credit quality purposes), but rather because the prepayment, yield, and price characteristics of the different mortgage types may vary widely from each other.

Different may be better; as examples the 15-year maturity and balloon-maturity mortgage securities generally carry less price risk than the 30-year securities we have examined. Tax-exempt bonds collateralized by residential mortgage securities often have lower *Better Rate* prepayment exposure because of the decreased ability of the low-income homeowners to obtain conventional refinancing. Adjustable-rate mortgages offer us the opportunity to enjoy increased yields during times of rising interest rates.

However, 15-year and balloon mortgage securities generally offer lower yields than do the 30-year securities. Mortgage securities collateralizing tax-exempt bonds often have lower prepayment speeds in general, thereby increasing price risk and decreasing flexibility. Adjustable-rate securities offer lower yields as well, and while their interest rates will rise with rising market rates, the rate caps may keep their yields below market and their prices discounted. The wide variety of agency pass-through securities do offer an array of differing opportunities. We just need to be cautious and make sure that we are knowledgeable about the advantages and disadvantages of the particular type we are considering before making our purchase decision.

Rearranging Risk: CMOs and REMICS

Most institutional investors are quite fond of the high-yield and high-credit quality aspects of mortgage securities, but not everyone considers all the other characteristics to be desirable. Some investors want short-, medium-, or long-term investments only, and not a mixture of all three. Other investors want variable interest rates, even if the mortgage securities themselves are fixed-rate. Many investors who are funding their purchases with fixed-term borrowings have little tolerance for prepayment fluctuations, and they want a more dependable principal payment schedule.

Collateralized mortgage obligations and real estate mortgage investment conduits accomplish the task of changing these mortgage characteristics through splitting out the total principal and interest payments from the mortgages to different investors in different ways. One set of investors own "desirable" classes (or "tranches") within the overall CMO or Remic, which may have interest rates that fall and rise with market conditions (called "floaters"), or may be shielded against all but the most extreme shifts in prepayments (called PACs and TACs). The desirable securities can offer us the best of both worlds, with all of the higher safety and some of the higher yields associated with mortgages securities preserved, and without some of the undesirable risk characteristics.

> "The purpose of CMOs and REMICS
> is to reduce risk."

Unfortunately, in order to reduce risk in some Remic tranches, we are forced to increase risk in other Remic tranches. Since we are not changing fixed homeowner interest payments when market rates rise and fall, we deliver floating interest rates that rise and fall with the market by creating mirror securities ("inverse floaters"), which are the direct opposite of our floaters. The rates of an inverse floater fall when market rates rise (thereby freeing up cash to pay increased floater interest payments), and inverse floater rates rise when market rates fall, the sum of floater and inverse floater interest payments remaining fixed like the underlying mortgages. We cannot reduce prepayment risk without changing homeowner behavior, so in order to reduce prepayment risk in some tranches we must shift and concentrate the prepayment risk to other classes, which are referred to by the euphemistic name of "companion" bonds.

"We Reduce risk in some tranches by Concentrating risk in others."

Inverse floaters and companion bonds are not "bad" securities per se, they usually carry especially high yields to compensate for the increased risk that they bear, and accepting the increased prepayment or interest rate risk in exchange for enhanced yields is a choice that knowledgeable and sophisticated investors often make. The danger is that less-than-knowledgeable investors may be drawn to these securities by their combination of high yields and high credit quality, and purchase them without realizing the potentially extreme interest rate or prepayment risks they are taking, risks that may prevent investors from ever realizing the high expected yields or even getting their money back if they bought the securities at a high premium (some of these securities have no principal attached at all, with their entire purchase price consisting of premium).

We cannot draw any definitive conclusions about the risk or return of investing in CMOs or Remics relative to agency pass-through securities, for the diverse world of CMOs and Remics includes higher and lower risk and return alternatives. The key difference between these two generic types of mortgage securities is the price of misunderstanding. Even if we do not fully understand how discounts or premiums work, or *Better Rate* prepayments, or the nuances of price risk, it is hard for us to get ourselves in too much trouble by buying near-par agency pass-through mortgage securities, indeed they are safer for us than virtually any alternative investment other than Treasury securities. With CMOs and Remics on the other hand, we can get ourselves in a great deal of trouble in a hurry if we do not understand the investment principles that underlie mortgage investing. Such securities should therefore be purchased only by investors who are comfortable that they fully understand what they are buying and what risks they are taking.

National Averages and Random Fluctuations

How pool ownership works is both simple to understand and crucially important to us as investors. When we purchase a $25,000, 8.00% Freddie Mac Participation Certificate (PC), we are probably not buying the same 8.00% Freddie Mac PC as our neighbor did the month before. This is because there are thousands of different 8.00% Freddie Mac PCs outstanding, just as there are thousands of 9.00% Fannie Mae MBSs and thousands of 10.0% Ginnie Mae MBSs.

When we purchase a particular mortgage security, we purchase an ownership interest in the specific pool of mortgages underlying that security, and no others. Let us say that the $10,000 PC that we purchase is part of pool number 101, which consists of 100 individual $100,000 mortgages, for a total of $10 million. Our $10,000 investment means that we own 1/10 of 1% (0.1%) of pool #101; and that we receive 0.1% of all principal payments and 0.1% of all pass-through interest payments from each of the 100 underlying mortgages. We do not get any share of the 100 mortgages underlying our neighbor's 8.00% PC.

Our concern is that when we looked at mortgage prepayments in previous chapters, we looked at smoothly changing monthly cash flows based on nice, round, even percentages. This is the conventional (and best) way of evaluating expected prepayments, and works reasonably well when we are looking at the economy as a whole, or at very large mortgage pools, or at portfolios that contain investments in a number of different mortgage securities. In practice, however, individual homeowners do not prepay 1% of their mortgage each month, they generally prepay either the whole mortgage or nothing at all.

In a small pool the results that we see will therefore look entirely different from smooth national averages. If our pool consists of 10 to 20 mortgage loans, it may be that one or two loans are expected to prepay in each year, which would mean that we as investors expect to receive 10 to 11 months of scheduled principal and interest payments, and during one or two months we expect to receive much larger payments as principal prepayments in full are passed through to us. It is also entirely possible that no loans will prepay in the year, just as it is possible that four to five loans may prepay. The smaller the overall size of the pool that we are purchasing a part of, the greater role random chance is likely to play in the size and timing of our pass-through principal payments. This random chance can work for us with higher-than-expected prepayments in a rising interest rate environment, or it can work against us with slower-than-expected prepayments. *The smaller the pool, the "lumpier" the cash flow and the greater the random fluctuations.*

There are several ways we can smooth out our cash receipts and reduce our exposure to random fluctuations. One method is to purchase only portions of very large mortgage securities, which have many underlying loans. Fannie Mae "Majors" and Freddie Mac "Giants" are each special categories of pass-through mortgage securities that are distinguished by their large sizes and national geographic diversity; a typical "Major" is over $200 million in size at origination. These securities tend to trade at slightly higher prices (and lower yields) than normal PCs and MBSs because of their superior prepayment predictability.

Another method we can use to increase the number of mortgages that underlie our investment is to purchase smaller pieces of more mortgage securities, thereby increasing the number of mortgages that underlie our investment. This method allows us to reduce our prepayment volatility risk, but it can be inconvenient in terms of the number of purchases required, as well as for the increased monthly effort to monitor our investments and annual tax work.

Tax Calculations

One final item that we may wish to consider before directly purchasing mortgage securities is the necessary tax calculations that must be performed. If we purchased our mortgage security at par, then our annual income, which we must report for tax purposes, consists solely of the interest income from the mortgage security—unless we sell our investment prior to maturity, in which case we must take into consideration the resulting profit or loss.

If, however, we purchased our security at a discount or a premium, then our tax reporting becomes more complicated. If we bought our security at a discount, and we are being repaid the principal at par, then we are earning an additional profit over the life of our investment that is equal to the dollar amount of the discount. Conversely, if we bought our mortgage security at a premium, and we are being repaid principal at par, then we are incurring a loss over the life of our investment that is equal to the dollar amount of the premium.

The preferred method for recognizing the discount profits or premium losses is to amortize them over the life of the investment, using a level-yield type of methodology. This concept involves making a reasonable prepayment projection, and then spreading out the recognition of profit or loss in such a way that the total taxable yield we report in each year remains level. Substantive prepayment changes may require a recalculation of the amortization schedule, a problem that can be minimized by purchasing near-par securities.

The above is intended only as an overview of the typical tax concerns that we are likely to face in purchasing mortgage securities. A tax professional should be consulted with regard to our actual tax filings, which could be an important consideration for some of us. In comparison to investments in limited partnerships, tax shelters, and S corporations, the tax considerations associated with investing in mortgage securities should be relatively simple for tax professionals to handle. If, however, our previous investments consisted of CDs only, and we do not use the services of a tax professional, investing directly in mortgage securities may require us to seek the help of such a professional in preparing our tax returns. (If, however, we are investing through a tax-deferred investment account, we do not need to calculate discount and premium amortizations annually.)

Mortgage Security Mutual Funds

There is a much easier way to invest in mortgage securities: mutual funds. When we purchase shares in a mutual fund that invests in mortgage securities, we no longer have to worry about:

- Seeking out information on mortgage security prices and prepayment rates.
- Negotiating with a broker for our best price.
- Purchasing poor securities on the basis of misleading prepayment assumptions.
- Selecting from among the wide variety of mortgage securities available.
- Getting accidently stuck with an inverse floater or companion bond.
- Random prepayment fluctuations in small mortgage pools.
- Immediately reinvesting our money every month.
- Investing retirement savings through regular small monthly deposits.
- Figuring out annual discount and premium tax amortizations.

As with other kinds of securities, mutual funds provide mortgage security investors with numerous advantages in the areas of convenience, professional management, and diversification. These advantages do not, however, come free, as we can expect to pay 0.5% to 1% or more of our annual mortgage security income in management fees and expenses, and possibly significantly more if we bought our shares from a mutual fund that charges a sales load.

Buying Mortgage Securities

Over time, these fees can have a significant impact on wealth accumulation, compared to how well we can do if we can invest and immediately reinvest in mortgage securities. However, the small investor who is accumulating wealth may however still be better off investing through mutual funds than direct purchases, if accumulating the assets to purchase a new mortgage security takes many months or even years, due to the advantage of immediately reinvesting in the mutual fund through a dividend reinvestment plan, with no interim loss of potential income in a low-yielding money market fund or interest-bearing checking account.

One difficulty in investing in mortgage security mutual funds is finding which funds invest in mortgage securities. While some funds prominently feature "GNMA" or "Mortgage Securities" in their names, most of the funds that are predominantly invested in mortgage securities do not refer to these investments in their names, perhaps for fear that these obscure-sounding names will scare off investors. Instead a variety of names like "Government Income," "Federal Income," "Government Securities," and "Federal Securities" are used, and the sponsors concentrate on advertising their high government-guaranteed yields. We don't find out that the fund is allowed to invest in Ginnie Maes until we open up the fund prospectus, and we don't find out that the fund is predominantly invested in Ginnie Maes and has been for years until we read the balance sheet at the end of the prospectus. Millions of us have in fact been investing at least part of our savings for years in mortgage securities, though we may not have all realized this was the case.

18
Winning with Mortgage Securities

Mortgage-backed securities are an ideal medium-term to long-term investment for individual investors. This is true for the millions of dedicated personal investors who have spent years teaching themselves about investments and investing; and it is even more true for the tens of millions of other investors who have never studied investment finance.

The highly advantageous nature of mortgage security investments for individuals is also something that is not yet generally accepted within either the personal investment or mortgage security investment communities. In this chapter we will review what we have learned in previous chapters and pull these concepts together to see not only why mortgage securities are uniquely suited for individual investors, but also why because of their very nature they are *more* suitable for individual investors than they are for the massive insurance companies, pension funds, and financial institutions that are the traditional buyers of these securities.

Simplicity

Mortgage securities are perhaps the most personal of all securities, and as such are among the very easiest to understand. The fundamentals of investing in mortgages are that we are loaning other people the money they use to purchase their homes. Period.

When we securitize mortgages, several other layers are added: a seller to find and create these mortgages for us, a servicer to collect the payments for us, insurers to protect the value of our investment, and a government-chartered agency to guarantee that full principal and interest on the mortgages will be paid to us. These enhancements are of critical importance to us, yet they do not change the underlying nature of what we are doing: we are lending money to purchase homes, and we receive principal and interest from homeowners until their mortgages are paid off. The factors controlling those payoffs are generally quite familiar to all of us who either have or had mortgages, or know people who have them. We all have *personal knowledge* of home mortgages.

This *personal knowledge* stands in marked contrast to the information required to understand almost all other kinds of investments (with the exceptions of federally guaranteed bonds and certificates of deposit). With virtually any other kind of investment, we are dealing with a myriad of specific and complex business risks that even the most financially astute among us are unlikely to have comprehensively explored.

Common stock is potentially lucrative, but how can we as individual investors reasonably predict the *future* market share or profitability trends for a particular company, if we are not knowledgeable of the business disciplines of marketing, operations management, or accounting? If we are not intimately familiar with that particular corporation or its industry?

How can we assess the likelihood that today's healthy appearing company will be able to pay interest and principal on its corporate bonds in another five years if we are not experts at interpreting balance sheets, income statements, and other financial statements? How can we *know* whether an early redemption can be forced on a high-yielding municipal bond issue through a means other than optional redemption if we don't know how to read and interpret bond official statements or trust indentures properly? If we buy only insured bonds in order to avoid credit risk, how can we *know* whether or not the insurance company itself is likely to be the next to follow Executive Life into bankruptcy?

Few have *personal knowledge* of corporate analysis. In the traditional investment world, we have grown used to layer upon layer of complexity, risk piled on top of risk. It is the accepted norm that there will be a vast gap between the average individual investor's knowledge of investments and corporate finance, and the minimum financial knowledge that is necessary to fully understand what risks and returns of a particular corporate stock or bond are important, let alone to independently assess whether the expected return is realistic or justifies the risk.

Are we as part-time investors better off purchasing an unfamiliar investment whose repayment source and characteristics we are personally knowledgeable about, or blindly accepting familiar but little-understood complexities?

Some of the greatest resistance to the idea of mortgage-backed securities being suitable for individual investors comes from within the mortgage security community itself. The professionals who work day-to-day in the institutional mortgage security markets live in a world of massive on-line computerized data bases, amid batteries of Ph.D.s and MBAs running sophisticated custom analysis software programs that calculate multiscenario holding-period returns and option-adjusted pricing spreads as they compete for the extra basis point in that day's $500 million issue. What possible place could an individual investor, who wants to invest $20,000 and doesn't know a future value from a modified internal rate of return, have in that complex world of high finance?

"Mortgage securities are considered highly complex and difficult to understand."

It is easy to look at all the Ph.D.'s and the sophisticated computer models, and draw the conclusion that mortgage securities are far too complex and mathematically difficult to be appropriate for individual investors. To do so however, is to miss the forest because of all the trees. All the equations and mathematical models are applied to mortgage securities *not* because they are so complex that we have to, but rather because they are so simple that we are able to!

There are so many intertwined risk factors and return potentials involved in corporate financial analysis that complex mathematical evaluation techniques are often of little practical benefit. What use are elegant equations if most of your assumptions are no more than educated guesses? Even if we had more-certain information, there are so many different variables to consider and their interrelationships are so labyrinthine that it would take a mind-boggling array of equations to represent the exact effects of a 1% change in interest rates upon the shares of an individual company. It is for this reason that traditional stock investing is sometimes considered as much an art as a science. The uncertainties overwhelm all attempts to precisely quantify the market.

In stark contrast, with mortgage securities we have pools of home mortgages; we have changes in interest rates with resulting reasonably predictable changes in prepayments, yields, and prices; and that is about it. It is this *simplicity* of having only a few variables and the *predictability* of these variables that makes the use of mathematically complex evaluation techniques worthwhile for mortgage securities.[1] Because such techniques can be applied does not however mean that they are required in order to invest in mortgage securities. Simplicity and predictability are the Essence of mortgage investing.

Mortgage securities *are* more complex than Treasury bonds or bank certificates of deposit. If however we need more yield, then *reversing the mortgage* is far more understandable for most of us than deciphering consolidated corporate financial statements, balancing earning growth rates versus dividend yields, or gauging the likely performance of the economy over the next decade. The *personal knowledge* that we have of home mortgages is sufficient reason by itself for us as individual investors to choose mortgage securities over more-traditional stocks, partnerships, or corporate bonds, on the grounds that reasoned understanding is almost always preferable to blind guesswork.

Higher Yields, Lower Risk

As commonplace as home mortgages are, mortgage securities are new territory for most individual investors, with new words to be learned and new concepts to be mastered. Is it worth our time to learn about these obscure investments?

Our answer has to be yes, for mortgage securities offer us not only the control benefits of personal knowledge, but also a combination of increased yield and reduced risk that cannot be found elsewhere.

As we learned in Chapter 2, through *reversing the mortgage* and turning the financial power of *snowballing stretched*-out interest payments away from paying down debts and into wealth accumulation, we can realize a 4-to-1, 10-to-1, or even 14-to-1 return on our *contractual* investments over the course of a 15-year to 30-year long-term savings plan.

Compounding Wealth Contractually

Inflation and taxes are twin drags on most investment portfolios, with taxes eating away at gains and inflation eroding purchasing power. Short-term treasury securities and bank certificates have trouble surviving these problems, and over time often have an effective negative return on an after-tax, after-in-

---

[1] Please note that for the discussion herein we have continued to treat all mortgage securities as being simple pass-through securities, usually the most appropriate form of investment for individuals. CMO classes do exist that are much more complex than that we looked at so far; however, the performance behavior of even the most arcane of CMO residuals can be more accurately predicted than that of the simplest of equities.

flation basis. As we learned in Chapter 3, mortgage securities offer the necessary yield we need to survive.

Surviving Inflation & Taxes

Monthly principal and interest payments may appear an inconvenience to some, and the percent or two rate advantage that mortgage securities hold over equivalent Treasury bonds may hardly seem worth the bother. However, as we saw in Chapter 4, monthly payments increase both flexibility and yield, and combining this yield enhancement with the interest rate advantage, we find that minor differences can compound to an ending wealth advantage of 50% or more.

Minor Advantages Compound to Major Dollars

At first glance mortgage securities might appear to be riskier than bonds, due to their long maturities and the negative way in which prepayments react to interest rate changes. Yet, as we found out in Chapter 13, the surprising truth is that long-term mortgage securities have much *less* price risk than long-term bonds. Indeed, mortgage securities offer a unique way to "beat the market" by allowing us to benefit from high long-term yields without taking long-term price risk.

"Beat The Market" With Short-Term Price Risk and Long-Term Yields

Reduced price risk is a wonderful short-term safety measure, but how about medium-term performance? As we found in Chapter 14, if we examine total performance inclusive of interest payments *and* price changes, we find that the combination of high yields and low price changes give us a security that excels if interest rate changes are only moderate, and has middle-of-the-road performance with extreme upward or downward price moves. High yields under reasonably stable market conditions are attractive and a good reason to invest in mortgage securities; however, the more important feature if we are trying to avoid risk is that mortgage securities over time are quite unlikely to have the worst relative yield performance.

Mortgage-Backed Securities Have the Least Risk of Generating the Worst Yields

When we look at long-term investing, we have to shift our perspective from that of individual investments to investment strategies, for the rate at which we can reinvest will be the single most important factor in determining our ending wealth. It is under these conditions that mortgage securities investments achieve their best performance relative to bonds or certificates of deposit. *No Choice* and *Better Home* prepayments, combined with monthly principal and interest payments, throw out enough cash for reinvestment at the new, higher rates that mortgage securities substantially outperform long-term and intermediate-term bonds if interest rates rise. The *No Telling* Face of Prepayments keeps enough cash invested at high levels for long enough so that mortgage securities will widely outperform short-term and intermediate-term bonds during a sustained fall in interest rates. Add in market-beating performance in stable interest rate environments, and we have an extraordinary tool for consistently building wealth in an uncertain future.

Mortgage Securities Perform Best Within a Long-Term Investment Strategy

The most complex component of mortgage security analysis for institutional investors is that of predicting and controlling exposure to prepayment changes. This unique aspect of mortgage security investing, and its impact upon price, yield, and cash flow, consumes the lion's share of the analytical resources that investment banks apply to creating and repackaging CMOs, Remics and other derivative mortgage instruments, and is also the uppermost risk factor that most institutional investors consider when they purchase mortgage securities.

The reason for all this concern is that an adverse change in prepayment rates which is annoying and inconvenient for the individual investor, can be dangerous and possibly deadly for the institutional investor.

> "The prepayment change that is annoying for the individual can be deadly for the institution."

This difference in magnitude of risk does not come about because adverse investment results for individuals are somehow less important than they are for large financial institutions, but rather because institutional investors are in an entirely different investment environment.

Winning with Mortgage Securities

Most institutional investors—such as insurance companies, banks, and savings and loans—are engaged in asset/liability management. They earn their money off the spread between the interest rate they earn on their financial assets, say 7.00%, and the interest rate they pay on their liabilities, say 6.00% (CDs and annuities are example liabilities). The problem with adverse prepayment changes is that with falling interest rates, mortgage prepayments speed up, and institutional investors find themselves having to reinvest money at 5.00%, for which they are *paying* 6.00%, thereby losing 1.00%. Conversely, with rising interest rates, prepayments slow down, the 6.00% liabilities mature and have to be paid back, and institutional investors find themselves having to borrow at the new rate of 8.00% to fund their old mortgage investment at 7.00%, again losing 1.00%. Worse, these investors are typically highly leveraged, with most assets being purchased with borrowed money. The change from a 1.00% positive spread to a 1.00% negative spread can over time severely damage or even bankrupt the institution. Leverage magnifies prepayment risk.

The attraction and the danger to institutional investors of purchasing mortgage-backed securities can both be found within prepayment risk. Because of prepayment risk, mortgage securities carry significantly higher interest rates than equivalent bonds. Mortgage securities are not bonds however, and adverse prepayment changes, magnified by leverage when the mortgage securities are funded by traditional liabilities, can be disastrous. The goal of many in the investment community, then, has been to artificially make bonds out of mortgage securities, and maintain the yield advantage while minimizing the prepayment risk.

The investment banking community has been working on this goal for a decade now, and overall has done amazingly well. Collateralized Mortgage Obligations (CMOs) were introduced in 1983, a new kind of structure that split apart mortgage cash flows into short-, medium-, and long-term groups (tranches), so that they could be matched to specific investor needs. The relatively simple early CMOs quickly evolved in a number of directions besides just splitting out principal payments sequentially: floaters and inverse floaters turned fixed interest rates into securities that moved with or against market rates. Interest-only and principal-only securities (IOs and POs) were created that carried the concepts of discount and premium mortgage securities to extremes: IOs received interest only and no principal, with their entire purchase price consisting of premium, while POs received principal only and no interest, receiving all of their yield from the recapture of discount. Prepayment risk was mostly pulled out of planned amortization classes (PACs), and shifted into highly volatile companion bonds. All of this was facilitated by Congress through the creation of a special tax vehicle called Real Estate Mortgage Investment Conduits (REMICS), which minimized issuer tax concerns.

There is, however, a fundamental limit to reengineering residential mortgages, in that prepayment risk cannot be eliminated (unless we change homeowner behavior); rather, it can only be shifted from one investor to another. No matter how brilliant the strategist, or how clever the structure, or how sophisticated the management strategy, the heart of the matter remains fighting the dynamic and shifting nature of mortgage securities in order to turn them into static, stable bonds. This transformation, inherently limited though it may be, has been responsible for the stratospheric rise of the mortgage security market from an asterisk in the textbooks two decades ago, to the $1.3 trillion dollar market of today.

Would it be better to just have an investor who could fully enjoy the benefits of the enhanced yield offered by mortgages securities, without being exposed to the risks of leveraged asset/liability portfolios? Thereby enjoying the benefits, but without nearly the danger? Should we change the product or change the investor?

> "Individual investors fully benefit from the yield, but face far less financial risk from prepayments."

We as individual investors *are* fully exposed to prepayment risk, just as are institutional investors. The difference lies in the impact of the risk: we get all our principal back, plus interest; however, our repayment in full tends to be sooner than we would like if rates are falling, and later than we would like if rates are rising. Not a bad risk as risks go, though we would still prefer to avoid it. However, it is by accepting this prepayment risk in exchange for enhanced yields that we as individual investors are able to achieve the market-beating performance demonstrated in Chapters 13-15. In every case, performance was calculated *after* fully incorporating the adverse changes in prepayments. This positive performance is entirely different from the risk/return situation that leveraged institutional investors face, for in their case shifting assets and fixed liabilities can lead to financial disaster in volatile markets.

Indeed, rather than benefiting by trying to force mortgages to behave like bonds in uncertain and changing markets, we as individual investors actually benefit from leaving untouched the monthly-pay, combined short/medium/long-term portfolio that is to be found within each mortgage security. In essence what we are doing is buying a "bond ladder" within each mortgage security, an investment strategy that is often recommended to protect the value of portfolios against an uncertain future. True, the composition of our bond ladder does shift against us with increasing short-term components when rates fall and increasing long-term components when rates rise, but unlike a bond ladder, every investment dollar is working for us at high, long-term yields.

Turning Disadvantages into Advantages

The last and most important characteristic of mortgage investing which we need to review is that of safety:

- **Safety** is the single largest motivation for individual investors to invest in mortgage securities.
- **Safety** is the feature that most distinguishes mortgage securities from many other, more-traditional investments for individuals.
- **Safety** is the reason why mortgage securities should primarily be purchased by individual investors rather than sophisticated financial institutions.

The formal study of finance is commonly referred to as the study of *risk and return,* with risk always being referred to first, and return being placed in second place. This stands in marked contrast to the way in which investments are often presented in advertisements, with sizzling yields presented in bold headlines and colorful graphs, and the legally necessary disclosure that there is some risk involved relegated to the fine print at the base of the advertisement page or television screen.

The practical difference between the two presentation priorities is profound. Both academic theory and common sense would dictate that the first thing we as investors should do is to establish our own acceptable risk level, and only then try to maximize return within the investment categories that do not exceed our own risk tolerance. Conversely, established and successful sales techniques within the investment industry call for enticing the potential customer first, and then after the customer is interested, letting him or her know that some risk is involved.

If we focus primarily on rewards first, then mortgage securities with their single-digit yields and obscure vocabulary are likely to be of little interest to the individual investor. Numerous impressive investment experts and firms can be found who will say that we should make 15%, 20%, 30% or more by purchasing their recommended stocks, buying real estate partnerships, investing in precious metals, speculating with futures or options, trading the market with their exclusive computer model, and so forth. What all these experts have in common are convincing reasons why what they are predicting *should* happen, what almost all lack is any certainty that what they predict *will* happen, or any guarantee that we will get our money back.

The wide gap between *should* and *will* has been demonstrated time and again in the investment world. No matter how profitable the trend or how widespread the enthusiasm, regardless of whether we are speaking of commercial real estate, junk bonds, silver contracts, the nifty fifty, or tulip bulbs, chasing high-yielding investments that *should* make us wealthy has instead all too often ended up making us poorer in the end.

Mortgage security investing is based upon an entirely different premise. First, we decide to limit ourselves to investments in which we can be assured we *will* ultimately get our money back (plus interest). Then we search for the best means of maximizing the cash we will be paid, and minimizing any price loss exposure should we have to unexpectedly sell our investments prematurely. This is the reason why we purchase mortgage securities: we *should* earn superior protection from price risk, we *should* have superior yield, we *should* achieve outstanding results over the long term, but most importantly, from the *Five Layers of Safety* we know we *will* get our principal and interest back. It is this certainty that most distinguishes mortgage securities from the wide range of other traditional investments for individuals which *should* return higher yields.

When we view investments from the perspective of risk and return, it is ironic that mortgage securities have become the investment of choice for many institutional investors while being considered somehow undesirable for individual investors. All the tools for reducing risk are available to major pension funds, banks, and insurance companies: specialized internal and external accountants, attorneys, and financial analysts; access not only to the publicly available printed media but also to the recommendations of numerous brokerage-firm research teams and real-time online computerized information bases; and the million and billions of investable dollars to diversify away much of the risk. Such investors do of course also purchase a variety of other investments, yet they have purchased well over $1 trillion of mortgage securities in the last decade, and the more they purchase, the more they like the highest yielding of the safe and certain securities. Despite the single-digit yields currently offered by mortgage securities, despite the increased exposure which leveraged investors have to prepayment risk, despite the long fall in mortgage rates that has triggered wave after wave of refinancings, institutional investors have grown so fond of the advantages offered by mortgage securities that they have bid the risk premium attached to mortgage securities over Treasuries down by more than half. If money talks, that is a trillion-dollar compliment.

In contrast, most individual investors have little knowledge of investment theory and practice. We generally have no direct access to the financial analysts, researchers, accountants, or attorneys; instead, we must often rely upon journalists' summaries of their understanding of the opinions of financial experts. Price and yield information is generally available to us within minutes or hours after the professionals receive it, but the implications of these changes may take days, weeks, or months to reach us. Individuals rarely have the financial resources to achieve what many experts would consider to be minimal prudent diversification (30+ different stocks), unless assets are held in the form of mutual funds.

Adding together the lack of investment knowledge, the lack of expert assistance, the delayed access to simplified information, and the frequent inability to adequately diversify, it becomes clear that stocks, real estate, corporate bonds, futures and options speculation, precious metals, and many other traditional investments for individuals are in fact far more dangerous for individuals than they are for institutional investors.

"Why are the least knowledgeable investors steered to the most dangerous investments?"

This is not to say that it is impossible for individual investors to "beat the market" in the more speculative arenas: many do, many do not. The question that we need to ask ourselves is how confident are we that *we* can beat the market? If we are not confident about our own ability to select among speculative investments where we risk losing everything, would we be better off in a safer place? Where we can personally understand our investments? Where we can earn advantageous yields? Where we *know* we *will* get our money back?

Investing our money can be seen as walking a tightrope, each of us balancing between risk and return as we edge forward. As mortgage security investors we carefully eye the rope ahead, trying to judge how many of our neighbors are likely to prepay their mortgages in coming years. We do well for several years, then interest rates suddenly and unexpectedly fall. We fall with them as our neighbors prepay their high-interest-rate mortgages and we are forced out of our high-yielding investment. We do not fall far, however, before we are caught by the net beneath us, our full investment principal with interest has been returned to us so we may start again. Climbing back on the tightrope, we reinvest our money and resume our investment journey.

The speculative investor walks blindfolded, unaware of how a decrease in pension fund capitalization rates can devastate a corporation's earnings, or of reports of the increasing oversupply of strip shopping centers, or of the relation between the value of the dollar and exports. The dollar suddenly soars in value, the shares of major exporters plummet, and the speculative investor slips off the tightrope as the value of his portfolio is sliced in half. There is no net, and it is a long fall, as he loses half of his savings in a matter of weeks, with no assurance he will ever get them back.

"Walking with or without a blindfold, working with or without a net, the choice is ours."

Investor Checklist

Selecting a mortgage security to purchase is a much simpler task than selecting a stock, or a corporate or municipal bond for one simple reason: we know that we will get our principal and interest back. Not having to worry about a company going bankrupt or losing market share eliminates most of the uncertainties involved in purchasing securities. In addition, mortgage securities are relatively similar to each other, for while different in some important ways, most mortgage securities have much more in common with each other than do stocks or bonds issued by differing corporations.

However, there are a few prudent steps that we should follow, in order to make sure that we are purchasing what we think we are purchasing, and that the price is as reasonable as we think it is. Before purchasing mortgage securities, make sure that you know the answers to the following questions:

1. **Who is the issuer?**
   The *issuer* of the security should be Fannie Mae, Freddie Mac, or Ginnie Mae. If not, then you are buying a different kind of mortgage security than those covered in this introductory volume, and you should proceed with caution. Some people will say that this is irrelevant because the collateral for the security is from the agencies, and the issuers themselves are just a legal technicality. *Not true.* There is a reason why someone went to the trouble and expense of creating an intermediate trust to stand between you and the mortgage securities and act as issuer. This intermediate trust may be reducing your risk, or may be increasing your risk; don't buy if you don't know.

2. **What is the name of the security?**
   The name of the security should be "mortgage-backed security," or "participation certificate." If the name is "Bond Class 4A" or "interest-only certificate," then you are looking at something else entirely. It could

be a good investment; it could be a bad investment; it is not a simple mortgage security of the type discussed herein.

3. **How much principal are you purchasing?**
Your broker should be able to tell you exactly how much premium or discount is within the purchase price that you are paying. Unfortunately, there are some who can be evasive in response to this question, particularly if the security in question is selling at a high premium, or has a fat commission built into its price (or both). If you have any doubts whatsoever about the security or the broker, *insist* upon an answer to the following question: "If every mortgage in the pool underlying the security were to prepay tomorrow, how much *principal* will I get back?"

If the principal you get back exceeds the price you paid (exclusive of accrued interest), then you are purchasing a discount security. If the principal you get back is less than the price you paid, then you are buying a premium security, and you *are at risk* for the entire dollar amount of that premium. This is not necessarily bad if the price is right and you know what you are doing. However, purchasing securities at high premiums is the most dangerous form of mortgage securities investing for investors who are not knowledgeable in the area.

4. **What is the weighted average coupon of the mortgages?** When looking at mortgage securities, we usually assume that the mortgage pools backing similar securities are themselves similar, and we are generally right. We can expect that the actual mortgages underlying a particular security will have interest rates that are 0.5% to 1.0% higher than the coupon of the mortgage security. Mortgage securities with 8.0% coupons are usually backed by mortgages with 8.5% to 9.0% interest rates; 8.5% security coupons are usually backed by mortgages with 9.0% to 9.5% interest rates. Keeping in mind that homeowners base their prepayment decisions on what *their* interest rates are, and not the coupon on the security their mortgage is in, we compare this mortgage rate estimate to what current mortgage rates are, and determine the likely prepayment speed of the mortgage security.

However, when it comes time to purchase a specific mortgage security, it is wise to double-check by asking what the "weighted average coupon," or "WAC," is of the mortgages underlying the security. Some mortgage securities are backed by mortgages carrying rates up to 2.55% higher than the security coupon rate, so that our 8.0% security may have

10.5% mortgages behind it (with the *much* higher prepayment speeds of 10.5% mortgages). A premium security with a WAC that is more than 1% higher than the security coupon has a lesser value, due to the higher expected prepayments than other securities with the same coupon (discount securities with relatively high WACs are *more* valuable for the same reason).

5. **What is the weighted average remaining maturity of the mortgages?**
   Most mortgage securities are created shortly after the underlying mortgages are originated, and the mortgages have similar maturities. However, some mortgage securities are created as a result of financial institutions restructuring their portfolios, and may have a wide range of maturities on the underlying mortgages. For this reason it is wise to double-check and ask about the "weighted average remaining maturity," or "WARM" (sometimes WAM), of the underlying mortgages. A short WARM (or WAM) relative to the maturity of the mortgage security increases the value of discount securities and decreases the value of premium securities.

6. **What is the pool size?**
   As is discussed in Chapter 17, prepayments are most predictable when we are purchasing part of a very large pool of securities, and least predictable when we are purchasing part of a pool that may contain only 5 or 10 loans. Ask what the original pool size was, what the current factor is, and what the current pool balance is (a pool with an original size of $10 million and a factor of 0.3 would have a current balance of $10 million times 0.3, or $3 million).

   If the current pool size is lower than $1 million, then the mortgage security is somewhat less valuable and should be available at a lower than "generic" price; this is particularly true if the current balance is under $500,000. If the pool is a "Major" or "Giant" or has a pool balance in the tens of millions, then it is somewhat more valuable, and will likely cost you more than the "generic" price you will find in the financial media.

7. **What is the settlement date?**
   Unlike most securities, mortgage securities usually have only one settlement date per month, with that date varying by security and month. Most trading (and price quotes) usually centers on the nearest delivery date. However, some securities are traded for delivery dates that may be one,

two, or even three months away. These securities usually sell at lower prices, because arbitragers have the ability to profit from earning long-term yields on short-term investments through selling the mortgage securities for a delayed delivery, and then borrowing the money to carry them at a cheap short-term rate. Make sure that your security is for the nearest delivery period, or that its price is lower if it is for a later delivery date.

8. **Are the price and prepayment assumptions reasonable?**
As is more thoroughly discussed in Chapter 17, it is a good idea to check the price of the security being offered to you, since mortgage securities are a negotiated market rather than an exchange. It is also good to check the reasonableness of the prepayment assumptions that your broker is using, as these assumptions may have a profound influence upon the yield shown for discount or premium securities.

Appendix

CPR and PSA Prepayment Speed Conversion Charts
(For mortgage loans older than 30 months)

Converting CPR to PSA			Converting PSA to CPR		
0% CPR	=	0% PSA	0% PSA	=	0.0% CPR
2% CPR	=	33% PSA	25% PSA	=	1.5% CPR
4% CPR	=	67% PSA	50% PSA	=	3.0% CPR
6% CPR	=	100% PSA	75% PSA	=	4.5% CPR
8% CPR	=	133% PSA	100% PSA	=	6.0% CPR
10% CPR	=	167% PSA	125% PSA	=	7.5% CPR
12% CPR	=	200% PSA	150% PSA	=	9.0% CPR
14% CPR	=	233% PSA	175% PSA	=	10.5% CPR
16% CPR	=	267% PSA	200% PSA	=	12.0% CPR
18% CPR	=	300% PSA	250% PSA	=	15.0% CPR
20% CPR	=	333% PSA	300% PSA	=	18.0% CPR
25% CPR	=	417% PSA	350% PSA	=	21.0% CPR
30% CPR	=	500% PSA	400% PSA	=	24.0% CPR
35% CPR	=	583% PSA	500% PSA	=	30.0% CPR
40% CPR	=	667% PSA	600% PSA	=	36.0% CPR
45% CPR	=	750% PSA	700% PSA	=	42.0% CPR
50% CPR	=	833% PSA	800% PSA	=	48.0% CPR

To convert a CPR Speed to a PSA Speed multiply it time 16.7 (1/.06)

Example: 10% CPR × 16.7 = 167% PSA

To convert a PSA Speed to a CPR Speed multiply it times .06 (6%)

Example: 100% PSA × .06 = 6% CPR

PSA Speeds can be converted to CPR Speeds during the first 30 months of aging by multiplying the CPR Speed times .06, then multiplying times the number of months since the mortgages were originated, and then dividing by 30.

Example: 100% PSA × .06 × 12 months aging / 30 = 2.4% CPR

CPR = Constant Prepayment Rate = Conditional Prepayment Rate.
PSA = Public Securities Association standard prepayment model.

Glossary

AAA & Aaa
The highest rankings of credit quality, as judged by the major rating agencies. Payment according to schedule is considered almost a certainty, though a few Triple-A securities do default.

Amortize (Amortization)
To pay down a debt under a scheduled *series* of principal payments. With amortizing investments we receive our investment principal back in a number of installments over time.

Basis point
A yield measure equal to one hundredth of one percent; 0.0001 or 0.01%.

Better Home prepayments
Optional prepayments triggered by homeowner moves to new residences. Better Home prepayments rise when falling interest rates lower the cost of new mortgages, and fall when rising interest rates increase the cost of new mortgages.

Better Rate prepayments
Refinancings of mortgages by homeowners to take advantage of lower interest rates. Better Rate prepayments are the most powerful form of prepayments. A surge in refinancings when interest rates fall can drastically accelerate the return of principal to investors.

Bonds
Interest-bearing securities that promise to pay principal and interest according to a contractual schedule. Bonds usually (but not always) pay interest semiannually, and all principal in a lump sum at maturity.

CMOs
See Collateralized Mortgage Obligations.

Collateralized Mortgage Obligations (CMOs)
Mortgage securities that are comprised of other mortgage securities, but which allocate cash flows differently to different investors. CMOs shift

prepayment and interest rate risks from some investors to other investors, and thus can offer either reduced or increased investor risks, depending on which class (tranche) of CMOs is purchased.

Compound interest
Interest earned through reinvesting interest monies already received.

Constant Prepayment Rate (CPR)
A prepayment speed measure which assumes that a constant percentage of the outstanding principal amount of the mortgage security prepays in each year for the life of the pool. A 10% CPR speed would project that 10% of the remaining mortgage balance would prepay in each year for the life of the security.

Coupon
The stated interest rate on a bond or mortgage security.

CPR
Abbreviation for Constant Prepayment Rate; also known as Conditional Prepayment Rate, as monthly prepayment amounts are conditional upon the amount of principal outstanding that month.

Credit quality
The relative likelihood that a borrower will be able to pay principal and interest as scheduled. A high credit quality borrower is considered to be very likely to be able to pay all principal and interest in full as scheduled, something which is considered doubtful for a lo- credit-quality borrower.

Discount
When we pay less than the face amount (or amount of principal outstanding) for a bond or mortgage security, the discount is the dollar difference between the purchase price and the principal amount. When we pay $9,000 for a $10,000 security, we are purchasing it at a $1,000 discount.

Discount security
Any security that has a market value less than the amount of principal outstanding; any security that is purchased at a discount.

Factor
The portion of the original principal balances that is still outstanding of the mortgage pool that underlies a mortgage security. If a security with an original balance of $10 million has a factor of 0.5, this means that

Glossary

$5 million in mortgage principal is still outstanding. Factors are reduced each month by the payment of scheduled principal on the mortgages, and can be sharply reduced as a result of prepayments.

Fannie Mae
See Federal National Mortgage Association.

Federal Home Loan Mortgage Corporation
A quasi-governmental agency chartered by Congress in 1970 for the purpose of making housing more affordable. Also known as Freddie Mac or FHLMC, it is one of the three major issuers of mortgage securities.

Federal National Mortgage Association
A quasi-governmental agency that was chartered by Congress in 1938 for the purpose of making housing more affordable, and was partially privatized in 1968. Also known as Fannie Mae, or FNMA, it is one of the three major issuers of mortgage securities.

FHLMC
See Federal Home Loan Mortgage Corporation.

FNMA
See Federal National Mortgage Association.

Freddie Mac
See Federal Home Loan Mortgage Corporation.

Ginnie Mae
See Government National Mortgage Association.

GNMA
See Government National Mortgage Association.

Government National Mortgage Association
A governmental agency chartered by Congress in 1968 for the purpose of making housing more affordable. Also known as Ginnie Mae, or GNMA. Ginnie Mae is distinguished from the other two agencies by its being an agency of the federal government whose securities are fully and directly guaranteed by the Treasury, and by the assumable FHA and VA mortgage loans that underlie its securities.

Guarantors
Used herein to refer to the three agencies, Freddie Mac, Fannie Mae and Ginnie Mae, that guarantee repayment of full principal and interest on their mortgage securities.

Holding period return
A yield measure which assumes that securities are held for a defined period of time (the *holding period*) and then sold. Holding period return takes into account the effects of purchase price, sale price, interest payments, interim principal payments, and the time value of money.

Institutional investors
Investors that are not natural persons, but are for-profit or non-profit entities that invest in securities. Institutional investors include insurance companies, banks, thrifts, pension funds, mutual funds, and investment companies, and are often characterized by large portfolio sizes and professional investment management.

Lags
The time between when interest begins accruing (or stops accruing) on the underlying mortgage, and when interest is paid to the investor. Lags vary between agencies and programs.

MBS
See Mortgage-backed securities.

Mortgage Securities
Securities that are directly or indirectly collateralized by or comprised of mortgages. While the discussion herein focuses on the most common kind of mortgage security — 30 year, fixed-interest-rate, agency mortgage-backed securities — the term is highly inclusive. Other kinds of mortgage securities include CMOs, adjustable-rate securities, mortgage collateralized bonds, multifamily and commercial mortgage collateralized securities, and private pass-through securities.

Mortgage-backed securities
This term generally refers to pools of mortgages that have been turned into securities. Each investor receives a portion of homeowner principal and interest payments equal to that investor's percentage ownership of the pool; with payment of the principal and interest guaranteed by a governmental or quasi-governmental agency.

Glossary

No-Choice prepayments
Mortgage prepayments that occur regardless of the current level of interest rates. Transfers or new jobs in other cities, divorces, foreclosures, fires, and flood losses are example sources of this kind of prepayment.

No-Telling prepayments
High-interest-rate mortgages that do not prepay even though they have been in a refinancing range for many months or even years. Waiting for anticipated moves, waiting for rates to fall further, or adverse changes in employment status or credit histories are common reasons for this kind of homeowner behavior.

Originators
The banks, thrifts, and mortgage companies that generate the documents and advance the monies to create or originate new mortgages.

Par
A security is said to be a par security, or to trade at par, when it can be purchased at its face amount. To purchase a security that has $10,000 in principal, for a price of $10,000, is to buy it at *par*.

Participation certificates
The name used by Freddie Mac to describe its version of mortgage-backed securities, also known as PCs.

PC
See Participation certificates.

Premium
When we pay more than the face amount (or amount of principal outstanding) for a bond or mortgage security, the premium is the dollar difference between the purchase price and the principal amount. When we pay $11,000 for a $10,000 security, we are purchasing it at a $1,000 premium.

Premium security
Any security that has a market value greater than the amount of principal outstanding; any security that is purchased at a premium.

Prepayment
When principal is paid on a mortgage sooner than contractually required, then a prepayment has occurred. Prepayments usually refer to paying off a mortgage in whole, though partial prepayments also occur.

Principal
   The face value or amount of a debt or security that must be repaid by the borrower, not including interest.

PSA prepayment speed
   The prepayment speed standard adopted by the Public Securities Association. The major difference between this model and the Constant Prepayment Rate (CPR) method is that the PSA model takes into account the reduced number of prepayments that occur in the first two to three years after mortgages are originated (see PSA to CPR Conversion Table in Appendix I).

Purchasing power risk
   The risk that the rate of inflation will exceed the earnings on our investments, leaving us with a real loss in terms of what our money will purchase, even though we have been making apparent profits. Purchasing power risk is particularly acute when we are paying taxes on our investment income.

Quasi-governmental agencies
   Agencies such as Fannie Mae and Freddie Mac that blend the characteristics of government agencies and private corporations. Chartered by Congress but "owned" by shareholders, these agencies have more flexibility and freedom of action than government agencies, and further benefit as their commitments are generally considered morally and implicitly guaranteed by the federal government. In exchange for these benefits, each agency is charged with serving the public purpose of making housing affordable to the public, and is closely regulated by Congress and the administration.

Real Estate Mortgage Investment Conduit (REMIC)
   A form of Collateralized Mortgage Obligation that carries significant tax advantages for the issuer.

Real return
   The real increase in spendable wealth which we realize from our investments on an after-tax, after-inflation basis. Real return is often negative for short-term, high-quality investments such as money market funds, Treasury bills, passbook savings, and 3-month CDs.

Realized yield
   See Holding period return.

Remic
See Real Estate Mortgage Investment Conduit.

Return
The yield that we realize from our investments.

Servicers
The companies that gather, process, and forward the homeowner mortgage payments each month. The servicer acts on the mortgage investor's behalf in making sure the house is kept insured, that taxes are paid, that late payments are collected, and that foreclosure occurs if payments are not made.

Snowballing
A term used herein to describe the growing speed and importance of interest on interest (compound interest) in increasing the value of our investment portfolios over time.

Stacking
A term used herein to describe the wealth-increasing cumulative effects of making a number of investment purchases over time, with total interest in each month being the sum of the interest earnings of each investment purchase.

Stretching
A term used herein to describe the wealth-increasing cumulative effects of making a single investment purchase, with that purchase generating income each and every month thereafter.

WAC
See Weighted average coupon.

WAL
See Weighted average life.

WARM
See Weighted average remaining maturity.

Weighted average coupon
The average interest rate on the pool of mortgages underlying a mortgage security.

Weighted average life (WAL)
A common method of measuring and comparing the expected length of our investment with different mortgage securities (prepayments make maturities of limited use). A weighted average life calculation tells us the average amount of time until we get our principal back. A mortgage security with an expected 6-year weighted average life is considered roughly equivalent to a 6-year bond, even though the mortgage security may have a maturity of 30 years.

Weighted average remaining maturity (WARM)
A common method for measuring the effective maturity of a mortgage security. Weighted average remaining maturity measures the average years until maturity for each of the mortgages underlying the mortgage security, and is a better predictor of cash payments than the contractual maturity of the security.

Index

A
Accountants, 63
Accounting, *see* Double-entry
Adjustable-rate
 loans, 207
 mortgages, 207
 securities, 208, 236
Adversity, 193-196
Aetna, 202
After-tax
 basis, 169
 yield, 22
Agencies, 66-71
 see Quasi
 standards, 69
Amortization, 4, 13, 18, 73, 75, 79, 81, 89, 117-119, 128, 204, 207, 212, 233
 see Planned, Targeted
Appraisal
 see Reappraisal
 report, 44
Asset/liability portfolio, 222
Audit, 63
Average life, 94, 124
 risk, 88

B
Balance, 75, 120
 sheet, 216
Balloon
 loans, 207
 mortgage securities, 208
Bank(s), 1, 7, 10, 44, 64, 93, 224
 see Foreign
 guarantees, 67
Bankruptcy, 42, 48, 50, 141
 risk, 4
Basis point, 233
Bear market, 54, 195
Beneficiary, 46
Better Home prepayment, 91-95, 96, 100-102, 120-130, 134, 139, 140, 150-152, 162, 166, 170, 177-179, 181-183, 220, 233
Better Rate prepayment, 95-97, 100-102, 120, 131, 133-140, 142, 150, 152, 170, 177-179, 181, 193-195, 207, 209, 233
Bill(s), *see* U.S. Treasury
Black Monday, 74
Bloomberg, 200
Boeing, 5
Bond(s), 2, 38, 39, 51, 52, 57, 63, 69, 72, 90, 105-108, 110-112, 136, 145-147, 150-152, 158, 160, 162-166, 168, 179, 180, 182, 186, 194, 197, 216, 219, 220, 233, 234
 see Companion, Corporate, Government, Junk, Mortgage, Municipal, Revenue, Tax-exempt, U.S.
 equivalent, 166
 holders, 63
 interest levels, 61
 interest rate, 160
 investment, 37, 157
 investor, 69

241

ladder, 222, 223
price gains, 170
rate, 106, 107
sales, 71
yield, 37, 57, 58, 60
Borrowers, 64
see Mortgage
creditworthiness, 44-45, 64, 106
Broker, 63, 201, 204, 212, 228, 230
see Securities, Stockbroker
Brokerage, 63
due diligence, 63
house, 202, 203
Bull market, 49, 54, 195
Buyers, 69, 106

C

Call options, 118
Cash, 35, 37, 45, 87, 108, 153, 157, 163, 178, 179, 183, 224
see Close-in, Faraway, Retirement
flow, 17, 79, 137, 149, 180, 211
payment, 110, 147, 240
return, 157
CBE, see Corporate
CD, see Certificate
Ceiling price, 139
Certificate of deposit (CD), 21-26, 29, 32, 52, 154, 195, 212, 218, 238
MBS comparison, 2-3
Citibank, 5
Close-in cash, 122-126, 129, 130, 146, 147, 149, 160, 161, 168
Closer-in cash, 124
CMO, see Collateralized
Collateral, 66
Collateralized mortgage obligation, 233-234, 238
CMO, 71, 199, 208-209, 220, 221, 233-234, 236
Commercial loan, 2
Commission, 7, 153
Common stock, 49-51, 195, 196, 216

dividends, 57
investment, 49, 50
Companion bond, 212
Company
performance, 50
risk, 4
Compounding, see Wealth
Compound interest, 12, 13, 15, 17-19, 234
Conditional prepayment rate, 234
Constant prepayment rate (CPR), 80-85, 93, 94, 102, 117, 123, 125, 128, 134, 137, 179, 202-204, 234, 238
conversion chart, 231
Consumer Price Index (CPI), 25
Contractual
documents, 69
document safety, 69-70
investment, 42, 218
maturity, 73
payment, 50
return, 11
Convexity, 152
Corporate
bond, 2, 3, 5, 42, 63, 68, 69, 97, 106, 200, 216, 225, 227
bond equivalent (CBE) yield, 37
bondholder, 141
debt, 67
losses, 48
managers, 63
stock, 216
Coupon, 113, 150, 229
CPI, see Consumer
CPR, see Constant
Credit
check, 44
history, 65
losses, 44
quality, 5, 205, 233, 234
risk, 6, 44, 216
safety, 5
Creditworthy borrowers, see Borrower
Currency

Index

fluctuation, 120
risk, 4
Current yield, 117-120, 125, 128, 143, 204
Curtailment, 76

D
Debt, 5, 18, 48, 88, 218, 233, 238
  see Corporate, Municipal
  service coverage ratio, 4
Default, 45, 47, 66, 68
  see Technical
Deficit, 47, 48
Delinquency, 99
Delivery date, 229, 230
Department of Housing and Urban Development (HUD), 67
Department of the Treasury, *see* U.S. Treasury
Discount, 100, 115-131, 151, 202, 206, 209, 221, 228, 234
  calculation, 105-114
  mortgage-backed securities, 141
  mortgage securities, 121, 127
  profits, 211
  securities, 117-118, 120, 136, 139-140, 206, 228, 229, 234
Diversification, 199, 225
  see National
Dividend, 33, 34, 50, 51, 56-58, 60-61
  see Common, Stock
  reinvestment, 56
  reinvestment model, 58
  reinvestment plan, 213
  risk, 4
  shrinking, 56-58
  yields, 57, 60
Divorce, 77, 237
DJIA, *see* Dow Jones
Double-entry accounting, 120
Dow Jones Industrial Average (DJIA), 190, 195, 196
  history, 53-56

E
Earning(s), 6, 141, 171
  see Interest, Interest rate, Reinvestment
  growth risk, 4
  interest, 18
Environmental risk, 4
Equity, 91
Escrow, *see* Insurance
Exxon, 106

F
Face value, 238
Factor, 73, 157, 163, 234-235
Fannie Mae, *see* Federal National
Faraway cash, 122-126, 129, 130, 146, 147, 160, 161, 168
Farther-away cash, 124, 146
Federal Deposit Insurance Corporation
  FDIC, 2
Federal Home Loan Mortgage Corporation, 66, 68, 235
  FHLMC, 48, 235
  Freddie Mac, 32, 47, 48, 66, 68, 93, 101, 106, 150, 205, 207, 227, 235, 236, 238
  mortgage securities, 77
  PC, 4, 43, 71, 102, 201, 206, 210, 211
  securities, 85, 102
Federal Housing Administration, 45, 76
  FHA, 45, 77, 84, 234
  FHA loan, 68, 77, 84, 85, 101, 102
  FHA mortgages, 73, 101
Federal National Mortgage Association, 66, 67, 235
  Fannie Mae, 47, 48, 66-68, 71, 93, 101, 106, 205, 227, 235, 236, 238
  FNMA, 48, 235
  MBS, 4, 43, 100, 102, 201, 206, 210, 211
  mortgage securities, 77
  securities, 85, 102
  stock comparison, 49-61
Federal Reserve, 67, 120
FHA, *see* Federal Housing

Index

FHLMC, *see* Federal Home
Fixed-rate mortgage, 11
Floater, 209
  see Inverse
Floor yield, 118
FNMA, *see* Federal National
Foreclosure, 66, 99, 237
Foreign
  banks, 7
  competition risk, 4
  currency fluctuations, 4
Freddie Mac, *see* Federal Home
Futures, 3, 5, 9, 225
  speculation, 41

G

General Motors, 5
Ginnie Mae, *see* Government
Glossary, 233-240
GNMA, *see* Government
Government
  bonds, 195
  guarantees, 48
  insurance, 45
Government National Mortgage Association, 2, 66, 67, 235
  Ginnie Mae, 2, 3, 47, 48, 66-68, 93, 106, 205, 213, 227, 235, 236
  GNMA, 48, 213, 235
  MBS, 2-4, 43, 68, 99, 102, 206
  mortgage securities, 77, 84
  prepayments, 101-103
  stock comparison, 49-61
Growth stocks, 120, 141, 155
Guarantee(s), *see* Bank, Insurance
Guarantor, 4, 64, 236
  fees, 93

H

Helpers, 63-72
Holding period, 160-163, 165-167, 170, 171, 180, 191, 236
  return, 236

  yield, 165
Home mortgage, 1, 9, 20, 33, 46
Homeowner, 64, 65, 67, 70, 74-76, 88, 89, 91, 95, 97, 98, 118, 120, 122, 125, 129, 130, 133, 134, 141, 162, 178, 182, 193, 216
  insurance, 45
HUD, *see* Department

I

IBM, 4, 5
Income, 22, 28, 30, 44, 65, 120, 211
  see Interest, Retirement
  statements, 216
  taxes, 27
  verification, 44
Indenture, 4, 69
  see Trust
Individual
  investor, 1, 7, 159, 215, 217, 218
  portfolio, 56
  retirement account (IRA), 22, 29, 30, 173, 180
Industry risk, 4
Inflation, 20, 25-27, 30, 31, 52
  rate, 6
  survival, 21-32, 219
Inheritance, 29
Institutional investor, 1, 63, 71, 222, 225, 236
Insurance, 3, 65
  see Government, Homeowner, Mortgage, Private, Property, Title
  company, 1, 7, 63, 142, 215
  company guarantees, 67
  escrow payments, 156
  layers, 46-47
  protection, 46
Interest, 5, 11, 12, 18, 33, 34, 52, 66, 71, 88, 105, 119, 141, 207, 224
  see Bond, Compound, Earning, Level, Mortgage, Pass-through
  earnings, 28, 29, 109, 160, 174

Index

income, 21, 70, 192, 211
on interest, 16, 37, 110
payments, 23, 48, 61, 63, 107, 109, 135, 156-158, 162, 165, 174, 183, 196, 208, 209, 219
savings, 13, 14
streams, 37
yields, 186, 187
Interest-bearing securities, 233
Interest-only securities (IOs), 221
Interest rate, 18, 50, 65, 71, 74, 75, 87, 88, 91, 92, 99-102, 106-108, 113, 115, 117, 120-127, 129, 134-137, 139-141, 147, 150, 151, 175, 181, 183, 185, 189-191, 193, 196, 197, 205, 207, 208, 210, 225 228, 233
earnings, 163
falling, 158-163, 178-182
investment, 90
level, 166
payments, 138
risk, 4-6, 35-39, 71, 234
speculation, 153
Intermediaries, 64
Intermediate trust, 227
Inverse floater, 209
Investment, 31, 34, 48, 50, 52, 54-56, 59, 87, 88, 91, 94, 105, 108, 112, 122, 135, 141, 150, 155, 156, 158, 176, 177, 180, 196, 197, 215
see Bond, Common, Contractual, Interest, Mortgage, Mortgage security, Reinvestment, Stock
alternatives, 41
company, 1
finance, 50
horizon, 52, 171
manager, 1
performance, 155, 157, 167
period, 163, 183
portfolio, 60, 61, 90, 141, 153, 218, 239
portfolio returns, 55
principal, 74, 77, 81, 82, 117, 120, 204

purchase, 239
risk, 42
strategy, 143, 154, 171, 178, 180, 182, 183, 195
yield, 31
Investor, 5, 17, 29, 30, 42, 48, 50, 54-56, 63, 67, 69-72, 106, 120-123, 125, 129, 130, 153, 208, 209, 217
see Bond, Individual, Institutional, Mortgage, Mortgage-backed, Mortgage securities, Nonprofessional, Professional
benefits, 17-20
checklist, 227-230
yields, 70
IO, see Interest-only
IRA, see Individual
Issuer, definition, 227

J
Junk bonds, 5, 59, 63, 74, 142, 224

K
Keoghs, 29
Knowledge, 69-70

L
Lag, 236
Lawsuit risk, 4
Leading indicators, 143
Lender, 64
  see Mortgage
Level interest rates, 166
Leverage, 221
Leveraged buyout, 63
Liabilities, 221
  see Asset/liability
Liquidation, 3, 75
Liquidity, 154
Loan, 44, 65, 68, 75, 77, 99
  see Adjustable, Balloon, Federal Housing, Mortgage, Veterans
Loan-to-value test, 99

Index

Lockout periods, 88
Loss swings, 127
Lump-sum payment(s), 19

M
Margin, 58, 135, 195
Market
  bid, 201
  rate, 50, 106, 107, 111, 126, 129, 139, 179, 180, 208, 209
  risk, 3, 4
  share, 216
  value loss, 113
  yield, 111, 135
Maturity, 33, 35, 82, 105, 109, 112, 118, 139, 145, 146, 149, 160, 204, 207, 233, 240
  see Contractual, Mortgage
MBS, *see* Mortgage-backed
McDonald's, 5
Money market fund, 29, 31-32, 154, 238
Monthly payments, 19, 66, 75, 98, 156, 185
  benefits, 33-39
  disadvantages, 33-35
  frequency, 37
Moody's, 5
Mortgage, 22, 38, 44, 64, 67, 77, 81, 84, 93, 97, 102, 137, 156, 175, 234
  see Adjustable, Collateralized, Federal Housing, Fixed-rate, Home, Private, Veterans
  borrowers, 45, 47, 66
  collateralized bonds, 236
  insurance, 45, 46
  interest, 14
  investment, 21, 22, 25, 35, 37, 82, 119
  profits, 24
  investor, 18, 19, 45, 46, 47, 48, 65, 66, 73, 95, 98, 99
  lender, 10, 12, 13, 44, 46, 64
  loans, 64, 65, 85, 94, 200, 210
  maturity, 77

note, 91
origination, 73, 77
payment, 11-13, 16, 20, 21, 33, 42, 64, 66, 99
pool, 48, 79, 80, 85, 99, 207, 210, 234, 239
portfolio, 146
prepayment, 75, 87, 91
principal, 13, 15, 20, 76, 179, 234
purchase yields, 32
rate, 26, 70, 89, 91, 93-96, 98, 126, 128, 134, 137
reversal, 9-21, 41, 42, 44-48, 74-77, 81, 87, 88, 90, 91, 95, 99, 117, 134, 194, 218
yield, 37
Mortgage-backed security (MBS), 1, 2, 5-7, 9, 25, 34, 39, 41-44, 49-51, 63, 64, 66, 71, 73, 74, 76, 77, 83, 84, 87, 92, 95, 105, 110, 112, 115, 121-123, 134, 138, 140-142, 145-147, 150, 152-154, 162, 165, 166, 169, 176, 178, 189, 220, 227, 236
  see Discount, Federal National, Government, Premium
  CD comparison, 2-3
  explanation, 4-5
  investor, 46, 79
  MBS, 1-3, 145, 147, 150, 151, 227, 236
  yield, 163
Mortgage-backed yield, 162
Mortgage securities, 10, 22, 27-29, 32, 35, 38, 39, 43, 51-53, 58, 61, 68, 106, 107, 112-114, 117, 125, 129, 136, 144, 150, 159, 160, 165, 166, 170, 171, 173, 175, 180, 183, 185, 186, 190, 191, 193, 195-197, 220-223, 227, 233, 234, 236
  see Balloon, Discount, Federal Home, Federal National, Government National, Par, Premium
  advantages, 215-226
  buying, 199-213

Index 247

choice, 6-7
investment, 158, 169, 192
investor, 35, 63, 163, 192
mutual funds, 212-213
risk, 5
selection, 205-206
varieties, 206-207
yield, 5-6, 103, 139, 191
Municipal
bond, 42, 48, 63, 68, 69, 97, 106, 200, 216, 227
debt, 67
revenue bond, 141
Mutual fund, 1, 2, 70, 154, 173, 174, 190, 199, 212, 236
see Mortgage securities

N
National diversification, 46-48
Negotiations, 49
New York Stock Exchange (NYSE), 67
No-Choice prepayment, 88-90, 93, 94, 96, 100-102, 115, 117, 118, 130, 220, 237
Nonprofessional investor, 4, 43
No-Telling prepayment, 97-102, 131, 137-139, 220, 237
Notes, 42

O
Obligation(s), 42
see Collateralized, U.S.
Options, 3, 4, 225
speculation, 5, 41
Origination, 73, 77
see Mortgage
Originator, 4, 64-66, 69, 237
Ownership interests, 49

P
PAC, see Planned
Par, 138, 158, 162, 202, 205, 211, 237
mortgage securities, 120, 121-127

securities, 120, 122-124, 127, 136, 206, 211
Participation certificate (PC), 68, 70, 210, 227, 237
see Federal Home
Partnerships, 3, 5, 42, 204, 212
see Real estate
Pass-through
interest payments, 210
securities, 70, 207, 209, 236
Payments, 3, 19, 34, 48, 70, 194, 210, 215
see Contractual, Interest, Lump-sum, Monthly, Mortgage,
Penny stocks, 204
Prepayment, Repayment
PC, see Participation
Pension fund, 7, 63, 142, 215, 224, 236
Planned amortization class (PAC), 208, 221
PMI, see Private
PO, see Principal-only
Pool, 210, 211
see Mortgage
size, 199, 229
Pooling agreements, 70
Portfolio, 171, 180, 185, 194, 210, 223, 236
see Asset, Individual, Investment, Mortgage
performance, 190
size, 236
Preferred stock, 69
Premium, 112-114, 115-131, 136, 204, 206, 209, 211, 228, 237
calculation, 105-114
MBS, 151
mortgage securities, 121, 139
price, 119
securities, 112, 118-120, 128, 138, 141, 206, 237
Prepayment, 50, 115-131, 146, 149, 150, 158, 166, 178, 183, 189, 195, 201, 217, 219, 234, 237

see Better Home, Better Rate, Conditional, Constant, Government National, Mortgage, No-Choice, No-Telling, Principal, Public, Refinancing
curve, 102, 133-142
definition, 75-79
fluctuation, 212
mastery, 87-103
mystery, 73-85
options, 118
penalty, 88
rate, 80-82, 92, 101, 120, 122, 123, 136, 137, 200, 212
risk, 5, 74, 114, 141, 206, 222, 224
shift, 4
speed, 74, 79, 80-85, 88, 93, 94, 100, 136, 199
comparison, 202-205
Price, 105, 108, 110, 111, 119, 121, 122, 124, 125, 201, 217
see Bond, Ceiling, Premium, Purchase, Sale, Securities, Share, Stock
determination, 201-202
effects, 129
gain, 55, 135, 180, 194
loss, 126
quote, 230
swing, 123, 170
volatility, 200
Price risk, 5, 111, 112, 136, 141, 143-154, 161, 169, 186, 187, 192, 206, 219
applications, 152-154
exception, 146-152
Principal, 10, 11, 18, 34, 50, 52, 66, 71, 73, 75, 79, 82, 83, 87, 88, 90, 92, 105, 106, 115, 118, 126, 128, 156, 158, 179, 196, 211, 219, 228, 234, 238, 240
see Investment, Mortgage
payment, 14, 33, 35, 79, 82, 117, 118, 125, 135, 173, 183, 210, 221, 233, 236

prepayment, 185, 210
purchase, 15
repayment, 17, 79
return, 115
Principal-only securities (POs), 221
Private mortgage insurance (PMI), 45
Professional investor, 142, 144, 159
secrets, 1-7
Profit(s), 21, 24, 60, 118, 121, 123, 124, 126, 127, 129, 135, 151-153, 157, 201
see Discount, Mortgage
Property
insurance, 45, 46
value, 45-46, 65, 99
Prudential, 202
Public Securities Association, 238
conversion chart, 231
PSA, 102, 202, 238
PSA prepayment method, 84-85
PSA prepayment rate, 84
PSA prepayment speed, 84, 238
Purchase(s), 16, 199
see Mortgage, Principal, Repurchase
price, 139, 156-158, 160, 163, 209, 236
Purchasing power, 6, 27
risk, 6, 238

Q
Quasi-governmental
agency, 236, 238
corporation, 67

R
Rate changes, 115-131
Rate of return, 6, 31, 52, 56
Real estate, 41, 59, 72, 142, 189, 195, 224
collapse, 74
partnerships, 41
Real Estate Mortgage Investment Conduit, 238
REMIC, 71, 199, 208-209, 220, 238, 239
tranches, 208

Index

Real return, 238
Realized yield, 136, 165, 238
Reappraisal, 75
Recession, 47
Redemptions, 4, 216
Refinancing, 79, 95, 99, 101, 133-135, 137, 139, 178, 233, 237
  prepayment, 98
  range, 136
Regulatory risk, 4
Reinvestment, 19, 176, 185
  see Dividend
  earnings, 176
  rate, 20, 174, 179, 182, 183
  sensitivity, 187
  yield, 183
REMIC, see Real Estate
Repayment, 13, 48, 158
  see Principal
Representation, 69-70
Repurchases, 76
Retirement, 31, 37, 39, 174
  cash, 31
  income, 30
  plans, 29
  savings, 174, 212
  savings plan, 22, 32
Return, 7, 11, 55, 60, 223, 233, 239
  see Contractual, Holding, Investment, Rate, Risk, Speculative
  on investment, 12, 117
Revenue bond, see Municipal, Tax-exempt
Risk, 7, 42, 51, 60, 105, 106, 199, 218-223
  see Average, Bankruptcy, Company, Credit, Currency, Dividend, Earnings, Environmental, Foreign, Industry, Interest rate, Investment, Lawsuit, Market, Mortgage, Prepayment, Price, Purchasing, Regulatory, Stock, Technology, Volatility, Yield
  profiles, 43

rearrangement, 208-209
return, 144

S

Safety, 68, 70-72, 223-226
  layers, 41-48, 64, 224
Sale price, 157, 158, 160, 163, 236
Savings, 12, 18, 27, 52, 174
  see Interest, Retirement
  plan, 31
  strategy, 171
Savings and loans, 7, 44, 64
S corporations, 212
Sears, 5
Securities, 26, 63, 93, 123, 128, 134, 149, 158, 166, 168, 169, 176, 180, 181, 186, 212
  see Adjustable, Discount, Federal Home, Federal National, Interest-bearing, Interest-only, Mortgage, Mortgage-backed, Par, Pass-through, Premium, Principal-only, U.S.
  brokers, 199
  Exchange Commission (SEC), 63
  fraud, 63
  name, 227-228
  prices, 106-114, 128, 129, 183
  yield, 37
Seller, 69, 106
Servicer, 4, 64, 66, 69, 70, 239
Servicing
  agreements, 70
  fees, 93
  rights, 66
Settlement date, 229-230
Shareholder, 49, 63, 238
Share, 50
  price, 49
Simplicity, 68, 70-72, 120-121, 215-218
Snowballing, 13, 15-18, 23, 24, 28, 31, 35, 37, 39, 75, 109-112, 157, 171, 175, 178, 181-183, 218, 239

Speculative return, 11
Stacking, 13, 14, 16-18, 23, 75, 117, 174, 239
Standard & Poor's, 5
S&P 500, 56, 190
Standardization, 68, 71, 72
Stock(s), 3, 5, 9, 34, 49, 50, 63, 68, 72, 158, 186, 200, 225, 227
 see Common, Corporate, Growth, Penny, Preferred
 appreciation, 58
 dividend yields, 57, 60
 GNMA/FNMA comparison, 49-61
 investment, 58, 156
 index investment, 58
 market, 49, 59, 61, 190, 196
 performance, 51-53
 price(s), 51, 60
 price performance, 60
 risk types, 4
 valuation, 51
Stockbroker, 7
Stretching, 13-18, 23, 35, 37, 75, 109-112, 117, 174, 239

T
TAC, see Targeted
Targeted amortization class (TAC), 208
Tax(es), 31, 156
 see Income
 calculation, 199, 211-212
 laws, 60
 rate, 29, 31
 shelters, 212
 special considerations, 28-29
 survival, 21-32, 219
Tax-exempt
 bond, 2, 3, 21, 34, 207
 revenue bond, 207
Technical default, 4
Technology risk, 4
Telerate, 200
Thrift, 1, 65, 236

Title insurance, 45-46
Tranches, 208
 see Real Estate
Trust
 see Intermediate
 company, 1
 indentures, 216

U
Underwriter, 64, 65
Underwriting, 101
 process, 65
 standards, 44
Unemployment, 154
U.S. Treasury, 48, 67, 151, 225, 234
 bills, 22, 26, 31, 52, 238
 bonds, 3, 48, 52, 58, 60, 105, 109, 147, 155, 176, 186, 196, 218, 219
 notes, 186
 obligation, 145, 151, 189
 securities, 67, 173, 209
 yields, 190

V
Veterans Administration, 45
VA, 45, 234
VA loan, 68, 77, 85, 101, 102
VA mortgages, 73, 101
Volatility, 5
 see Price
 risk, 211

W
WAC, see Weighted average
WAL, see Weighted average
WAM, see Weighted average
WARM, see Weighted average
Warranties, 65
Wealth, 24, 27, 56, 59, 61, 192
 accumulation, 21, 23, 28, 29, 173-187, 213, 218
 accumulation history, 190-193
 compounding, 11-16, 218-219

Index

building, 9-20
Weighted average
coupon (WAC), 200, 228-229, 239
life (WAL), 4, 82-83, 240
remaining maturity (WAM/WARM), 200, 229, 240

Y

Yield, 18, 22, 25, 34, 42, 48, 52, 105, 109, 110, 112, 119, 125, 130, 143, 144, 149, 151, 152, 176, 181, 191-193, 202, 204, 208, 217-220, 223, 224, 239
see After-tax, Bond, Corporate bond, Current, Floor, Holding, Interest, Investment, Investor, Market, Mortgage, Mortgage-backed, Mortgage-backed security, Realized, Reinvestment, Security, Stock, U.S.
curve, 186
differences, 203
enhancement, 37
fluctuations, 170, 205
level, 176-178
measure, 233
performance, 167, 195, 219
risk, 88, 141, 205, 206
risk comparisons, 167-171
risk reduction, 155-171
swings, 169

About the Publisher

PROBUS PUBLISHING COMPANY

Probus Publishing Company fills the informational needs of today's business professional by publishing authoritative, quality books on timely and relevant topics, including:

- Investing
- Futures/Options Trading
- Banking
- Finance
- Marketing and Sales
- Manufacturing and Project Management
- Personal Finance, Real Estate, Insurance and Estate Planning
- Entrepreneurship
- Management

Probus books are available at quantity discounts when purchased for business, educational or sales promotional use. For more information, please call the Director, Corporate/Institutional Sales at 1-800-998-4644, or write:

Director, Corporate/Institutional Sales
Probus Publishing Company
1925 N. Clybourn Avenue
Chicago, Illinois 60614
FAX (312) 868-6250